The All-Everything Operating System

IBM i for Business Means Business!!!

BRIAN W. KELLY

Copyright © 2009, 2016 Brian W. Kelly

Editor Melissa Sabol
Author Brian W. Kelly

Title: The All-Everything Operating System

All rights reserved: No part of this book may be reproduced or transmitted in any form, or by any means, electronic or mechanical, including photocopying, recording, scanning, faxing, or by any information storage and retrieval system, without permission from the publisher, LETS GO PUBLISH, in writing.

Disclaimer: Though judicious care was taken throughout the writing and the publication of this work that the information contained herein is accurate, there is no expressed or implied warranty that all information in this book is 100% correct. Therefore, neither LETS GO PUBLISH, nor the author accepts liability for any use of this work.

Trademarks: A number of products and names referenced in this book are trade names and trademarks of their respective companies. For example, iSeries and AS/400 are trademarks of the IBM Corporation and Windows is a trademark of Microsoft Corporation.

Referenced Material: The information in this book has been obtained through personal and third party observations and copious reading over many years. Where unique information has been provided or extracted from other sources, those sources are acknowledged within the text of the book itself. Thus, there are no formal footnotes nor is there a bibliography section.

Published by: LETS GO PUBLISH!
P.O. Box 621; Wilkes-Barre PA 18503
Brian P. Kelly, Publisher
Plains, Pennsylvania
brian@brianpkelly.com
www.letsgopublish.com

Library of Congress Copyright Information Pending

Book Cover Design by Michele Thomas

ISBN Information: The International Standard Book Number (ISBN) is a unique machine-readable identification number, which marks any book unmistakably. The ISBN is the clear standard in the book industry. 159 countries and territories are officially ISBN members. The Official ISBN For this book is:

978-0-9802132-8-7

The price for this work is:	$18.95 USD

10   9   8   7   6   5   4   3   2

Release Date: 2009, July, 2016

Dedication

To Joseph and Peg McDonald

Great Friends of IBMi

And

At the Top of My Best Friend's List!

Acknowledgments

I would like to thank many, many people for helping me in this effort.

I would first like to thank my immediate family, starting with my lovely and dear wife, Patricia, followed by my oldest Son, Brian, youngest son, Michael, and lovely daughter, Katie. Pat, by the way is also as lovely as a bright and sunny day.

In every book that I have written or have edited, I publicly acknowledged all of the help that I have received from many sources. Some of these wonderful people are still on earth and others have made their way to heaven.

I would like to thank many people for helping me in this effort. I appreciate all the help that I received in putting this book together, along with the 66 other books from the past.

My printed acknowledgments were once so large that book readers needed to navigate too many pages to get to page one of the text. To permit me more flexibility, I put my acknowledgment list online at www.letsgopublish.com. The list of acknowledgments continues to grow. Believe it or not, it once cost about a dollar more to print each book.

Thank you all on the big list in the sky and God bless you all for your help.

Please check out www.letsgopublish.com to read the latest version of my heartfelt acknowledgments updated for this book. Thank you all!

In this book, I received some extra special help from many avid Lets go Publish! supporters including Bruce Ikeda, Dennis Grimes, Gerry Rodski, Wily Ky Eyely, Angel Irene McKeown Kelly, Angel Edward Joseph Kelly Sr., Angel Edward Joseph Kelly Jr., Ann Flannery, Angel James Flannery Sr., Mary Daniels, Bill Daniels, Robert Gary Daniels, Angel Sarah Janice Daniels, Angel Punkie Daniels, Joe Kelly, Diane Kelly, Brian P. Kelly, Mike P. Kelly, Katie P. Kelly, Ben Kelly, and Budmund (Buddy) Arthur Kelly.

Table of Contents

Chapter 1   What Is The All-Everything Operating System?...... 1
Chapter 2   The Value of Great Operating Systems................... 15
Chapter 3   Does an Operating System Add Business Value? 31
Chapter 4   Where Did IBM i Come From? 49
Chapter 6   IBM i -- The Unsung Operating System!................ 91
Chapter 7   Brief History of Computers from IBM Rochester 103
Chapter 8   IBM Power System with IBM i............................. 151
Chapter 9   Autonomic Computing from the Start................... 163
Chapter 10 Advanced Computer Science Concepts in IBM I... 177

Advanced Computer Science Concepts:

Chapter 11 Integrated System Functions............................. 183
Chapter 12 High Level Machine Interface............................ 203
Chapter 13 Single-Level Store 225
Chapter 14 Object-Based Architecture 243
Chapter 15 Integrated Security 251
Chapter 16 Integrated Relational Database 263
Chapter 17 Integrated Business Language Compilers............ 277
Chapter 18 Consistent, Intuitive Control Language 297
Chapter 19 Integrated Transaction Processing..................... 323
Chapter 20 All-Everything OS: Extra Ingredients 341
Chapter 21 The All-Everything OS in Perspective 367
Song: Eggplant That Ate Chicago 399
Other Books by Brian W. Kelly 401

Preface:

It is my pleasure to write about IBM's finest operating system. It is even more of a pleasure to have the person responsible for the architecture of the System/38, AS/400, and System i, as well as the now champion IBM i operating system, the all-everything operating system, included in this book. Check out the Foreword and check out Dr. Soltis's books when you have the opportunity.

Though I have met Dr. Frank Soltis and have spoken to him one on one and he knows me and I know him, I continue to be in awe of him because of what he created. And, quite frankly, because of the way he carries himself, you'd never know he is who he is. I am impressed with the IBM i operating system and the person, Dr. Frank G. Soltis, identified with most of the special parts of the machine. And, ladies and gentlemen, most of the overall machine from the 1978 System/38 to the current IBM Power System with IBM i is software. Thus, most of the machine is the all-everything operating system.

For the many years that Dr. Soltis worked for the IBM Corporation, IBM knew how special a scientist, an engineer, and a person he really is. For IBM it had to be like Clark Kent showed up for work every day but they really knew who he was. As IBMi's Chief Scientist, Dr. Soltis used creativity, knowledge, a major sense of confidence and sheer genius along with some wonderful friends, Dick Bains, who is now with the Lord, Roy Hoffman, others, and a great sense of self, to create the best, yet least sung operating system in the galaxy.

Yes, the galaxy includes IBM, Microsoft, HP, SUN, Linux, Unix, and all phenomenally functional yet otherwise simplistic architectures. And, no, to this day, nobody has built anything finer than that which a young Frank Soltis and his friends, mostly in their twenties and thirties, were able to create into the best operating system in the universe. As the limits of single processors are clearly in sight, it makes the IBM i operating system even more needed to move the world into the future. As you will learn in this book, most operating system vendors are trying to patch and extend their inefficient creations of the past into the future and so far it is not working. Without about twenty-five more years work, it isn't going to work. You already know their names.

Without even reading the first chapter of the book, you have already discovered that the all-everything operating system is an IBM product. Even before Bill Gates was a teenager, IBM had released the very first sophisticated business operating system. Just like Gates' first operating system, this guy was called DOS for Disk Operating System and it was used to power IBM's first chip-based computer, the IBM System/360. Along with DOS/360, IBM also announced OS/360, a phenomenally more capable operating system that would run on its larger models. Eventually DOS grew up to become z/VSE and OS became z/OS

In 1972 Big Blue introduced virtual memory into the operating system environment with a version of the operating system known as OS/VS1. The "VS" was to designate the idea of virtual storage. IBM was not the first to use virtual storage, but it was the company to perfect it for large scale business computing. With all of this success, IBM had become the premiere operating system builder in the world. In many ways, once IBM had passed Univac in the early 1950's it was clear sailing for the company's commercial data processing systems from then on. There are few who would argue about IBM's quality or IBM's service in the computer field and it says something for the all-everything operating system that it sits on the very top of IBM's achievement list.

I will save most of the goodies about the subject of this book until the book proper, but you know already that the operating system of which I write has struck me as so elegant and so powerful that I was compelled to label it the all-everything operating system. It just happens to be available only from IBM. If your curiosity abounds out of control to know why anybody would select an IBM operating system as an example of an all-everything operating system, I urge you to feel free to digress from this Preface and go directly to Chapter 1 and you will learn enough to know why this unique operating system helps businesses to be successful.

I surely hope that you like this book. I have been in the computer industry as an IBM insider for 23 years and following my career with IBM, I have been mostly independent, providing consulting services for clients in many industries. I confess to be an addict of the type of no-sweat computing that IBM brought forth in 1969 with its System/3 small business operating system called System Control Program or SCP. I have remained an addict while IBM introduced its "Future System" project in 1978, with the System/38 CPF operating system, the great grandfather of the all-everything operating system,
IBM i.

The "Future System" was laden with such advanced computer science operating system concepts that the IBM Power System running the IBM i operating system today is still futuristic in its capabilities. It even tricked IBM. It was so complex in its internals that in order to achieve ease of use externally, the company could not make it all work on schedule. This forced IBM's Chairman at the time, Frank Cary, to postpone its initial delivery date so that the Lab could have the time to make the system work. Knowing how much IBM hates to miss deadlines, you can appreciate all the special ingredients that had to be right for the Company to release this baby.

IBM wanted the system to be known for its facility, not for how many reboots an average technician could perform in an average work day. In other words, unlike other operating system vendors, IBM decided to make the hardware and the operating system, from the chip to the user interface, work together before it made the new operating system available for all of us to use. When the "Future System" was made available, thanks to a yeoman IBM effort, it worked like clockwork.

Few would expect that any operating system originally built in the late 1970s would have advanced integrated design characteristics better than all of today's competing platforms as well as the most advanced operating system research projects. Yet the 21st century all-everything operating system, based on the 1978 "Future System" tops the charts in terms of innate advanced computer science capabilities. If IBM made more hoopla about its major achievements in technology in the fashion of Microsoft, we'd surely all know about the all-everything operating system by now. But IBM is substantially more humble than Microsoft and the company reserves its messages about its business operating systems for the business marketing channel, not the consumer channel.

I wrote this book so that everybody, from consumers to business people, can know about the all-everything operating system. Far from "legacy" as it is referred to by the unknowing, the all-everything operating system is exactly that. It is all-everything. Moreover, it is not a one size fits all take-it-or-leave-it proposition. It runs on hardware of all sizes and on each size, it is integrated with the chip functions. There are sizes from very, very small to humongous behemoth. It is so granular that it can do computing jobs for very small businesses and very large businesses and those in-between. Regardless of its size, its ease-of use personality and advanced software capabilities are unmatched.

The story of the all-everything operating system is worth telling and it is worth hearing. If you are a business person thinking about getting your first computer to run your business, or you have a PC server or multiple servers, or even if you have a full IT department, this story is worth your time. For the technical at heart, there is enough information about this special operating system that by reading this book you will have a much better appreciation for how well it gets its work done, and I would expect that you will be duly impressed. In a nutshell, this book is your best bet to understanding what the all-everything operating system is all about and how it can improve the bottom line for your business.

This book is very easy to read. Each chapter is written as a self-contained essay that gives historical background and / or technology information about the all-everything operating system. By looking at the table of contents, you can pick the essay that you want to read first and then go right to it and it should make sense. Of course, you might want to read in sequence with Chapter 1 first to get a feeling of the machine, its relevance, and its value to business. Either way, I predict that you will enjoy this book. Thanks for taking it home with you.

Brian W. Kelly
Wilkes-Barre PA

About the Author

Brian W. Kelly retired as Assistant Professor in the Business Information Technology (BIT) program at Marywood University, where he also served as the IBM i and midrange systems technical advisor to the IT faculty. Kelly developed and taught many college and professional courses in the IT and business areas. He is also a contributing technical editor to IT Jungle's "The Four Hundred" and "Four Hundred Guru" Newsletters.

A former IBM Senior Systems Engineer, he has an active consultancy in the information technology field, (www.kellyconsulting.com). He is the author of sixty-seven books and numerous articles about current IT topics. Kelly is a frequent speaker at COMMON, IBM conferences, and other technical conferences and user group meetings across the United States.

The All-Everything Operating System originated with the System/38 back in 1978. It is only coincidence that in its original version it happened to be Mr. Kelly's 38th published book.

Foreword

Presented by

Dr. Frank G. Soltis, IBM i Chief Scientist

When I first began to design computers for IBM, the idea of software compatibility was not very important. If software had to be rewritten in order to run on a new generation of computers—that was okay. Business users in the 1970s made it clear to IBM and other computer vendors that compatibility was important. Their major investments were in software applications, and these applications had to run on the next generation of hardware. Not only did existing applications have to run, they had to run faster.

The requirement to reuse applications for scientific computing, especially for supercomputers, did not exist until very recently. Rewriting applications for a new generation of scientific computers was the norm. Even in the Unix world, software compatibility was not too important until business users began to use Unix. Now, whenever IBM announces a new Power System model, there is always a statement that the new model is "binary compatible" with the previous models. This statement is aimed at Unix users to assure them that older applications can still run without having to be rewritten or recompiled.

As hardware technologies continued to evolve, hardware vendors have been able to increase performance, increase throughput, increase capacities and add new functionality to our computer systems. In order to fully use the new hardware, application programs generally need to be rewritten. However, as long as older applications still see some performance improvements when running on new hardware, there is little incentive to rewrite the old applications.

A great example of this reluctance to rewrite old applications is the move from 32-bit computing to 64-bit computing. Computers with 64-bit hardware have been available since the early 1990s. Today, computers from mainframes to PCs have 64-bit hardware. Although it took nearly 15 years to accomplish the rewrite, 64-bit operating systems are now available for every major hardware platform. Applications are another story.

Very few 64-bit application programs exist today. Unix, Windows and even mainframe computers overwhelmingly run 32-bit applications on 64-bit hardware. There is, of course, one glaring exception. All IBM i applications run as 64-bit applications, but that's another story. For the rest of the industry, the move from 32 to 64-bit software will take at least 25 years, and possibly longer.

What if moving to new hardware did not improve the performance of existing applications? Worse yet, what if performance was degraded unless the applications were rewritten for the new hardware? This could be a disaster for both computer vendors and users.

Surprisingly, this is exactly what could happen in the computer industry over the next couple of years. There is still much debate about exactly what will happen, but many in our industry are convinced that a major rewrite of all applications is the only way forward. Let me explain.

The Core of the Problem

Ever since the first microprocessors emerged in the early 1970s, the way to increase performance was to make chips that had smaller and smaller features and that ran at higher and higher clock speeds. Higher clock speeds mean that all programs, old or new, see some performance improvements.

This approach to microprocessor design ended a few years ago when the size of the transistors on a chip became so small that much of the electricity pumped into those transistors leaked out, producing a large amount of heat. By this time there were also so many transistors packed tightly on these chips that the total heat generated could not be simply carried away. Some chip makers believed that without very sophisticated cooling mechanisms, clock speeds above five gigahertz would melt the silicon from which the chips were made.

The result was chip makers stopped increasing clock speeds. This is not to say that advances in silicon technology and chip design ended. Indeed, Moore's Law, which says the number of transistors on a chip doubles every two years, is still very much alive. What has changed is the way chip makers are using those additional transistors predicted by Moore's Law. Those additional transistors are now being used to increase the number of processors, or "cores," in the chip. Chip maker Intel, for example, predicts that in the not too distant future we will see chips with hundreds of cores inside.

Eight is Enough

While multicore chips may have solved some problems for the chip makers, they are creating enormous problems for almost everyone else in the computer industry. System manufacturers, operating system designers, compiler writers, application writers and users are all affected by the decision to implement multicore chips. Single-threaded applications -

those applications designed to run sequentially on a single processor - do not benefit from running on multicore chips. These applications must either be rewritten for multicore chips, or at the very least, recompiled with a compiler that is designed specifically for parallel processing.

By most estimates, greater than 90 percent of all applications today are single threaded. Rewriting or recompiling these sequential applications to run in parallel will not be easy. Most software experts agree that somewhere between four and eight is probably the maximum number of cores that can be used by existing applications. Going beyond eight will require fairly radical redesign for applications. And yet, chip makers are bound and determined to go well beyond eight cores as the only way to increase performance.

New development tools to deal with what some authors have called "the multicore menace" are rapidly being developed. A myriad of new languages and tools designed specifically for parallel programming are appearing almost daily. Microsoft, for example, has already released several new parallel-programming tools and a new programming language, called F#. Intel, HP and several other vendors have also released new programming tools and languages for multicore chips.

Many new parallel-programming languages that were originally created for programming massively-parallel supercomputers are also being proposed for general-purpose use. Two of those languages, Erlang and Clojure are dialects of Java that enable applications to be distributed across thousands of cores.

To further complicate matters, many computer professionals believe that multicore chips, as they currently exist in conventional general-purpose processors, will not survive much longer. They point out that the problem with a large number of cores on a single chip is the inability to feed data to all of the processors. The number of connections to the chip is not increasing, meaning that the bandwidth to off-chip memories is limited. Hardware vendors, for example IBM and Intel, are proposing to stack memory chips above their processor chips to increase the number of connections to the chip and thus increase the memory bandwidth. This too is not a long term solution.

The biggest news for computer hardware may be the many specialized processors that are designed specifically for parallel processing. One example is the Cell chip from IBM, which contains a Power processor and eight special-purpose processors designed for parallel processing. Created originally for gaming platforms, where intense graphics and real-time responsiveness are extremely important, these chips are now being used for a variety of applications, including supercomputer applications. It will not be long before multicore chips include a variety of different processors for specialized functions.

Intel has recently announced that it too is exploring system-on-chip designs - complex microchips that perform specialized tasks on top of general-purpose computations. Programming these "hybrid architecture" chips will not be easy and will require new programming tools.

About the only thing that is clear about the future of multicore chip development and the software technologies that will be used to create applications for massively parallel chips is that there is no clear future. While it is imperative that the computer industry moves quickly to identify effective tools and techniques that can be used by software developers to create future parallel applications, there is no indication that this will happen soon.

High Productivity Computing System (HPCS)

One of the most exciting projects in parallel processing was started a few years ago by the Defense Advanced Research Projects Agency (DARPA). It is called the High Productivity

Computing System (HPCS), and its goal is to provide a totally new generation of high productivity computing systems that can be used for a wide variety of applications. The reason for the need to create a new generation of computers is because of the way parallel applications are written today.

Using layers of abstraction to hide complexity and to greatly enhance programming productivity has long been a staple of commercial programming. Commercial applications written in assembly language disappeared many years ago. Yet, in the world of programming highly-parallel applications, programmers are still living in the stone age and using what amounts to parallel assembly language. The new languages and tools being developed for multicore chips are trying to raise the level of parallel programming, but they still have a very long way to go.

Because parallel programming languages and tools are very primitive, programmer productivity is very low. Also, whenever a new generation of hardware emerges, entire applications have to be totally rewritten. There is no ability to reuse existing applications on the new hardware. HPCS is intended to solve the productivity and the reuse problems. To solve these problems, DARPA funded research efforts in three companies: Cray, Sun and IBM.

IBM's Programmable Easy-to-use Reliable Computing System (PERCS) project, funded by DARPA, is an attempt to create a highly adaptable computing system that configures its hardware and software components to match the application demands. Working with Los Alamos National Laboratory and 12 major universities, IBM's goal is to create systems that automatically analyze the workload and dynamically respond to changes in application demands by reconfiguring its components to match application needs.

The PERCS project uses a combined hardware-software design methodology to integrate advances in chip technology, architecture, operating systems, compilers, programming languages and programming tools to deliver scalable systems that will provide an order-of-magnitude improvement in development productivity for parallel applications by 2010.

To accomplish this, PERCS includes a new open-source, object-oriented language called X10, innovative middleware, and new programming environments that will be supported by hardware features to automate many phases of the program development process. Some of these components are already available. Other features will be delivered in 2010 with IBM's Power 7 processors.

While the goal of HPCS is to meet the need for commercially successful petascale computing systems for high-end users in government, science and industry in 2010, IBM has a broader goal in mind. The technologies created for PERCS will be implemented in future versions of Power Systems intended for commercial applications.

End of Multicore Computing?

It should now be obvious that the computer industry will likely see major disruptions in the next few years. Reprogramming applications for multicore chips will not be easy. Up to about eight cores, operating system enhancements and compiler improvements are probably good enough to provide sufficient performance improvements for most of today's applications. Beyond eight cores it is not obvious that conventional applications will see any benefits and may even see reduced performance.

As more and more cores on a chip compete for the same data, there comes a point where adding another core will actually slow down the application. Even with all of the efforts being expended in rewriting existing applications for multicore chips, there is the strong possibility that multicore computing in its present form will not survive for more than a few years.

Because of the limitations with multicore computing, many computer scientists, especially those in academia, are not only predicting the end of multicore computing, they are predicting the end of conventional computer architectures like Intel's X86. They argue that the X86 architecture was never designed for parallel processing and that a multicore implementation is just a short-term fix.

Many of these same computer scientists are now calling for the creation of a new stable and enduring computer system architecture that will support massively parallel processing. Perhaps the new system design will look something like the one being created for IBM's PERCS project. Perhaps it will be something else. There is no shortage of proposals for what the future system design should be. There is, however, agreement that it will be very different from today's design.

One of the primary goals of almost all of these future system design proposals, whether it is IBM's PERCS or any of the others, is to enable the reuse of existing applications. In other words, the goal of any new design is to be capable of incorporating future hardware and software technologies with minimal impact on existing applications.

Futuristic Design

Does this sound familiar? The goal for a future system design is technology independence. This should not come as a big surprise. The software development investments that have already been made in applications for everything from supercomputing to business computing are far too valuable to simply throw away. The next generation of computer systems must find a way to protect those investments.

As Mark Twain once commented, "History does not repeat itself, but it does rhyme." There is a certain amount of satisfaction knowing that concepts such as technology independence that emerged in the 1970s are once again being revisited. Viewed as a radical futuristic concept when it was first introduced in the IBM System/38 back in 1978, technology independence with its ability to incorporate new hardware and software technologies without impacting existing applications has clearly stood the test of time.

That original design of the System/38 did not stand still. More functionality continued to be included, and in 1988 the ability to run applications from the System/36 was added. That merging of two systems resulted in the System/38 being reintroduced to the computing world as the AS/400. The new AS/400 became an instant success with businesses of all sizes.

In 1995 IBM introduced the first 64-bit Power processors into the AS/400. Thanks to its technology independent design, not a single line of application code had to be modified or even recompiled for the new hardware. No other system has ever been able to move applications to a totally new processor architecture without requiring massive application changes. The AS/400, which was subsequently renamed to iSeries, System i and finally IBM i, stands alone in this regard.

IBM i today has that very same technology independence that has protected the application investments of hundreds of thousands of businesses all over the world for more than 30 years. Moving to new generations of hardware and software over the years has never required rewriting or even recompiling applications. Even the move to the first commercially available multicore chips in 2001 did not require application changes. Those same applications that moved seamlessly from one computer generation to the next will continue to move forward in the future. No other computer system can match this record.

Maybe the world is finally ready for some of this "radical" thinking. The HPCS project from DARPA is certainly trying to find ways to avoid having to rewrite applications every time the hardware changes. Microsoft and Intel are putting out new tools as fast as they can to protect their investments in X86 hardware and software, even if the whole concept of multicore chips might be flawed.

And, let's not forget about productivity. IBM i and its predecessor systems were designed from the very beginning to make writing applications far more productive than conventional computer systems. Integrating many of the components needed by the application, such as a database, into the operating system is one way to improve productivity. Single-level storage, where all storage is treated as memory, is another. Built-in security and virus resistance also can make life a lot easier for application programmers.

If as many believe, the computing world is at a turning point because of the limitations of multicore hardware, then maybe, just maybe, a futuristic design such as the IBM i is the answer. While it is highly unlikely that the IBM i design will be the only answer, it is comforting to know that IBM i will be there to meet the needs of business computing well into the future.

I wish you well in your future endeavors and I am pleased that you have an interest in IBM i.

The Best,
Dr. Frank G. Soltis

Dr. Frank G. Soltis Biographical Information + more.

If you ever happen to have the opportunity to hear Dr. Frank G. Soltis speak, it will be a memorable moment indeed. Several years back, my neighbor, who has a hard time powering on his twenty + year old IBM ValuePoint PC with its 10 GB of disk storage, accompanied me to hear Dr. Frank speak at the Delaware Valley Computer Users Group (DVCUG) in historic Philadelphia. A Real Estate expert and College Professor by trade, my neighbor, Professor John Anstett, was thoroughly impressed with Dr. Soltis, as a speaker and for his ability to put difficult notions into simple terms.

The architectures that he designed for IBM i do exactly that. They take very complex capabilities, assure it's the system and not the user that manages them, and then they present themselves to users in the easiest way possible. Without stealing anybody's thunder, "it's so easy, a caveman can do it!"

When Dr. Frank G. Soltis speaks, the world listens. He is regarded throughout the world as one of the most significant computer scientists of the twentieth and twenty-first centuries. He is recognized as the "Father of IBM i" as it was his work from his Ph.D. dissertation research that served as the basis for his creating the most revolutionary computer architecture of all time. His work led to a totally new breed of computer system, beginning with the 1978 IBM System/38 and culminating with today's IBM Power System with IBM i. He is a folk hero to the expanding IBM i community, and rightfully so.

During the last decade he led the effort to define the architecture of the 64-bit PowerPC processors used in the IBM iSeries and pSeries servers. As the IBM Chief Scientist for IBM i until his retirement December 31, 2008, he was responsible for defining the future directions for IBM systems.

As part of the future, he directed IBM's best and brightest engineers in the creation of the IBM Power 6 driven IBM Power System and the design for Power 7, Power 8, and later chip offerings. Though IBM i is his first love, Dr. Frank helped IBM make IBM's new Power 6 - driven hardware system, the best hardware in all of IBM for Unix (IBM's AIX), Linux, and of course, IBM i. For all of these operating systems, and for all of those chips, Dr. Frank Soltis found room on the chip for those items in the OS that were needed to make that particular OS more special on IBM Power. Since IBM i is already special, that's like having a special chip to make special OS functions even more special.

This book describes in detail many of the innovative and advanced computer science principles developed by Dr. Soltis and made operational in the IBM i line of computers. Advanced notions such as single level storage and the technology independent machine interface, both were brought forth under Dr. Soltis's direction.

His work continues to have a major influence on IBM's advanced computing efforts. Dr. Soltis travels the world speaking on IT trends and technology advancements. In addition to his research, he is a Professor in the Department of Electrical and Computer Engineering at the University of Minnesota where he teaches graduate courses on high-performance computer design. Dr. Frank G. Soltis is an award-winning author with several books, technical papers and other publications to his credit. He holds more than 25 patents and published invention disclosures related to computer systems. In his spare time he enjoys working on and racing Porsches with his sons.

To find two of his best-selling books, *Inside the AS/400*, and *Fortress Rochester, The Inside Story of the IBM iSeries*, just type the title into your favorite search engine. Both are available at Amazon and Google.

Thank you, Dr. Soltis for investing your valuable time in this project

Chapter 1 What Is The All-Everything Operating System?

The All Everything Machine!

A few years back, I wrote a book that even IBM liked. The book was called The All-Everything Machine, a catchy name that well explains the popular AS/400 heritage line, which has been described often as IBM's best computer ever. I was willing to "loan" IBM the "all-everything" name for a while but Big Blue had other naming missions in mind. With all of the product renaming going on at the time, my thoughts were that the AS/400 heritage line should have a spiffy name that separated it from all other machines. All-Everything Machine as a name surely would have done that!

By the way, that book was one of my most successful ever. Among the many who bought it, IBM purchased 500 copies for their operation in Milan, Italy. I offered to accompany the books on their trip to Milan but I did not get to go. I'll let you all know on my Web site if I get to follow this book to some exotic IBM site worldwide. I am very travel-ready.

IBM no longer has an all-everything machine per se. There was a big hardware change in early 2008. The bottom line on the change is that IBM succeeded in changing the machine so that the AS/400 operating system (i5/OS at the time) was no longer needed to run the new hardware. The AS/400 name itself had been replaced by iSeries in 2000, followed by i5 in 2004 and finally, the System i in 2008. During this time, IBM's customers had been able to run Unix and Linux as a guest operating system on i5/OS but i5/OS was always needed. Since 2008, this is no longer true. Any of the operating systems can run on the new hardware without IBM i having to be the lead dog.

IBM had previously succeeded in putting all of the System i pieces needed on the Power 6 chip. This includes the advanced i5/OS RISC instruction set (now IBM i) along with the native System/36 instructions. Additionally, IBM added the 32-bit Unix/Linux and 64-bit Unix/Linux instruction sets. From Power 4 to Power 6, the chip hardware was able to run Unix, and Linux but it needed i5/OS because the I/O adapters behaved differently from pre Unix models. i5/OS had provided a nice virtual environment in which Unix and Linux could run.

On the same line in Rochester, Minnesota, IBM manufactured both the pSeries units, which were Unix and / or Linux only, as well as the iSeries units. Just a few things separated the p units from the i units. One major difference was the input / output processors. The i units always had very intelligent controllers (microcomputers) that were used to offload the main processor(s) for peripheral operations. These input / output processors were called IOPs for short. When the main processor wanted to write to disk, for example, it sent the buffer load to the IOP along with instructions and then went on to the next task on the system. On the i units, when the IOP was finished with its work with the database, it would gently tap the main processor on the shoulder and let it know that it was done.

Unix and Linux did not need assistive input / output processors. They worked with a form of direct I/O. So, in Unix, the processor would stay engaged while the input / output operation was occurring. Instead of the IOPs, the final hardware change was to add smart input / output adapters to the system. Now, all aspects of the same hardware can support Unix, Linux or i5/OS. The newer and faster IOAs work well with any operating system used on the Power platform.

Separate the All-Everything OS from the All-Everything Machine

In essence, IBM took its all-everything machine and separated the hardware from the all-everything operating system. Additionally, it took its p series machines and separated the OS from the hardware. The result is a new and improved system that can run any of the operating systems equally well. There no longer is a need for a System p set of hardware and a System i set of hardware. One set of hardware runs all the operating systems. This is a great technological achievement. After creating this new hardware box, IBM had to give it a name that was reflective of its capabilities. It was neither a System p nor a System i, yet it was both.

The merged System i and System p box was introduced as the IBM Power System. It is a cut above the old p and i models as it uses IBM's newest and fastest Power 6 chip technology. It was announced to be a new generation of systems unifying the former System i and System p product lines. As part of the new packaging, IBM's integrated operating system formerly known as i5/OS was renamed as IBM i. Some in IBM call it just, "i." Along with the name change came the logo and the logo tells a lot about the mission of IBM i. The Logo says, "IBM i for Business."

Figure 1-1, Dr. Frank Soltis Introduces IBM i and the Power System

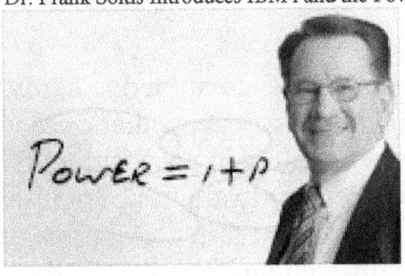

The hardware platform is absolutely outstanding and it represents everything that the AS/400 heritage boxes ever

thought of becoming. It is the hardware for the all-everything operating system (IBM i) as well as the Unix and Linux operating systems. When it runs IBM i, it is actually a better version of the all-everything machine than the one I introduced to IBM in Milan in 2005. But, since hardware and OS are no longer one, as they had been from System/38 to the System i, the one uniquely identifiable aspect of the former all-everything machine is its operating system, the all-everything operating system, IBM i (i for Business).

Figure 1-2 IBM i for Business Logo--All-Everything Operating System

The New Power Equation

The New Power Equation for i Clients

This major new platform provides a compelling new choice for companies of all sizes. The new IBM Power Systems have unified IBM's highly successful integrated platform, IBM System i™, with its fast growing UNIX® operating system platform, the IBM System p™, which also ran the open source Linux OS. So, from an IBM hardware perspective, the company created a great name for a product. Who can argue with "The IBM Power System" as a powerful name? I know of nobody complaining about the quality of the platform name. It is catchy and to say it again for effect, it is quite "powerful."

From an IBM perspective, creating one hardware system to run three major operating systems that once were tied to specific hardware is a win-win proposition. Everybody has won. IBM's advanced hardware has been improved and it does its job even better and faster. All three operating systems run equally well on IBM's most advanced processor chip, the IBM Power 6. There are no constraints left and there is no reason why the new Power Box cannot run any of the three operating systems anytime.

The IBM marketing team likes to point out that it is now even easier to take advantage of a single, energy efficient and easy-to-deploy platform for all of your UNIX, Linux and IBM i applications. By the way, there are over 15,000 available across all three operating platforms and you can still run all three operating systems together sharing one processor. And if you like, IBM i can be in control of all three. So, nothing was lost in the transition. Flexibility was gained and a better name was brought forth for the Power 6 based hardware.

If this book were about hardware, there would be an awful lot to talk about. Along with the new IBM Power Systems hardware in the traditional shaped IBM black boxes, Big Blue also brought forth a very impressive combo blade server. It is one of several new blade servers that IBM announced but, it is actually a technological phenomenon unto itself.

The new IBM BladeCenter® JS12 comes with industrial strength virtualization provided by a new firmware facility called PowerVM™. Six different blades with each blade having up to four processors can share the virtualized I/O subsystem via the new virtual technologies. A number of Intel and AMD X64 blades were announced concurrently enabling this combo box to run Windows, Unix, Linux, and IBM i on multiple processors on multiple blades sharing the same storage area network. Being a tech guy for so many years, I am hard to impress. If I were not writing about the all-everything operating system in this book, I would be telling you even more about this first foray into blades for Power 6 and IBM i. This is the first of many to come so, be ready to be impressed.

IBM designed the new systems and the combo blade servers to help its small and mid-sized clients focus on running their businesses instead of their computers. Since many IT shops use Windows, Unix, and Linux, having one box that runs all three equally well helps make it easier for the business. So, there is no longer a need to fight heterogeneous computing.

IBM's hardware offerings are now built to make them all run in harmony and peace. Blade Center has achieved much of this in its first outing. Watch for more.

System i Shops Have Nothing to Fear

To many who had watched the IBM System/38 become the AS/400 and then continued to watch as it became the System i platform, the elimination of an integrated platform name for the hardware and the software may make it seem that the all-everything machine has gone away. This is not true. The all-everything machine is no longer a single named entity. It is now a combination of the best hardware IBM makes (IBM Power Systems) and the best operating system IBM makes (IBM i.) It is as good as ever and with Power 6, it is even better.

IBM's investment continues in the platform. Even before the hardware merge of April, 2008, by the time March 2008 had rolled around, IBM had already made available its major new version of the all-everything operating system with many new and powerful enhancements. It was released as IBM i 6.1, and according to industry experts, with the investment shown in this release, IBM again demonstrated that it will continue to deliver and enhance the integrated operating system that AS/400™, iSeries and System i clients have valued for well over two decades.

As you will learn in this book, there are many, many reasons why, now, though separated from a hardware platform per se by name, this newly named advanced operating system called IBM i has become even better, warranting its description in this book as the all-time best, the all-everything operating system. Just as I called the all-everything machine a treat back in 2005 with my book of the same name, the all-everything operating system is even a bigger treat. Eggplant anyone?

He Thought Chicago Was a Treat!

In the 1966 song by Norman Greenbaum titled: "The Eggplant that Ate Chicago," an Eggplant comes in from Outer Space and lands in Chicago. That's Chicago, as in Illinois, as in the home of the 44th president of the United States. Fortuitously for him, as the song goes, upon landing, the amorphous Eggplant thought Chicago was a sweet treat, "it was just like sugar." This song comes to mind again as I think about the best way to introduce the all-everything operating system.

If an alien race came to earth and evaluated our state in computer evolution and picked a winner, it would be the IBM i operating system, a.k.a., the all-everything operating system. The IBM Power System hardware from which the OS gains some of its integration strength would win, the all-everything operating system would win and if somebody could convince the aliens to pay for what they take, IBM would win as they would make a lot of dough. If our friend, "the Eggplant" were part of the alien expedition, it's a sure thing that he would find that the IBM i Operating System is really sweet.

> Note; for you Eggplant lovers, I have included the words to this 1966 hit at the back of the chapter.

Hardware

Though the OS is no longer packaged with the hardware, the hardware is fully enabling and continues to facilitate the integration with the IBM i operating system. If any combination of hardware and operating system ever came close to pure business value it would be the all-everything operating system on the IBM Power System. Since 1978, IBM has been packaging instructions on the chip and in firmware as it created the most advanced complete system in the universe.

With regard to hardware scalability, reliability, availability, security, ease of use, flexibility, self-management, self-diagnosis, and much, much more, the Power System with IBM i has been and will continue to be a winner in every category. It is the only server / operating system combo today that supports applications and data using 128 bit addressing with security integrated into the machine. But, who's counting?

Software

Carrying the facilities even further, the power of this box has always come from the operating system. With regard to software scalability, reliability, availability, security, ease of use, self-management, self-optimization, and self-diagnosis, again, IBM i would be the winner in all categories. Throw in an integrated relational database, integrated transaction processing, built-in productivity tools, development tools, middleware, and even more and, to borrow a phrase, it's all shock and awe. Mostly awe.

The IBM i OS has it all. In fact, it is the only operating system that fully supports applications with 128 bit addressing running on 64-bit hardware. As a point of note, its predecessors, i5/OS, OS/400, and CPF (System/38), had been doing that for almost thirty years. The earliest versions of CPF and OS/400 used 48-bit hardware running at an abstracted 128-bit software level.

Yes, the capabilities of an all-everything operating system do exist on planet Earth and through its great grandparents, CPF, OS/400, and i5/OS, they have been here since 1978.

The all-everything operating system removes real software limits as to the number of jobs, threads, transactions or data that can be active in the system. Even an Eggplant could tell that there isn't another operating system on the face of the earth that comes close.

Unmatched Elegance

The Secret is now out. The all-everything operating system is an IBM OS called IBM i and it is designed for business. Of course, I do not expect anybody to take my word for that, so I have fourteen more chapters in which to tell you about the past, the present and the future of this remarkably advanced, powerful, and durable operating system.

For a commercial operating system to be the one and only all-everything operating system, it would have to have an internal elegance unmatched by any other hardware/software combination, and better than that, it would have to be miles and years ahead of anything else that has ever been built. If distance were a real factor in computing, the IBM i operating system would register at many times the distance from the sun and back. It would be way ahead of its competition if for no other reason that its address / pointer space is so humungous.

While other platforms continue to struggle with addressability and forced software rewrites for upgrades, IBM i software, like the Energizer Bunny, just keeps running and running and running, even as the underlying architecture and the hardware change. Time is a real factor and as you will see, the IBM i is more than thirty years ahead of the competition. Nobody can touch it. But that is not all, as hard as it may seem to believe, the competition still is not catching up because, quite frankly, it would cost them too much.

There is a saying in IBM i user circles that only IBM could have afforded to build a system with internal integration of chip functions and software that is so rich in advanced computer science. In many ways, this explains why no other OS vendor, including the mighty Microsoft, has ever, nor can ever, take on the task of building such an advanced operating system from scratch. They simply cannot afford it.

In Chapter 10, you will learn in detail about the advanced architectural underpinnings of IBM i. It's a good read for the neophyte and the expert alike. In Chapter 10, you will see how the six fundamental advanced computer science concepts upon which IBM i is based make the platform the all-everything operating system. No other vendor, at any time, has ever come close to building an all-everything operating system and the reason is simple. They cannot afford the unique combination of chip-enabled functions and the advanced software architecture that is at the heart of this operating system.

Computer Science Research Project

Some might argue that the closest thing to IBM i is an experimental "machine" developed at University of Pennsylvania, which later moved to the laboratory of John Hopkins University. It is called EROS, which stands for Extremely Reliable Operating System. You can learn more about the capabilities of EROS at the following URL:

`http://www.eros-os.org/`

> Note: In all fairness and for full disclosure, EROS is no longer an active project and has been succeeded by Coyotos and CapROS, neither of which have reached any measurable commercial success. Their concepts are based on those in EROS and thus this discussion about EROS continues to have merit.

Unlike the IBM System i, AS/400, System/38, as well as the IBM Power System with IBM i, EROS, for all its goodness, is not integrated with a machine or a chipset. It is just pure software. EROS and its successors are more or less experimental operating systems used for pure research into several of the most advanced computer concepts that have ever been brought forth by the computer science community. These include object orientation, single level store, and security capabilities.

EROS and its successors run on standard fare x86 / x64 boxes from 486 up. Because EROS is just an experimental OS, it does not have its own hardware base and thus it is not and cannot be a fully integrated machine. Intel has not added capabilities and instructions to its chipsets to better support EROS. Additionally, EROS cannot have a fully developed technology independent machine interface, integrated transaction processing, or an integrated relational database.

Compared to the IBM i operating system, available since 1978 in one form or another, EROS is a partial implementation. EROS and its successors, however, is the closest thing out there. All of these advanced computer science notions are explained in Chapter 10.

Though special indeed and the basis for EROS sponsor Jonathan Shapiro's doctoral thesis, the project was nowhere close to making it to commercial prime time. Your neighbors won't be getting one in the near future or the distant future. The same goes for EROS' successors. However, and I repeat, it is the only operating system other than IBM i, even in experimental stages, that attempts to use the most advanced computer science concepts as its basis. Windows and Unix and Linux and Solaris don't even bother. They'd have to be rewritten to participate in this advanced computer science game and this will never happen. For as often as Microsoft rewrites operating systems, you would think they would work to get it right once and for all.

Having the most advanced experimental OS projects in the world, studied at the most prestigious computer science academic institutions in the world, as the closest thing to the all-everything operating system can give IBM a great sense of accomplishment. IBM has taken the advanced concepts and used them as the basis upon which to build IBM i as a commercial quality product. That means that IBM i has implemented, commercially, the facilities about which OS projects such as EROS continue to dream. The designers and builders of IBM i in Rochester, Minnesota should take a great sense of pride in this accomplishment. IBM i is no ordinary operating system.

Research vs. Reality

Yes, you heard me right, the closest thing to an IBM i is a project in a research lab that just needs a few more billion in research dollars to become a real commercial operating system. However, nobody, including Bill Gates, is lining up with those billions. Meanwhile, this humble OS called IBM i, built in an IBM Lab located in Rochester Minnesota, originally intended for use in small to medium sized business, has all six of the most advanced computer science attributes ever conceived. And the boxes that this OS runs on go from mom and pop size to systems larger and more powerful than mainframes.

While the theorists were theorizing, IBM actually built a machine and an OS, thirty years ago, that does all of the things that were in their theories plus lots more. The IBM Power System hardware that is used with IBM i is the tenth generation of this technology and it is without doubt the finest computer science machine and OS combo that has ever been built. The most advanced computer science research projects in the world are not as far along as the IBM System/38 that was announced by IBM way back in 1978.

Unmatched World Leadership

The integration of chipset functions on the IBM Power Systems and the IBM i OS lead IBM and the rest of the world in advanced computing.

Viva La Eggplant

By the way, Norman Greenbaum, the Eggplant song's writer also had another outer spaced theme hit, "Sprit in the Sky," which was very popular. In Figure 1-3, we show the Amazon.com picture of Greenbaum that you get when you click on the "Eggplant that Ate Chicago" in his Spirit in the Sky album. And, now, the sweet all-everything operating system is at its lifetime sweet spot, just waiting for the Eggplant invasion. Before I present the words to the song, I thought you would like to see the picture of Greenbaum checking out nature. Here is a YouTube link, so that you can listen to this long forgotten, yet wonderful oldie:

Figure 1-3 Norman Greenbaum Waiting for the Eggplant

http://www.youtube.com/watch?v=b-Lc0Lra9cI
Words to song second last section

Chapter 2   The Value of Great Operating Systems

Who Cares?

To many business people, it really does not matter that there is an operating system under the covers of their business computer. They know next to nothing about it and care nothing unless it does not work. So, if the operating system were the all-everything operating system, it still would not matter -- even if it were the best at everything that it does.

On the other hand, if the user of the system had some computer savvy such as the infamous "computer people" or they were a knowledge worker in an organization in which information was key, they would notice if the all everything operating system were in charge. The fact is that most business people just are not interested. They do not care about the special features of the OS. They don't even want to know that there are even more benefits when the OS is combined with the IBM Power System hardware. They do not have the time and to repeat, they simply do not want to know what makes the all-everything OS so special. Their business is business, not Information Technology (IT).

However, to the extent that having a particular operating system feature adds real business value, and not having it subtracts from business value, there would be interest. The fact is that there are plenty of reasons for business managers and entrepreneurs to want to know more about their business operating system. This chapter demonstrates the value that an all-everything OS can deliver to a business. .

Who Needs the All-Everything OS?

In the rest of the book, while examining the notion of the value of an operating system to a business, and how to realize its value, I hope to whet your appetite for the all-everything operating system by outlining a number of business benefits for a company using the IBM i OS. Following the business value factors, for the technical at heart, there is plenty of opportunity to examine an exhaustive list of technical capabilities and benefits that are associated only with the all-everything operating system.

We discussed in Chapter 1 that in early 2008, IBM introduced a new all-everything operating system called IBM i. This all-everything operating system runs on IBM's newest Power Systems machines. These were introduced at the same time that the former IBM System i and System p boxes were sent to pasture and the new iteration of the operating system was christened as IBM i.

So, there is no longer one term to describe an all-everything machine in IBM. That being said, it is OK to use the OS name, IBM I, in its place, just as we might use the term Windows machine. Though this work horse using the best hardware and best OS no longer has just one name, it is lots more capable and more powerful than the whole team of what is now known as the Stella Artois Clydesdales.

Generic Value of Computers

> Note: I would like to acknowledge the fine works of Paul A. Strassman, former VP of the Information Products Group at Xerox Corporation. Paul A. Strassman has written a number of IT Management books and has expressed concerns regarding attempts to quantify IT value. He is a refreshing author and his many books, including **Information Payoff**, McMillan, 1985, have helped convince me and many others that we have been right all along.

There is no question that in the 21st century, operations in most large corporations would rapidly grind to a halt if their computers ceased to function. The sustenance of all advanced information-oriented societies now rests on the proper functioning of small and large processors that control everything from electric power, telecommunications, financial services, and energy-supply enterprises. We are quite vulnerable to a deliberate attack on the very software that operates our information infrastructure in the form of information warfare or hackers with a mission.

But, do not fret. As bad as it is for IBM that nobody even knows about the impregnable AS/400 heritage machines and now the IBM i operating system, nobody knows enough about what the all-everything OS is all about to even consider an attack.

Large and small systems and desktop PCs are only tools. Though business blessings do come forth from these tools, the blessings are not unqualified. You may have witnessed in your own career seemingly identical machines with identical software performing admirably in one company, yet when deployed in another organization they actually make things worse. A quick investigation into the matter and more than likely you would find inferior management and personnel without proper training. It all starts with management in just about anything.

Better Management Makes a Great System Even Better

If a company puts out a bum product, management must take the rap. Likewise if a company cannot use IT effectively, management again must take the rap. Certainly computers enhance sound business practices, but they also intensify inefficiencies whenever the user community is disorganized and unresponsive to customers' needs.

Ironically, the best computer technologies will always add unnecessary costs to a poorly managed firm. The problem is not the inherent capabilities of the technologies, which may be in a word, overwhelming. The problem, historically, is management's inability to use the tools effectively. For instance, there have been various studies by think tanks that contend that as much as seventy percent of IT projects have not delivered their expected benefits. Since this is true, why would we not see more firings in these industries? Perhaps failure is expected.

A major cause of the failings of companies is well documented. Many organizations have been unsuccessful in integrating the results of their efforts into day to day work processes. In reviewing these findings, a number of top corporate executives share the same opinion.

CEOs and COOs and even CIOs complain that there is no correlation between IT expenditures and corporate profits. Yet, sometimes in some companies there appears to be and actually there might be a correlation. How can this be? Though "all men are created equal," the human condition permits and delivers broad variances in our performance in given areas. If the machines are the same and the software is the same, then the problem is with the human beings. The problem is with the bodies and minds, the feet and hands and arms and legs, starting with management and working down. The key point here again is that it starts with management.

Douglas McGregor's Theory X and Theory Y models of management style suggest that there are some managers who trust and give general direction and there are others who have none too little trust and they give micro-directions. Business productivity has roots in well organized, well-motivated, and knowledgeable people who understand what to do with all of the information that shows up on their computer screens. This would be a Theory Y type management scenario. Such excellence does not prevail so frequently in Theory X businesses and that may explain why in a number of companies, there is no correlation between IT expenditures and profit. In those companies, it is unrealistic to expect that computerization could ever change that.

Prove the Relationship

In Theory Y organizations, business executives, as well as computer experts, typically recognize that the fortunes of the enterprise originate with the people who administer, coordinate, and manage employees, suppliers, and customers. Let's say that on the average, the cost of computerization equals less than one-fiftieth of revenues (<2%). Therefore, it does not make sense for top management to demand that the IT Manager prove how computer budgets relate directly to profits. The best that the implementation of a fully functional computer system can provide is to make the knowledge workers be more effective and more efficient – whether there is a correlation to the bottom line or not. And, of course in most cases there is but, it is difficult to track.

The experts suggest that this relationship between corporate profitability and computer spending has been like this for quite some time. It is not a recent phenomenon. From this, it is easy to conclude that it is unlikely that any direct relationship between computerization and profitability will magically appear in the future. Computers are only tools for change, hopefully for the better. However, observation shows that identically trained people in different organizations can come to opposite conclusions from an examination of data obtained by identical means. What matters then is not the provision of information on a computer screen. Good software can do that. What matters are the knowledgeable actions workers take with the information they are given.

There is no question that all computer systems, if deployed properly, have a great potential to provide information. However, because of the human condition, managers may very well misuse that potential. Thus, one might conclude that the effective and profitable use of information technology does not begin with a better understanding of hardware or software; it comes from knowledge workers having a better understanding of their respective organizations, their goals, and their strategies.

As a concluding thought on the business value of IT, it is still propitious to align IT with the business. It does not matter what technology is in play. Once aligned, the measurements are not so simple. You can forget about productivity, improved customer satisfaction and quality as IT measurements. The way to measure IT's alignment with business goals is to gauge IT's impact on the one metric that matters most to CEOs and shareholders: net cash flow. The bottom line is that alignment comes down to accounting and "the bottom line." It's that simple.

The Feature du Jour Approach to Computer Selection

What does all this have to do with an all-everything operating system? We're working up to that. Let's first look at a few typical scenarios and issues that may be at work in companies that do not have the luxury of using an all-everything operating system.

A risk in the deployment of IT is the notion of the system or feature du jour. There are such systems out there, and you probably know of them. They change their features and their look and feel every couple years and then by pulling support or by psychologically swaying the masses that their old wares are inadequate, they get to sell the same thing, new and improved, again and again and most often for more money. Rarely do businesses fight back. However, perhaps even this paradigm may be changing as the recent introduction of Windows Vista and it's gratuitous differences for the sake of difference caused many companies to push back, stop, and rethink their plans. Microsoft changed its ways and now with Windows 10, there are few complaints.

Most businesses are not in the computer business and their executives do not want to be in the computer business. So the executives rely on a team of inside employees and outside consultants. Most of these have been certified to protect the business opportunities of the computer company however, and not the opportunities of the business firm.

Unfortunately, this certified team is not certified to find the best solution for the company and most of the time, they are not even so inclined. They know one thing and the one thing they know is what they ultimately recommend and it is what the company ultimately buys. They believe they are right without even looking elsewhere. The all-everything operating system is rarely considered, as the certified experts in most businesses are certified in making Microsoft products work, not in what may ultimately be the best course of action for the business..

Give Me Exactly What I Know!

What often happens in these ad hoc scenarios is that companies end up with a proliferation (mish-mash) of incompatible systems that rapidly grow obsolete as the business or organization changes. Strassmann calls these the 'build and junk' solutions. In these situations, there is often no room for new thought because the pattern of computing, successful or not, dependable or not, has been in place for some time and the voices supporting that equipment, the change brokers in the organization, actually do not want to change themselves.

Thus a truly innovative and affordable solution – software and hardware -- would be left on the table because it would not be compatible with the current mindset of the firm's IT advisors. In many ways, that is why the all-everything operating system is not so well known in many small to medium sized businesses. It does not matter how good it is. Nobody wants to hear about it - even the very IT advisors on whom the organization depends.

In addition to the mindset that espouses the short term "build and junk" solutions that continually patch one deficiency and create another, there is a similar mindset with software function that has been delivering its payday for years without issues. Because anything that has been running on a computer for more than five years can be disparaged as "legacy" by the young Turks who often provide the prevailing thought in small to medium sized businesses, companies often find themselves pushed to eliminate the old and move on with the new, just because it is "new." What's wrong with "build and keep?"

More often than not, new means Microsoft and anything else is old. Microsoft, of course does not like to tell you that its own OS roots are well over 25 years old. Despite the pressure to replace, there is hard evidence that older applications and platforms still work fine and it is not hard to find them providing value every day in most organizations. However, if you will pardon me, it is not politically correct.

Coincidentally, software built for the great grandfather of the IBM i OS, over thirty years ago, still runs on today's all-everything operating system. And, believe it or not, it is difficult to convince some people that this is an advantage, not a disadvantage, no matter who is doing the talking.

Before we get a little deeper into the notion of Business Value, let's talk about an industry that needs the most productive and the most reliable computers in order for its business to function. This industry has to keep track of every penny and nothing, and let me repeat, nothing, can go wrong. Already, if you know something about Windows servers, you are saying to yourself that such units need not apply in this industry and for the most part, they don't.

The Casino Industry Demands Technology Excellence

If you own a casino in Las Vegas, you are more than likely a millionaire but that's not what this book is about so we won't go there. To protect your millions and the millions more that you hope to collect, you have little concern about hurricanes or even blizzards in the Las Vegas desert community; but, you certainly are concerned every day and every night that operations continue to function. So, from your computer systems, you demand continuous availability, a must in the round-the-clock casino industry.

So, how do Casinos prevent a shutdown? The answer is simple. As part of their overall system strategy, they use the all-everything operating system running on IBM Power System hardware and they have been doing so for about 20 years. It all started in Atlantic City and in Chapter 15, I have included an interview with a friend of mine and former fellow IBM Systems Engineer, Bob Morici. Bob designed and implemented the first high availability systems running back then using the all-everything operating system for Bally's in Atlantic City. News spread like a contagion and the AS/400 became the go-to machine for casinos across the world.

Does uptime matter to a business? Ask Steve Wynn of the Casino with the same name. One of the few defections to Windows, Wynn, reportedly a friend of billionaire Bill Gates, chose Windows for his casino solution. This was widely reported by the press and if successful, it was feared that other IBM i installations might also follow. Many saw this as an inevitable erosion from IBM technology to Microsoft.

Nobody is talking about this openly but the rumor is that a few years ago, not too long after the Wynn was up and running without any IBM i units to protect it from disaster, the whole shebang went down deader than a door-nail. As noted previously, the casino gaming industry requires stable, secure, and scalable solutions and infrastructure to support their mission-critical, 24/7 operations, and before Wynn, the go-to system had always been the IBM Power system running IBM i.

After Wynn selected Microsoft and Intel, business was not quite as certain for IBM's marketing teams. But after the rumor was spread, that the Wynn was down hard and for forty hours their people could not even book a guest into their hotel and their registers could not open for money, the word was that operations were in chaos. I've hear nothing about this since and have had no verification but I had heard it from an IBM guy as I recall at a seminar. If this is true, I can see why IBM would use this event as its reference event for those who might stray from the high availability, all-everything operating system environment. Having my own experience with Windows, it certainly is believable.

IBM i Runs 96% of Las Vegas

The fact is that the IBM i operating system and IBM Power System hardware runs 96% of Las Vegas. In addition to reliability in the OS and the hardware, a duplicate system mirrors transactions in real-time and tapes go out 24-by-7, in armored trucks, to a facility unknown even to the IT directors. I would not even know how to find the name of this facility but, I know it exists. You can bet the backup company also uses AS/400 heritage technology

Though seemingly impregnable, nobody actually thinks that that the solid performance of the IBM i operating system and the casino software environment means that the hardware systems, operating systems, and application systems are invulnerable. But, it would take something like a 9/11 attack to create a major issue and even then the off premise backup tapes would save the day. IT managers challenged for an answer to this potential danger suggest that they would get another Power System from IBM almost immediately and they would get it running in a fallout shelter if real disaster ever happens.

The Venetian is an example of IBM i reliability with multiple AS/400 heritage systems that run the hotel, casino, slots, inventory, purchasing, reservations, financial, accounting, payroll, as well as time and attendance applications. There is no way that a manual processes can duplicate the automated ones that perform specially designed functions such as tracking guests' room accommodations, gaming-table winnings, loyalty-points accumulations, comp-cards, and personal preferences such as the type of meals or entertainment individual guests enjoy. The system really "can't" go down but if it does, even without a natural disaster, there is a disaster.

AS/400 heritage systems with IBM i have a history of better than 99.5% availability for one system. With mirrored disk drives this is substantially increased closer to 99.9% This may be OK for some, but if a system were down for a half day, or forty hours as was rumored to be the case of the Wynn a few years back, it really could be devastating. The losses from manual processes and procedures would add up very quickly. Consequently, casinos most often run two IBM Power Systems with IBM i, rather than one. This pushes availability through the roof or as the math majors would say, it asymptotically approaches 100% availability.

The integrated database on the system and its advanced binary radix tree and other indexing schemes even keep the indexes available for instant retrieval. Unlike other systems, they do not have to be constantly shut down for rebuilding. So, a casino player can be sure that his or her loyalty cards or as casinos call them, comp cards, are updated instantly and the database is always up-to-date on both machines simultaneously. You know that if you are a playing customer and you don't get your points on your account immediately, you start losing faith and it impacts how happy you may be in continuing to play at a particular casino. So, to keep the smiles, updates are instantaneous and simultaneous.

They Run their Business on IBM i

I have my own experience in the Casino Industry as I had the pleasure of providing advanced education to the IT Directors of the Circus Circus properties in Las Vegas and Lake Tahoe several years back. Circus Circus has recently been taken over by MGM/Mirage but, they still use the IBM i platform to keep their casinos running. Having five IT Directors in the same room is a challenge for anybody and teaching these top dogs in their field anything they do not already know is another challenge. Yet, none of these directors were challenged when they offered the ultimate compliment for the all-everything operating system driving their business systems. They quickly noted, "We run our business on it." That says it all.

They also took note that system packaging is self-contained, highly reliable, and it reduces their most critical cost – people. It is easy to manage because it is so tightly integrated. This reduces the people cost and the people cost is the highest cost in running just about any service business so, casino IT managers choose the IBM i platform not just because it does not go down. A pencil doesn't go down either but I would not run my business on a pencil. Casino IT Managers like the IBM i platform because it has unique properties that enable them to devise better solutions to run the business, implement those solutions, and be assured of continual high performance and of course, availability.

Keep Your Wallet Open

The fact is that it is the tight, sometimes hard-wired, integration between hardware, operating system, database, and applications that permits the most demanding IT clients to avoid management costs that can be ten times the cost of the system. Numerous Las Vegas IT Directors note that it is their humble opinion that if they were forced to use Unix or even the Windows platform, the IT cost would be ten times higher because of all the people involvement -- involvement that is not needed in an IBM i shop.

IBM i IT Directors in casinos and in other industries will tell you that each IBM Power System running IBM i typically carries an up-front price of a few hundred thousand dollars. The up-front cost of Intel hardware is less but when the Windows licenses are added up, the cost gets closer but, is still typically less than the more reliable IBM i hardware and system software.

On other platforms; however, as well known by savvy and experienced IBM i IT Directors, the management, development, and maintenance costs often end up costing millions of dollars each year. Again, seven times the cost of an IBM i shop for those who are counting.

IBM i has become the de-facto high-availability operating system and server system for the Las Vegas and the Atlantic City casino industry because it is designed to run packaged applications with minimal programming and maintenance. Even the larger Casinos often managed by Native Americans choose the IBM i way. The Mohegan Sun at Pocono Casino near my home town of Wilkes-Barre, PA, for example, is proud to use IBM i and IBM Power Systems technology, and their IT staffs are relatively small when compared to other major companies.

Agility is Important to Casinos

Making the AS/400 heritage machines the best choice for the long haul is its flexibility in responding to new requests for data from its integrated database. One of the factors pressing on this industry, as it has for many others, is the constant and vigilant attention that casinos must pay to regulatory compliance. Unlike the financial auditors in the collapsed US financial system who seem to have been on vacation the last several years, the auditors from the Nevada, New Jersey, and other state gaming commissions don't mess around, and they are always trying to get new information. Because of this, their regulations change quite frequently.

Non-compliance is not an option so this task keeps IT staffs on their toes. Thus, the scalability and flexibility of the IBM i platform is a high priority item. Add the strength of IBM as a partner to the casino industry and you have an unbeatable team. The IBM i systems perform as expected, 24 by 7 by 52, so that the casinos can serve not only the regulatory bodies that license them but also, the players and the guests who provide the revenue, all in a way that helps differentiate them as leaders in their market. IBM i's powerful development tools also enable casino IT shops to keep providing more service with the continual mission of outpacing the competition. For the casino industry, that is pure business value.

IBM i Apps for Casinos Provide Value

Software vendors such as Inter-American Data for hotel applications, Stratton Warren Software for inventory management, Infinium Software for financials, and Agilsys for lodging management, have for years been writing low-maintenance products that run on the IBM i systems. IBM i fits perfectly into the casinos' game plans. By selecting IBM i, casino operators have shown that they would rather spend money on promoting their gaming properties than on staffing for IT. They might even tell you that you can bet the house on that.

Betting the House

Whether the mission is a system that is good enough for casinos or a system good enough for any business from Hospitals to Banks to any business needing a good ERP or CRM platform, IBM i more than gets the job done. Forget about the feature du jour style of computing when with IBM i you get a platform and a means of creating and using applications until the applications no longer make sense for your business. That's when to change, not when Microsoft needs to sell its next OS version.

Regardless of what industry your company may play in, knowing that the casino industry by more than 19 to 1 pick the IBM i style of computing because it delivers the bacon and it does not go down, you might want to ask yourself what kind of business value that provides. Platforms that are not available when you need them do not serve the needs of the business. Not only does IBM i provide value to casinos and other industries which choose its style of computing, it does so with one of the highest availability ratings of any system in the universe. There's another thing on which you can bet the house and you can bet you will win great value for your bet.

In the next chapter, we discuss some specifics about the kind of value that you can expect from the best business operating system in the business, IBM i (for Business).

Chapter 3   Does an Operating System Add Business Value?

Realizing the Benefits of Computing

The chanting by industry analysts for years, "not to worry because computers deliver competitive gains, speed up business transactions, increase customer satisfaction, deliver superior quality, and lead to improved profitability," has become generally accepted wisdom. But sometimes, if the applications are not hosted on the right systems or servers, regardless of the quantity or quality of the chanting, the benefits are never realized. Gaining the benefits from your system or server is not a given. When you do not gain from your computing experience, quite often, it is because the operating system has major limitations and does not offer you the benefits, the scale, and the reliability to meet your needs.

The question as to whether IT provides business value as noted in the prior chapter has spawned much activity in management circles over time, and even more just recently. The question is not how much return on investment for projects, and especially information technology projects, is provided by IT, but whether there is any ROI at all for IT efforts. Many of the managers and academicians and analysts who have offered their thoughts on the subject seem to have concluded that as necessary as it is, IT implementations often do not add to business value in any meaningful way. It's almost like how the opposite sexes sometimes describe themselves. You can't live with computer systems but, you also can't live without them.

Strassmann affirms this thinking. The theory goes that as IT analysts and technicians streamline a given area of the firm using technology, a significant portion of the ROI, if the project is successful, comes about because the productivity cogs of the former system have been eliminated, and these could theoretically have been eliminated without the use of major technology.

I do not share this doom and gloom view of the inherent value of IT. However, there are many very poor implementations in businesses for many different reasons. In my own backyard, I have observed companies and organizations in which managers could not accept that a desktop PC was not intended to be the IT panacea server for the organization. At about $1500 per box, it would be nice if that was all that needed to be successful. Rarely to never could such a small investment bring home huge technology benefits. And it doesn't happen with the next $1500 purchase either. In fact, the truth is that it never happens, regardless of the number of 'servers' the company buys.

I tell my clients and my students and you will hear it in this book, "The system makes a difference." And I also tell them "Not all computer systems and operating systems are created equal." You'd think that they would already know that but, the fact is, some just don't. Today, very few people in my industry even use the word "system" to refer to the computers and operating systems that are used to run the business from the back rooms of the organization. Instead, they call them *servers*. Even IBM, for a number of years used the word server in their terms, but in the last several years, Big Blue has gone back to basics and a system is again a system.

A system is much more than just a server and IBM has always made systems. A system, in its most simple definition, is a group of interrelated parts working together as a whole. An IBM Power System running IBM i is a full system with an all-everything OS and it is also a very capable server for multiple purposes. Any other "server," especially a Windows server is merely a component within a system. However, such a server, or even a desktop client masquerading as a server, is often sold as a do-it-all server. My experience is that all is well in this environment until you want to do something else – then you need a second server. Then, a third... Soon, just like that, you've bought the farm.

The Other Side of the Mountain

So, we might conclude from our reading so far in this book that there is business value to be gained from good IT investments. However, without a hefty fee, even Lloyds of London will not assure that any value will be realized. Nor can they!

So far, for example, we have learned that the management of the organization and their expressed desire to succeed in IT projects has a major bearing on IT success or failure. We have also learned about Strassmann's notion of 'build and junk' solutions. Additionally, we learned that there are times when the IT professionals in an organization have more important things on their agenda than the welfare of the firm. Unfortunately, they may not even know it. A simple self-test for these IT folks would be if every decision they make favors their personal certifications.

Please know that I am not trying to cast aspersions on the character of IT personnel. However, I am a believer in the philosophy espoused by the great U.S. General George Patton who once said, "When everyone is thinking the same thing, somebody is not thinking!" I submit that many of the Windows certified experts, systems programmers in my personal vernacular, remind me of the little boy who never saw the other side of the mountain. Because he liked the side of the mountain he was on, he concluded (imagined) that the other side of the mountain was ugly and barren and not worthy of even visiting. Yet, he had never seen that side of the mountain.

I run my personal business on two desktop PCs. One is backup for the other. I would love to have a business large enough to be able to afford an IBM Power System with IBM i and some businesses automating integrated software. I know the platform and I know how much better life could be for me at tax time and at other times when I would like a snapshot. But, I live on the leeward side of the IT mountain- thankful for every macro Excel provides. I, too, use the Microsoft style of computing for the simple things necessary to run my very small one-person consulting business. And, of course, I have helped my clients install Windows servers both inside the IBM i complex and externally. Though I know where I want to live, I do feel I know both sides of the mountain.

Many of my peers stay on the Microsoft side of the mountain or the Unix side of the mountain. They know nothing about the IBM i side and they never care to find out. Instead, they have concluded, just as the boy on the "good side" of the mountain, that there is no reason to even know what is on the other side. Because they have already thought it through and because neither IBM nor the Windows dominated press gives them any reason to look any further than Redmond, Washington for their business solutions, they choose not to look at IBM i. It does not matter if IBM i is the best possible solution to so many ills that their company may be facing. They will never know that the all-everything operating system may be the perfect solution.

Thus, in most Windows shops, the continual demand for funding is for more Windows servers, faster servers, and more people to support the servers. Obviously, for them, just like the boy on the good side of the mountain, there is no other way.

However stacked the deck may be in favor of Microsoft and Intel in most IT shops today, I would not be telling the full truth if I ignored the fact that this results from there being no compelling reason to look at an IBM i platform as a real business solution for small businesses. Most businesses who should be driving their IT shop with an IBM i based system have never heard of the AS/400 or IBM i. The "uninformed" Microsoft certified IT staff sees no value in messing up the mix by looking at non Microsoft servers even if there may be the possibility for management to better realize the rewards of their investments.

Quite frankly, I can't blame the Windows certified professionals out here. They really don't know that there is better water to carry than Windows if that is their only game. Again, that's why I wrote this book. I expect and to a lesser degree hope that the Microsoft side will want to know about the all-everything operating system so that they can advise their management that there is more out there than that to which they are accustomed... and it may even be lots better.

The system actually does make a difference.

ERP Provides Business Value

The business value factors and the technical factors that we are about to discuss and which are highlighted in this book differentiate an IBM i based system from all other systems. It is no wonder that the all everything operating system is the dominant platform used for Enterprise Resource Planning (ERP). It is the best environment and ERP is the defining business application for most companies. It is the all-everything application and it is not too coincidental that the most implementations and the most successful ERP implementations run on the IBM Power System family of computers with IBM i as the main operating system.

> Note: What is ERP?-- Enterprise Resource Planning is software that provides a business management system as a solution that integrates all facets of the business, including planning, manufacturing, sales, and marketing. As the ERP methodology has become more popular, software applications have emerged to help business managers implement ERP in business activities such as inventory control, order tracking, customer service, finance and human resources. IBM i based systems are the industry leaders in providing ERP solutions to small to medium sized businesses. Yet very large companies, such as Costco and

Nintendo of America have also found the IBM i platform perfectly suited for their business needs.

ERP and IBM i -- Unbeatable

ERP is now being hailed as a foundation for the integration of organization-wide information systems. ERP systems link together the operations of entire organizations, such as accounting, finance, human resources, manufacturing, distribution, and more. Moreover, they also connect the organization to its customers and suppliers through the different stages of the product or the process life cycle with Supply Chain Management (SCM) and Customer Relationship Management (CRM).

ERP systems come with many modules. However, the most significant modules, where the majority of business value is achieved are as follows:

1. Inventory Management and Control
2. Order Entry
3. Billing / Pricing / Accounts Receivable
4. Purchasing / Accounts Payable / General Ledger
5. Production Management
6. Human Resources / Payroll

Besides all the benefits of the individual modules, and despite how a given company does business, the overall benefit attributed to an ERP package is the connectivity of information. In other words, the modules, when deployed are integrated such that the output of one module - order entry for example, feeds many others, such as billing, inventory control, accounts receivable, and sales applications. There are no rough edges. Each module knows how to "talk" to each other module, and the modules understand each other. That's integration and there is a whole lot of business value to that notion alone. Considering that the "i" in IBM i means integration, it is easy to see why IBM i is the preferred platform for ERP.

The Benefits of ERP and IBM i

In addressing the notion of the business value of a computer system, it makes sense to see what software that machine is running. Since most companies that automate do so to help their business run more smoothly, the typical business applications such as order entry, billing, account receivable, etc. are most often first to be implemented.

This is how it is regardless of whether the applications are part of a big ERP system or not. Therefore, we can say that the business value of any computer system is the value provided by its applications, such as ERP. So, rather than begin a discussion about system oriented features that provide business value, we can simply use the benefits of ERP systems as our guide to business value. After all, it is the combination of the ERP system and the IBM i operating system that bring those business benefits home.

Four generic objectives that companies have, when they implement ERP, are as follows:

1. To improve responsibilities in relation to customers
2. To strengthen supply chain partnerships
3. To enhance organizational flexibility
4. To improve decision-making capabilities

From these objectives, companies have more specific motivations. Though these motivations do not equate to hard dollars, the most common generic reasons for which businesses implement ERP are as follows:

1. Need for common platform, (such as an IBM i based system) with the intent to replace innumerable smaller systems (such as Windows servers).
2. Process improvement expected from the implementation
3. Data visibility that could be used to improve operating decisions
4. Operational cost reductions
5. Increased customer responsiveness in operations
6. Improved strategic decision making

Moving down the chain of rationale, for implementation, there are five major and specific reasons why companies undertake ERP projects.

1. Integrate financial information
2. Integrate customer order information
3. Standardize and speed up manufacturing processes
4. Reduce inventory
5. Standardize HR information

Knowledge of the generic benefits to be gained by companies that have already implemented ERP systems is often the main reason that drives other companies to an ERP implementation. These benefits include the following:

1. Improved Work Process
2. Better customer satisfaction
3. Better customer service
4. Fewer complaints
5. Better quality (less rework)
6. Increased access to data for business decision making
7. Increased control of work processes by staff
8. More timely information
9. Greater accuracy of information with detailed content.
10. Improved cost control
11. Improved customer response time
12. Efficient cash collection
13. Quicker response to market conditions
14. Improved competitive advantage
15. Improved supply-demand link
16. Integration with eBusiness

When a company completes an ERP implementation with an IBM i based system, after the startup issues are resolved, the benefits quickly begin to accrue. Benefits are in many different areas since ERP is as far-reaching as an integrated application set. There are way too many applications and their associated benefits to list in this book. However, the major benefits that add to the business value in the operations and financial areas are as follows:

Operational

1. Reduction in inventories
2. More inventory Turns
3. Lower carrying costs
4. Reduction in total logistics cost
5. Fewer stockouts
6. More efficient picking
7. Reduction in manufacturing cost
8. Reduction in outside warehousing
9. Reduction in procurement cost
10. Increased production capacity
11. Improved order cycle time / accuracy / cost.

Financial

1. Increased shareholder value
2. Reduced assets deployed
3. Increase return on equity
4. Improved cash flow

Added Value Adds to Profits

Now, we are talking. Business managers understand those things that add value by increasing profits, whether they manifest themselves as opportunities to gain more business or they manifest themselves in lower cost through operational and financial efficiencies. When these benefits are quantified, they become a real value that is added to the firm. But, with an IBM i, all-everything operating system running on the IBM Power System, that's just the beginning

The ERP application benefits can be accrued on any computer system but because of the large system function and ease of use characteristics of IBM i, any software project is more likely to be successful and it is more likely to cost less and be live sooner than on any other platform. It's also a fact. Surveys show that IBM i ERP implementations are completed significantly sooner than those on other systems.

Whether the application is ERP or CRM (Customer Relationship Management) or SCM (Supply Chain Management) or eBusiness, or simply Human Resources or

Payroll, the IBM i OS adds additional value to the business. This value does not come from the application software. It comes from running the software using the IBM i operating system rather than Unix, Linux, or Windows. It comes from the business being able to quickly react to the unexpected. In other words, IBM i plus ERP equals business agility.

Besides the list I am about to show, one of the most well-known aspects of the IBM i operating system is that its development tools help programmers and implementers get new work up and running more quickly and they help the team maintain existing work in a highly productive fashion.

This helps businesses customize new strategies to beat the competition, have those plans implemented in software sooner and with a higher probability of success, on a system that stays up to continually provide business value, and after all that still costs less to achieve. IBM i even works on weekends and at night when the IT guys in Windows shops are applying the latest fix packs.

Change is Constant

My experience is that even with a fine-tuned packaged ERP solution, one of the biggest software libraries on a well-used business system is the "change library." There will always be changes in a dynamic business and there will be lots of changes over time. With IBM i, it is a documented fact that you can develop applications or change applications five to ten times faster than on any other system. On other platforms, IT shops are cautioned to not make changes that can help make the software run better for the organization. So, on other platforms what you see is what you get, even if you know you need something else.

IBM i enables your staff to react to your competitive environment and augment the benefits of any package that you choose to run. If applications can be completed quicker, then their benefits are obviously accrued faster, and the firm benefits from the better method sooner, not later. Moreover, because it is finished sooner, it costs less to build. So, benefits more quickly roll in and costs are reduced when the all-everything operating system is in play.

IBM i or Server Farm—You Make the Call

Another of the biggest values that IBM i adds to the business is that it can run the whole business on just one machine, thereby saving both hardware and implementation dollars as well as the support personnel that are required for a server farm. The next biggest value that IBM i supplies is that it just does not go down. We highlighted this in Chapter 2 in the section about casinos. Because the machine does not go down, and the operational environment is less complex than a farm of finicky Windows servers, your critical business applications are always available. Downtime can be an extremely costly factor to a business depending on technology to survive.

Downtime is one of the main costs that should be taken into consideration during a system and software evaluation. An average ERP implementation for example, on a non-IBM i server would experience 2.8 hours of unscheduled downtime per week and according to a recent survey of 250 Fortune 1000 companies, industry analysts have reported that the average per minute cost of downtime for an enterprise application is as high as $13,000. Considering that a Power System with IBM i has a yearly average downtime of just over five hours, there's a lot of money to risk by not using an IBM i System.

Dennis Grimes, former CIO of Klein Wholesale Distributors, which, at the time was the fifth largest candy and tobacco wholesaler in the US, explains it this way:

> "There is a tremendous time savings because the system does not go down and force us to scramble to get our orders out and our work done. There is virtually no system down time, no restarts, and no calls at night or weekends. Applications just run and run and run. Forget it's there! No time spent on getting things to run right. The machine is self-optimizing.
>
> We have Windows servers also and the IBM i unit has them beat by far on economies of scale: It can run many things without choking. I only need to manage one system. It is even easy for me to add capacity on demand.
>
> We have our box on the Internet. Nothing is impregnable but this baby is tough to crack. I know of no other system that can't be hacked. Security is just part of the whole package. You just get it. The IBM i operating system doesn't have the open doors like other systems."

Being able to develop and maintain applications in short time frames and run multiple workloads on multiple operating systems on the same machine with just one processor (or 64 if you need them) along with always being available for action, are major business values for an IBM i system. But, there are a ton more.

The following is a comprehensive but not exhaustive list of the added value that a company gets from running its ERP, CRM, HR, or any other application on an IBM i system:

Factors that Add Business Value with an All-Everything OS

1. IBM i is designed for small to medium businesses, not as a toy for the desktop.
2. Working with IBM as a trusted partner
3. Unsurpassed competitive edge
4. Best tangible ROI
5. Quickest investment recovery (less than a year)
6. Elimination of multiple, underutilized servers
7. Highest level of integration
8. Outstanding performance
9. Best Security – no hackers, no viruses
10. Runs core business applications and eBusiness on same machine
11. Deploy new applications quickly

12. Fastest ERP implementation
13. Highest customer satisfaction
14. Intuitive management tools
15. Fastest speed to market
16. Greatest business agility
17. Reduced complexity
18. Enables change quickly
19. Highest IT staff productivity
20. Reduction of technical and administrative costs.
21. Free, integrated DB2 relational database
22. Free, integrated transaction processor
23. Free packaged Web servlet server for eBusiness
24. Free PHP and MySQL package shipped with OS
25. Simplified IT infrastructure
26. Best usability characteristics (ease of use)
27. Highest user productivity and effectiveness
28. Easiest, least costly implementation
29. Lowest cost of ownership
30. Non-disruptive business growth (virtually unlimited)
31. Seamless, streamlined upgrades
32. Long lasting software solutions
33. No need to buy new packaged software when IBM i is enhanced
34. Lower implementation time and costs
35. Most dependable, flexible, affordable
36. Zero downtime (99 44/100% uptime)
37. Fewest unplanned outages
38. Simplified maintenance.
39. Best service team in the world (IBM)
40. Etc...

That is an awful long list of value items. Each has an impact on the business. By running your business with the all-everything OS, you get to enjoy these benefits as a by-product. With any other OS solution, these benefits do not apply.

Technology Value

To the technical team, the above list would appear to be fluffy kinds of things with little substance. Yet, there is a story behind each and every one of the business value factors that are shown in the above list. It is tough, however, to digest that whole list, and it is tougher to believe that there are actually many more items that can be added to the list. Yet, there are.

The above business value factors are achievable, however, because of what IBM builds into IBM i.

Now, let's look at the technical features of the IBM Power System with IBM i compared to the Unix, Linux, and Windows platforms. There may be a commercial machine out there that has implemented one or several of the below features of the system, but no other system has more than a few. The technical factors that bring the business value factors to the forefront are listed below. Please note that this is not a complete list of features and functions but it is a pretty large list nonetheless.

Power System (AKA iSeries) Technical Factors

1. Implements IBM's FS (Future System) technology
2. Most advanced computer science technology in the Industry
3. Tenth generation of 64-bit RISC computing
4. Advanced autonomic computing
5. 30 year old software runs without recompilation
6. Manages up to thousands of disk drives as one image
7. No need for C,D,E,F drives
8. DB file placement auto-optimized for performance
9. Allocates file space as needed on multiple drives
10. No need to move or split files on different drives
11. Provides internal SAN for multiple OS environments
12. High Level Machine (hardware abstraction)
13. Technology Independent Machine Interface (TIMI)
14. No recompiles-- migrations from S/38, AS/400, iSeries, i5

15. Object based
16. Single level storage
17. Capability based addressing
18. Integrated DB2 Universal Database
19. Pre-integrated database, middleware, and operating system
20. Automated database reorganization
21. Integrated transaction processing
22. Tuxedo and CICS not needed
23. Runs many applications at one time without crashing
24. No server farm required
25. eBusiness and ERP on same server
26. Outstanding performance
27. Integrated performance collection
28. Integrated Apache HTTP in OS package
29. Standard WebSphere in OS package
30. Integrated dynamic workload management (self-tuning)
31. Workload integrity
32. Integrated resource management
33. Integrated backup
34. Continuous operations with "hot site" failover
35. Runs up to four different operating systems concurrently
36. IBM i, Unix, Linux can share one processor
37. Integrated resource virtualization
38. Integrated security facilities
39. Virtual high-band integrated network
40. Share single physical storage pool
41. Multiple subsystems
42. Resource balancing (automatic and manual)
43. Continuous 24 X 7 operations – no disk defrags needed
44. Share resources and maximize CPU utilization
45. IBM Virtualization Engine
46. Increases server utilization rates
47. Logical partitioning (Up to 10 partitions per processor)
48. Heterogeneous workloads
49. Advanced server consolidation
50. No assembler language needed
51. Programming independence from machine implementation and configuration details

52. High levels of integrity and authorization capability with minimal overhead
53. Efficient support in the machine for commonly used operations in control programming, compilers, and utilities
54. Self-generating, self-adapting object code based on technology independence
55. Efficient support in the machine for key system functional objectives, such as data base and dynamic multiprogramming
56. Underlying technology change does not translate into the need to recompile applications or disruption to the business.
57. Five to ten times programming productivity advantage
58. Compilers are database and transaction processing aware (not an afterthought)
59. Enhanced IT productivity
60. And more!

From my IBM experience, I am convinced that I would be able to deliver a 1/2 day or longer presentation about the IBM i OS on Power with just these topics. However, I would admit that more than likely it would just scratch the surface of the topics in the above technology list. That's how powerful the platform is.

If you spent the time to burrow through this list, and you are a technical person, you are probably impressed with the IBM i on Power technology. There really is lots more to tell you though, and throughout the book, you will be exposed to more of the technical magic surrounding the IBM i OS platform. Because I have written this book so that a business person or a technician can read it; however, the level of detail in this book does not approach what you would find in a technical manual or a technical book.

Moving On

So, hang on, the plot has been revealed but, the best is yet to come. Stay tuned for a number of chapters that bring forth even more exciting goodies about the all-everything operating system.

If I am a bit too superlative in my remarks for your taste, permit me to apologize in advance. I believe in what I say but, I do not expect the reader to share all of my opinions or my enthusiasm. So, I hope you hang in there with me.

Whether you are a business person, an IBM i person, a Windows person, a Unix / Linux person, or a mainframe person, there is lots in this book for you. No, you're not going to learn which bit to turn on in the PSW to make the system purr like a kitten, but you are going to learn about the computer science attributes that make the IBM i platform more of a system than you have ever been exposed to in the computer industry.

And, if you can get through that, you'll learn how a system using those advanced attributes makes life better for the IT staff as well as for the whole business organization. Everywhere you look in this book, you will learn about the value that an IBM i system adds to the organization.

Chapter 4 Where Did IBM i Come From?

No Secrets Please

There is no better kept secret in the computer industry than the new IBM Power System with IBM i. It comes from IBM, the all-time leader in advanced computer and supercomputer technology. Adding secrets to secrets, another secret about IBM i of which most modern computerists are unaware is that IBM has created this platform from the chip to the OS as the finest, most architecturally elegant, most usable, most productive, and most affordable computer system of all time.

This phenomenon in the computing industry gets a software and hardware rebirth every few years just like clockwork. Its most recent re-birth was in early 2008, though the all-everything operating system and the rest of the full package have advanced underpinnings that go back well over thirty years. That's an awful long time for any company to keep any secret. With the IBM Power System as IBM's premiere hardware offering today, IBM is expected to reveal all of its secrets as eventually even its mainframe systems will be running on this same internal hardware. When IBM chooses to make its big splash, Big Blue will begin to focus on claiming the proceeds from the many years of advanced development that recently culminated in its new IBM Power Systems running IBM i. There is lots more to come.

That's what this book is all about.

Not only has IBM kept the secret but with the all-everything operating system, it has continued to keep the lead. That is noteworthy, but not quite as noteworthy as the fact that the machine's architecture was conceived and delivered over thirty years ago and is still the best technology that anybody has ever built.

In the 1970's leading up to the announcement of the IBM System/38, Dr. Frank Soltis, recognized globally, as the Father of the AS/400 and IBM i was the key player in bringing IBM i to life. Soltis, who served IBM as its Chief IBM i Scientist until his retirement in late 2008, assured that Rochester Minnesota, not Endicott or Poughkeepsie NY, where the mainframes lived, would bring the world's best technology to life in a package that was affordable by most reasonable sized businesses. By the way, Dr. Soltis is so tuned into the notion of an all-everything operating system that he agreed to write the Foreword to this book.

Using its 30-year old "nobody else can afford to build one" architecture, IBM continues its technology lead by far compared with all the other platforms of today, including the mainframe. One would have to conclude that IBM is about 30 or so years ahead of its competition and that's before you factor in that during the thirty years since the all-everything operating system's conception, IBM has not stood still. Each and every year, more and more capability and facility has been built into the all-everything operating system. Now, I am not suggesting that the IBM Power Systems with IBM i is 60 years ahead of the competition but, that is where the math logically takes you.

IBM i: Easy to Use & Hard to Forget!

If I had never worked with other computers, mainframes, 1130's, System/360 model 20s, Unix, Linux, PCs, etc..., I probably would not have appreciated what a solid system the AS/400 heritage line has been right from the beginning. The Rochester Minnesota - built "small business computer line" from which the IBM Power System with IBM i was spawned has always been unusually easy to work with. In every other computer platform, especially the earliest models, there were cryptic codes to decipher and continual puzzles to solve just to get the machine turned on. Programming for these behemoths was and for the most part still is even worse.

Of them all, at least before I worked with Unix, I felt that the mainframe was the most cryptic of the cryptic. Technicians carried special green cards with codes and hexadecimal translations galore in order to program properly on a mainframe. At the time I learned it, I was convinced that the mainframe had been slapped together by bit- head engineers, who expected just other bit-head engineers to work with it. Real people need not apply. Even today, I have great respect for the technical acumen of the professionals who know the mainframe and who make it hum for very large organizations. They know what they are doing. Then again, they must.

When IBM introduced the first ancestor of today's Power System with IBM i as the System/3 in 1969, it was remarkable. It was as if IBM had sent all the geeks home that day. There were no strange codes that were indecipherable. No IBM green "HEX" card was needed. Programming the System/3 was almost as easy as speaking in English. Maybe not that easy; but, it was easy. IBM had succeeded in using high tech engineers to build a system for regular people. The operating system (SCP as it was initially called) was not very advanced, but it was very simple to use. I don't know how they did it, but they did. IBM has kept the principle of small system ease of use in the product all the while continuing to add large system function. IBM i is the beneficiary of all those years of building OS function.

System/3 was just a start, but it was a good start. From that moment on, the IBM Rochester style of computing became contagious. Rochester wares were the most popular computers in small businesses for decades. Each and every Rochester computer was built on the principle of great function with no pain. Each model was substantially better than the preceding machine and IBM business customers just gobbled them up; consequently, their businesses grew unimpeded by technology and reboots.

IBM i for Small and Large Businesses Alike

Today, the IBM Power System with IBM i is positioned to be sold to small businesses to medium sized businesses to the largest businesses in the world. As a family of systems, with various sized models and various costs, it handles workloads from the size of just bigger than mom and pop organizations to 95% of the Fortune 500. IBM has recently labeled its Power System with IBM i as a "mainframe for the masses" because it gets as big as a mainframe but it can be used effectively by a small business.

This book walks you through the story of the all-everything OS from the very beginning until today. In addition to telling a powerful, compelling story, it describes in layman's terms the technology and computer architecture innovations that are part of every Power System with IBM i. When you finish this book, you will understand why IBM is proud to have built the finest operating system in the world, and you may just find a place for a particular size one of these rascals in your own business.

For the most part, this book reads as a series of essays. Each of the chapters is built as a short story unto itself, with the sum of the chapters telling the story of the all-everything operating system. For the most part, you can pick up any chapter and read it without having to read a prior chapter. However, you may want to read these early chapters first to get a perspective on what the IBM i operating system is all about and its relevance in IBM history.

This book presents the IBM all-everything operating system, its underlying superiority, its rapid customer acceptance, the IBM development history, and the IBM all-everything operating system's probable future starting with the new IBM Power System hardware line.

This is not meant to be a technical book at a low detailed level. It is written for those who have some or little technical background, who may know lots or nothing about an operating system. However, there are a few chapters in which I do get just a little bit technical, hoping that I can show the reader in reasonably simple terms how the IBM Power System with IBM i, when in control of your business operations, offers superior, one of a kind capabilities. It is a special system with a long and successful tradition.

When you finish reading this book, regardless of your technical competency, you will have a good idea of a number of unique computer science architectural attributes from which any computer system, from any vendor, can benefit. You will also understand how those attributes can help any company, such as yours, preserve its software investment and permit the upgrading of hardware and software without forcing a rewrite or a re-build, or a re-purchase. You will learn that no other computer company, of software or hardware heritage, ever created a machine with all of these advanced architectural attributes. Not only this, but no computer company has yet to be able to adopt even one of these powerful notions into their computer systems and operating systems of today.

This book is written then to teach you what is unique about the IBM I operating system and why it is the all-everything operating system. It demonstrates why the parts that are unique, are also good, not bad; and why you should demand these facilities in any platform in which you choose to run your business. Remember, the system actually does make a big difference in the overall value of IT to your business, and there is no system that has ever been made that delivers value better than the IBM Power System running the IBM i operating system. In this book, you will learn why!

Chapter 4 Appendix: Twenty Questions

There Could Be a Lot More

When I was first trying to create a compelling Chapter 1 to help the reader gain interest in this book right from the beginning, I started to ask myself a number of questions. These are the questions I would ask somebody who was suffering from any of a number of IT maladies prevalent in non IBM i IT shops. The maladies include "no perceived business value disease," "system down disease," "where's my information disease," and of course the killer, "Microsoft myopia staff disease."

These questions are not subtle, and for the most part, they are answerable by a simple yes or simple no. In each case; however, a situation is portrayed that (a) you either do not have an IBM i IT environment or (b) you can have only with an IBM i IT environment. The list of questions is not exhaustive; but, there are enough to keep you busy in a very productive exercise, if you have the time.

So, without further ado, here are the twenty questions plus a few more:

Business Value Questions:

1. Are you suffering from more customer complaints because your customer, product, inventory, and shipping information are not available to your customers when they want it and the way they want it?

2. Are you losing customers because your systems are not available or are not accommodating when your customers need information or responses?

3. Would you like to be able to reduce the breadth of knowledge that you need or would need to keep your IT infrastructure up and running?

4. Would you like never to hear (again for some) those words, "the server can't do any more. We need another server, and another..."?

5. Would you prefer to get your IT work done without a major hardware and human resources investment in a server farm?

6. Would you like to be able to contain and manage the cost and the increasing complexity of your IT deployments rather than be forced to add the next server, and the next, and the next?

7. Would you like to be able to reduce your required IT people skill level and cost and not require so many high priced IT staffers just to have your server(s) operational and ready for work?

8. Would you feel better about your IT investment if you did not need a plethora of skills just to keep your server(s) up and running?

9. Would you like your IT staff or existing person in the organization (depending on your business size) to be able to perform IT related jobs with more flexibly and with less essential knowledge pigeonholed in individual staffers?

10. Would you like to be able to reduce (perhaps to one) the number of boxes and operating systems, and database packages and achieve the requisite savings in IT personnel costs?

11. Would you like your business database to be there when you need it for every transaction and every query?

12. Would you like to be able to have a comprehensive, information-laden database without the requirement for a high-priced database administrator?

13. If you already have a computer server that has not quite measured up, would you like to get it right this time, rather than hearing a bunch of sales pitches each ending with, "Of course it will do that" when, in fact, it cannot?

14. Would you like to get out of an environment where you need a new server and a backup server for every new application or new function that you need to run your business?

15. Would you like to not have to pay for the associated increase in server support people, to take care of your growing number of servers?

16. Wouldn't it be nice if there were one server that, without breaking the bank, was able to absorb all of the work from all of the other servers and grow with you from just a few to several hundred to several hundred thousand users – without having to scrap the machine, add servers, or start over?

17. Would you like to have an all-in-one all-everything machine solution designed to address the business, technical, and financial pressures faced by all small to medium sized businesses, rather than an IT environment that creates more pressure than it relieves?

18. Would you like to have a server with security and management capabilities that is a direct descendant of mainframe offerings with a long history in the marketplace?

19. Would you like a server that was designed and built with the facility and the agility to provide your firm a means to secure revenue opportunities that might otherwise be unavailable or technically problematic in a world with small Windows, lots of hackers, and limited support people ?

20. Would you like a server that is not subject to intruders, hackers, spyware or the infamous virus du jour?

21. Would you like to have a server platform in which your software does not have to re-written or re-purchased every five years because the new server or the new operating system line can't run it, or can't run it at full speed?

21. Would you like to hear "yes" when you ask your IT staff if your server has the ability to handle high workloads and data processing chores that offer your company (and other small and mid-sized firms) the technology needed to seamlessly work with robust enterprise computing environments at a fraction of the cost, even though your business is not gigantic and your pocketbook has limits.

22. Would you like to have an IT environment that lets you live comfortably, like the big guys live, without having to pay big guy prices?

23. Would you like to have a server built by a company that knows that smaller and mid-sized companies have concerns and needs that are unlike their larger cousins, because they live with constrictions and limitations on the small servers that are not usually found running larger enterprises?

24. Would you like a server that can provide you large enterprise function with small system ease of use and small system cost?

25. Is it upsetting to you that the business-critical nature of technology for the SMB market mirrors the IT reliance of

larger enterprises, yet so far your IT tools have fallen far short of doing the job and providing business value?

26. Does it bother you that SMB companies such as yours must deal with similar issues of IT complexity, yet are challenged to find a way of achieving success with the economies of scale issues in the small multi-server IT environments?

27. Have you been forced to say no to important IT projects that can grow your business because at a hypothetical $70,000 annual cost for a single IT staff member? Has it become clear that IT growth, despite its potential long-term competitive advantage, is simply beyond the reach of your company as well as many other small and mid-sized firms?

28. Would you like to have a server about which IBM, the leader in server technology says: "IBM Power System with IBM i is a premier business system designed to help you to improve productivity while reducing costs and complexity?"

29. Would you like a server that can achieve significant cost savings for your organization either by never needing a server farm or by consolidating the industry-standard Intel servers running Microsoft Windows and / or Linux onto one server?

30. Would it not be great if the data center architecture enabled a consolidation server, such as an all-everything OS running on an IBM Power System, that in one processor could run additional operating systems in series, i.e., first as a Unix server, then as a Linux server, etc…? Even a Windows Server? How about all at the same time?

31. Do you find it a challenge for integrating business functions in the typical server environment that requires the execution of applications running different operating systems in parallel on many different servers?

32. Can you see how it would save lots of additional systems and thus lots of money to run all integrated business functions on one integrated operating system, such as the all-everything machine (IBM i), that permits many operating systems to run along with it in just one machine?

33. Would you like to have a system that can run Linux, Windows, Unix, and OS/400 under one set of covers with support for NetServer using virtual Ethernet and Microsoft Peer Networking, as well as Samba, enabling cross talk between operating systems under the same set of hardware covers?

34. Would you like your organization to benefit from unprecedented levels of reliability, scalability, and a high level of system integration?

35. Would you like additional savings to come from reducing system administration head count and avoiding the operational costs associated with server downtime?

Technical Questions:

36. Would you be able to achieve additional productivity with a system that provides its own virtualized storage area network, supports multiple file systems and multiple operating systems over the same disk storage?

37. Would you like a system that is programmable in both computer science languages, C, C++, Java, as well as business languages such as COBOL and RPG IV?

38. Would you like to work in a transaction processing environment that enables interactive and Web programs to be developed in 1/5 to 1/10 of the time of conventional systems?

39. Do you want to say no to disk fragmentation and reorgs?

40. Do you want to say no to ever running out of space on one disk while the system has many empty disks?

41. Do you want to say no to rewriting applications and splitting disk files because you, not the system, must manage disk space utilization?

42. Do you want to be able to migrate your software applications, when necessary, to the next generation of computing without having to scrap them, rewrite them or even recompile them?

43. Do you want to say no to placing files on specific disks and specific locations for performance reasons?

44. Do you want to spend time typing data definitions into your programs when IBM i programming languages can bring in the data descriptions from the database automatically?

45. Do you want a system that provides everything that you can run on a PC without having to worry about having to do the CTRL-ALT-DELETE dance to solve crashes or deal with virus attacks?

46. Would you like a machine with a documented average up-time of 99.98%?

47. Would you like to have a machine that can easily convert from the older technology, such as 48-bit CISC hardware, to newer technology, such as 64-bit RISC, without having to recompile your programs?

48. Would you like to be able to perform Concurrent Maintenance on your system without having to bring it down?

49. Would you like to be able to backup your system while it is active? In other words, would you like to be able to

preserve data and programs without having to perform a shutdown of your server to do your backup?

50. Would you like to bring data down naturally from the system to MS Excel and other applications from one or more DB2 Universal databases using ODBC, SQL or OS/400s built in query and SQL?

51. Would you like to have up to 60 Windows NT4.0/2000/2003 servers, controlled and administered by one server rather than a farm of independently supported Wintel boxes?

52. Would you like to be able to carve out up to ten partitions (each treating the partition as one whole machine) on a one processor server?

53. Without purchasing expensive virtualization software, would you like to run with virtualization always on, providing the highest possible utilization of your computer resources?

54. Would you like to be able to tune and auto tune the operating system in ways that are impossible with Windows and Unix boxes?

55. Would you like programmers to be able to develop new applications or change existing applications 5X to 10 X faster on your server?

56. If you did not think of a business information need at the time you bought your major software package, would you expect that your IT staff will be able to get you this information from your current system? Do you think they should be able to get you information that is needed, but the item was just not on the software checkmark list when you bought the package?

And the Answer Is

Of course, the answer is that most business managers want a computer that provides productivity and efficiency and results without pain. Quite frankly, technical people aren't really interested in hurting themselves to get a computer job done either. Getting major business value from your production IT server should be easy and it is easy with the all-everything operating system, IBM i

Chapter 5   Voices of Users, Analysts, and Industry Experts

Users Know Best!

There is nobody who knows the value of IBM i better than somebody who uses it day in and day out. So, rather than continue with twenty questions or get into the technical details of the machine, I thought it would be a good idea to round up some of the good thoughts of AS/400 heritage users, analysts, and worldwide industry experts. This assemblage of spokespersons for IBM i does so of their own free will because they have a story to tell that they believe it is worth hearing. I might add that it should be worth your time to hear what they have to say.

I asked each to provide me with one to two pages. As you will see, some comments are shorter than a page and a few are a bit longer than two pages.

Most of the analysts, consultants, industry experts, and even IBMers have a background in working with IBM i and AS/400 heritage customers and thus their point of view represents observations of IBM i family customers in action over the years. So as not to leave the reader with just the voices of the pundits, however, I went half way across the country to get a perspective from a bone fide user who happens to have experience with two different IBM i machines in his own home town.

The writings of the individuals in this fine group are provided immediately below. The format of the rest of this chapter then will be to highlight the name of the person, followed by their story in their words. At the end of the stories, there is a short biography of each of the writers. I hope you enjoy their musings and I hope that it gives you a real perspective on where the IBM Power System with IBM i, the great grandson of the famous AS/400, came from, and what a fine machine it continues to be. And, as you will see, to get to the root of the family tree, our esteemed "panel" will take you back to 1978 when IBM was first introduced, but under a different name.

Jim Sloan, Jim Sloan, Inc.

JS: "I knew the System/38 when it was just a piece of paper. It was amazing in its conception but, it seemed terribly slow in developing. Major IBM development managers fended off the IBM Company just to be able to produce the product. That was a terrific political success though from first-hand knowledge, I know it was very difficult to pull off.

I must say that with all that we put in the machine, it was incredible that it worked as well as it did. The fact that something so large with so many different players (hardware, software, support etc...) can come together is a tribute to good management and lots of effort.

The biggest problem that the system had from the get-go was that it was underpowered hardware-wise. Making up for the lack of hardware power on the early System/38 was a major accomplishment. Of course, with the AS/400 and the i5 and now, the IBM Power System, all the power issues have been fixed.

I am in the development area and so I don't have customer testimonials or customer war stories to share but, this was and is a terrific system. Ironically, after spending so much to make the system work, IBM tried to kill it. And I don't mean just once or twice. In the end, each time, customers saved the product. They would come back to IBM and just not let the company discontinue a system that was so vital to their business."

BK: "How do you see the product now and into the future?"

JS: "It is one heck of a good product. It is a terrific product with terrific acceptance but for some reason IBM just does not market it aggressively. I do not know why they don't market it. They just don't. I would hope that changes and IBM highlights the system once again."

BK: "Though I don't share this opinion, there are some folks in the industry who say that Windows has taken over and even if IBM chose to go after small businesses, as it once did with System/32, System/34, and System/36, it is probably too late for the IBM i product line to make an impact."

JS: "It is never too late if IBM chose to market the machine as it should. It would be successful indeed.

The box has been good to me in many ways and I sure have had a good time working with it. I have been working on this for over thirty years and it has been wonderful to me. Considering that I worked with it from when it was just a piece of paper, that's a long time."

Skip Marchesani, Custom Systems Corp

"Sure, I can tell you the most outstanding attribute of the iSeries and AS/400 and now the IBM Power System with IBM i. It has rock solid reliability and availability, unsurpassed in the industry, and there are systems out there that have run non-stop 24 by 7, 366 days a year, for years at a time. More and more shops are noticing that when their other servers are misbehaving and failing, the iSeries or AS/400 or IBM Power System with IBM i continues doing its thing every day, day in and day out."

" Years ago when the AS/400 first came out, a large national insurance company installed about 10,000 of the smallest models in their remote sales offices all across the US. About every three years, a systems technician would visit each remote office to check on and do maintenance on the AS/400. On one particular visit to one of the remote offices the systems technician asked to see the 'office computer.' The office manager showed him a PC sitting on a desk. The tech explained that the PC was just a workstation and he needed to see the system (AS/400) they were connected to. The office manager just shrugged and pointed to the other two PCs on desktops in the office.

Finally, the system technician traced the twinax cable connection (wires from PC to AS/400) to a point where it went thru a wall in the back of the office. He asked what was behind the wall and got more shrugs. The entire office staff had turned over in the last year. He went next door and asked to see the wall next to this remote office but there was nothing to see. He went back into the remote office and knocked a hole in the wall with a hammer, and saw the AS/400 humming away in what the building superintendent said had formerly been a closet."

[They had walled it in and it was still running the business.]

"I once had a conversation with a database manager for a large government facility on the West Coast. This person, who was in charge of all kinds of servers - Ingress, SQL Server, Sybase, Oracle, etc... had a total of five people on his staff counting himself. I asked him how much time the AS/400 database took to maintain. He said no more than 1/10 of one person. I asked him how much attention the other machines required. He started to ramble - or so I thought. He likened the AS/400 to a daycare child who comes in each day and you tell him what to do and he goes and does it and you don't see him again until the end of the day when he gets picked up. He likened the other kluge of databases to the hyperactive kids who get dropped off without their medicine. They are in your face, literally from the moment they arrive until they are dragged out at the end of the day."

"One time I was teaching a DB2/400 class and a student asked why Oracle DBAs make so much money. Before I could answer, another student volunteered that Oracle is such an inferior product that it takes a full time, highly skilled, highly paid DBA to keep it running."

"Oracle is good example of an inferior product with outstanding marketing. It's absolutely amazing that companies like Microsoft and Oracle can develop products that have very serious shortcomings, but their marketing is so outstanding that in spite of themselves they create a very loyal following. DB2/400 (aka DB2 for IBM i) is a functionally rich, standards compliant, object-based relational data base product. And, it just doesn't break! But, IBM's marketing is such that the industry is not aware of it."

Al Barsa Jr., Barsa Consulting Group

Several years ago, long before his untimely death on April 4, 2008, Al Barsa provided me with this story to share about the Unique AS/400 model set. I used it in my previous book, The All Everything Machine and I include it in this book because it is still relevant and Al would be proud to have it here.

Al Barsa was a friend of mine and many in the AS/400 heritage community. This picture is from a Web site established in his honor: http://www.mr400.com/Al.html. Al Barsa loved the AS/400 and IBM i technology with a passion and his many award-winning presentations were done with enthusiasm and a sense of right.

Figure 5-1 Al Barsa, Mr. 400

Note: Though this is the text of the audio taken from IBM Legends of iSeries # 0213, Al Barsa lived through this ordeal and was the "IBM Rep" in the story. The first paragraph here is the story as transcribed from the IBM videotape. This is followed by Al's personal comments about the incident.

"Like I was saying, this IBM Rep shows up at this NY labor union to do a checkup on their IBM server. The thing is nobody knows where the server is! I mean nobody has ever backed it up. No one even knows if it is in the same building, so they start tracking this cable. They go up one corridor, down another corridor, and they go round a lot of corners. I mean it's wrapped around... It goes up one floor. It even goes through this ventilation duct. Finally, the cable leads to a storage closet two floors away. The door is locked. Secretary says nobody has been in there in over six years. Somebody figures out that the super two buildings down might have a key. They get inside. It's like a blast furnace. It's so hot... the tech guy gets a nose bleed. Evidently, a power outage two years ago knocked out the AC. But the server [AS/400] in that closet rebooted [by itself], and got back to organizing and running that union [with no manual intervention and without anybody knowing]. Are you following this? Six years, no attention, no maintenance, and a 140 degrees virtual oven..."

Al Barsa offered a few casual comments about the video:

"Look at this video. It's a fairly true story about me! In late 1999, I was doing last minute Y2K stuff at some of my accounts in NYC. While I was engaged in this process, one of my clients took me up on the offer and wanted to make sure their system had been prepared for the millennium.

So, I showed up in my Brooks Brothers suit, no hat. The missing system in the story is absolutely true, and the super was from that building, not one or two buildings over, and he had a key ring that must have been 18" in diameter!

He found the key to the closet in no more than 30 seconds (much to my dismay).

The system was a B30 [old AS/400 model] that had gone through a blackout two years earlier, and rebooted because the system value QPWRRSTIPL had been changed to '1', but the air conditioning never recovered.

The story about me getting a nose-bleed is absolutely true."

Bob Warford, Labette Community College

Electrical Failure

"One night, the city of Parsons, KS, lost all its electrical power and when the batteries on our UPS got low, the IBM AS/400 shut down as it was supposed to.

When we came in to work the next morning, we found the IBM AS/400 was not running. This caused a lot of excitement. We could see that the lights on the control panel were on, but we could not figure out why the IBM AS/400 wasn't responding to the system console or workstations.

After a lot of looking and research, we finally gave up on trying to find the problem ourselves and called IBM Tech. support. The first question they asked us was "Did you press the white start button?"

Talk about feeling dumb. No, we hadn't pushed the white start button and yes, the IBM AS/400 came right up when we did.

To be fair to my staff and me though, because we are not dumb, we had never shut down the IBM AS/400 without instructing it to do an automatic restart and IPL so no one on my staff had ever seen the IBM AS/400 down. Not since the day it was installed.

To be truthful, no one on my staff had ever even started the IBM AS/400. The technician who installed it turned it on during installation and there was never a need to turn it off and there was never a time when it had had a problem that would take it down.

I think it is pretty impressive that a computer could run two years and never be down."

Six Days Down in Twenty-Five Years

"We (Labette Community College) bought our IBM System/34 in 1980 only because the IBM sales representative signed his name to provide several reports that our president at the time wanted. Although we were only buying a small IBM System/34 and a $500 student management system that didn't have the required reports in it, IBM fulfilled the sales representative's commitment and developed the reports for us. We had an IBM SE on campus most of the first year.

I believe the sales representative decided to work for someone else shortly after the sale was completed. I never heard what happened to his supervisor who also signed off on the reports.

When the college finally got a grant in 1986 that provided the funds to replace the IBM System/34, we migrated to an IBM System/36 because the IBM System/34 had only had one day in six years that it had been down. In addition, all our data and software migrated to the IBM System/36 without having to make any changes. It took one night to do the total migration.

In 1998, when the college got another grant, the decision was made to switch to an IBM AS/400 for the same reasons we had switched to the IBM System/36. In the twelve years we used the IBM System/36, we had only had three days we could not run and all of them had been in the last year and were problems relating to the diskette magazine drive. Actually we were able to run, we just couldn't backup.

All of our existing software also ported without any major problems. The only problems dealt with the IBM AS/400's library lists and duplicate program and menu names in the production libraries. The IBM AS/400 migration started at 4:30 P.M. on Friday and for all practical purposes was completed by 1:30 P.M. on Sunday. This included unpacking the computer and configuring all the workstations and printers.

The reliability and compatibility of the IBM System/34, IBM System/36, and IBM AS/400 has just been phenomenal.

To be honest, we did have a problem with the IBM AS/400 this fall. Something went wrong in the power supply and when the system did its scheduled shutdown and restart; it could not come back up. The technician who repaired it said he had never seen that problem before. That resulted in the AS/400 being down for two days while we waited for parts.

I would say that six days down in twenty-five years is pretty good. Although we did have other service calls in that time, there was none that prevented us from completing our work.

As far as software compatibility goes, what other computer system can say what I can about the IBM system? I still have a few of the original programs from the original student registration system that was purchased in 1980 running untouched. Although the IBM migration utilities recompiled the load members and we are still running some things under 36 emulation, we have not had a need to change the source code.

As you can tell, I like IBM AS/400s.

Someone really needs to help IBM do a better sales job on the IBM AS/400 [IBM i marketing] because the IBM AS/400 is really a wonderful machine."

Doug Hart, Whitenack Consulting

"The System/38 was developed from the IBM "Future Systems" project. This heritage continues today with advanced OS features that continue to place this system at the front line of business systems.

For me being "old school", I still find the strength of the AS/400 line being the backbone of a company's computing platform. The integrated database, security and communications facilities give the system a consistent standard in which all the operating components work flawlessly. A business' primary applications (Accounting, HR, etc...) today must be available full time. The AS/400 with its 99.999% up-time rating gets the job done.

Today the i5 line using the Power 5 processors [and now the Power Systems line with the Power 6 processors] has outstanding performance. The systems are truly scalable from quite small to the most powerful of platforms. With advanced functionality such as Logical Partitioning (LPAR), the sophistication and state of the art capabilities of the line continue to lead the industry.

IBM's group in Rochester Minnesota that develops the system understands both their customer's needs and the future directions for computing. As I follow the evolution of the line I'm continually impressed with capabilities of the product."

Ken Anderson, Quadrant Software

"The IBM Power System with IBM i: The greatest business machine money can buy.

I first met Brian while attending the NY IBM users group. My company had been invited to present to the group on the benefits of Electronic Document Distribution in an iSeries/i5 Enterprise. The interesting thing was that I showed up 2 hours early, before anyone had a chance to get there. I cordially asked the front desk where the user group meeting would be held. After she led me to the room, the only thing there was a copy of a new book Brian had written about IBM's relationship with the iSeries (before the i5 was announced). (I'd recommend the book to any IBM i shop I might add). I read about 50 pages and realized that we were on the same page. I think most IBM i shops I meet think I'm too young to know anything about IBM i, but once they hear me speak, they are amazed that the black box has made friends with some (not enough) in my generation as well. So, when Brian approached me to add a comment to this book, I jumped at the chance.

I don't want to tell any war stories. It's not that I don't enjoy hearing about the i5 box that was sheet rocked into a wall and continued to run for 5 years, or Dr. Frank [Soltis] describing what a great customer Microsoft was on the platform and how they replaced a couple black boxes with lots of NT servers. I do. I love them. Rather, I want to describe how one mid-twenties guy was converted and what I think needs to happen to convert EVERYONE else.

Because you see, it's not the decades experienced IT Director or CIO that is going to ensure that this box continues to run SMBs all over the world. It's not the diehard programmer who came up on the 34, 36, and recollects using punch cards and tubes back in the day. Those people already love IBM i. It's converting the people, like me, who learned right out of the gate you press start to turn off your PC.

First off, I have to admit I was VERY skeptical the first time I saw the mean green screen. I remember thinking it looked like the computer James Bond used to look up spy information. You remember, back when it was still amazing that "M" had installed that phone in a car. I thought as most right out of college people entering the working world do. After all we are conditioned to believe that Windows is the only OS out there. Every program you are taught or use is NT based. "People still use these?" I thought.

But over the years, I have had the opportunity to meet hundreds of IBM i customers and talk to literally thousands of them over the phone. In every possible industry from manufacturing, healthcare, distribution, insurance, food, city government and even police stations, customers were using the platform for every conceivable computing purpose. And they were using it with half the staff and twice the reliability of anything else out there.

I guess I will tell one story. And this is just one of many I have that all begin and end the same. I have a friend/customer named Rick. Rick came aboard as IT Director at a division of an IBM i shop where each division has the autonomy to choose what they want to run for applications etc... The business had significantly changed since the decision was made to bring in the 400 initially, and Rick was brought in as part of a new ERP project.

Rick hated the 400 right at the beginning because of all the reasons most folks in his position do. It seems expensive to buy apps, maintenance fees seem high, it seems old, etc... It really boils down to simply learning something new. But, Rick has something that I think is a prerequisite for anyone that does well in IT, an open mind. If one is intent on getting rid of IBM i system for something else, they will and have. It's much more difficult if you approach it with an open mind. So he decided to allow IBM i-based apps, in with all the others.

He did painstaking tests on all of them. I remember him measuring how fast the order entry folks could enter an order in each candidate's application (a nightmare for sales people like me, I might add). And each time I spoke with him, he was a little less harsh on the black box. Until, finally, a year later, they had made a decision. He chose an application I know only lives on in the IBM i family, and I flat out asked him how he arrived at that, since it was no secret that he had no great affinity for the IBM i family.

Rick said, Ken, "I tried every possible justification, every ROI calculation, but they all came up the same. The total cost of ownership with this thing is simply lower than anything else I could get my hands on. I can run everything on the same machine. I can do multi-company, different languages, I can even partition. It runs email too." Rick wasn't ready to admit he'd been converted, but I knew, that was his way of saying he'd been wrong at the beginning.

And it's hundreds of these types of stories that got me where I am today. And if I hadn't seen it with my own eyes or heard with my own ears, I would have put up the wall and gone on thinking there is only one choice out there. And so would Rick.

But because of my job, I have the opportunity to see so many different kinds of businesses and how they operate. It is much more difficult for someone straight out of college to do the same thing. So how do we convince them? IBM can't do it. I think they need to learn it themselves. By exposing WHY you love the platform and really show them what this thing can do, it will happen on its own. Rick had to learn it on his own and so did I. The die-hards that simply crammed it down my throat could have never convinced me of anything other than, "they like it because it's all they know". It was only after real life examples and real ROI that I came to realize, if you are running a business vs. downloading .mp3 files, and surfing web pages, the Power System with IBM i is simply the best business machine money can buy.

So I challenge any IT executive out there, to show the accounting folks how you arrived at that native IBM i payroll solution. Or the downtime figures of someone who chose the other. Or to bring the Jr. Programmer into the ERP selection process and show them how many less IBM i systems you need to run 5 companies vs. how many you need with the "other" choices out there. I'm not in my mid-twenties anymore, but, I like to think I'm carrying the torch a little further than those before me can. And if I can, I hope I'll be converting a few in the generation to take my place, along the way.

One last thing- While sitting at home the other night watching the latest primetime show, LOST, I almost fell out of my chair. It cut to commercial and one of IBM's latest campaigns came on. Although I love the new ad campaign, it always annoys me that the IBM i is never part of the puzzle. It's hard enough for IBM i shops to get the budget to buy the new Power System with IBM i they want or my products from Quadrant (hopefully you all will), without IBM highlighting every other server, but no IBM i on TV.

There's Linux and global services; but, never anything on the do-everything machine. Then, it happened. The best consolidation platform in the world was the message. It wasn't like the Sox winning the World Series or anything

(I'm obviously from Boston). We have a long way to go for that again. But, it was a little like the late inning rally when Boston was down to the last out and losing to the Yankees in the ninth inning of the 2004 ALCS- a little glimmer of hope. Maybe they are finally getting it, I thought. Getting what thousands of SMB's all over the world already know. The Power System with IBM i is simply the greatest business machine money can buy."

Dave Books, Former IBM Systems Engineer

"One of IBM's best kept secrets is the incredible reliability of the AS/400. I did some work with the Rollins Company here in Atlanta. They are the parent company of Orkin Pest Control, among others. Orkin has a small AS/400 in each of its four hundred plus branch offices. They're controlled from Atlanta. Critical information is downloaded to a large AS/400 here each night. Thus there's no need to back up the individual AS/400's at the branch level.

Last year, I was talking to one of the support reps on the Orkin help desk. He told me about a call he got from an Orkin branch manager. As the manager described the problem he was having, the support rep became more and more convinced it was an AS/400 hardware problem. The support rep called IBM hardware support and they dispatched a CE to fix the problem.

When the CE arrived at the branch office, there was no one there who knew where the AS/400 was. It had been rocking along doing its job with no attention from anyone for so long; no one was currently working, in the branch office, who had been there when it was first installed. The IBM CE and the branch manager literally had to go around the office opening doors until they finally found the broken AS/400. Fortunately it was fixed quickly and was back in normal operation. The support rep who relayed this story to me thought it was an incredible testimony to the day-in, day-out dependability of the IBM i family."

Bob Cancilla, Formerly of Ignite/400

"There may be some concern and question about the future of the machine within IBM, but not about the machine. As you well know, the machine and its software gets better and better exponentially. Talk about the world's best kept secret!

IBM recently bragged about the big deal they did with eBay selling them AIX or Linux (non IBM i) based machines with WebSphere. It was a very huge sale. I think that IBM did the customer a giant disservice by not selling them on IBM i based technology. The Power System with IBM i could have reduced the staff and administrative nightmares that eBay must suffer from by an astronomical numbers! I would bet you could probably run the entire eBay network on three of the big IBM Power Systems with IBM i with total replication and redundancy creating an environment that would never fail. Furthermore, the total environment could be managed by a handful of people.

But, IBM's Software Group sells WebSphere Server (WAS) by processor so, they sold a lot of copies of WAS, ND, and machines and other supporting software and hardware and the CIO of eBay seems to love having a huge body count to administer his kingdom. Too bad the CEO wasn't aware of iSeries [IBM i]; she might have had a different opinion. "

Sr. Marketing Manager at IBM Software Group

A friend of mine (your author BK) who spent many years in iSeries activities had this to say in an email note to me just recently:

"A while back.... I was creating my own list of why I love iSeries [i5]... even though I had been away from that division for 4 years.

I looked up the OS vulnerabilities and IBM i had only one recorded vulnerability (and it wasn't even on the IBM i partition) vs. hundreds and hundreds on other operating systems. Check it out at: www.securityfocus.com

The IBM i platform uses I/O Adapters (IOA). IBM i offloads this work to the IOA's freeing up the CPU(s) to run many more applications. This is not how other servers operate.

Automatic Load Balancing - IBM i creates one large disk pool that automatically balances content across all disk heads for maximum performance. This means you never need to know where your data is, therefore negating the need for a $100K+/yr. Data Base Administrator. I remember one of my old roles at a previous company was to keep track of where and how objects were stored for my department. And it was a big job. It is hard for non-IBM i folks to realize that is not necessary. It took me 6 months after my arrival at IBM to understand why that role is not needed with IBM i- BIG money saver for iSeries owners.

Again around Data - IBM i allows you to create data spaces that can be dynamically added to MS Windows or Linux partitions. Because these spaces are dynamic and not fixed (like adding a 120GB Hard drive to a PC for extra space), disk space is maximized and not wasted. Then you get the benefits of having this data under multiple disk heads. All this equates to lower TOTAL cost of ownership.

For writing Java Applications, the IBM i Java Virtual Machine is embedded in the Machine Interface (closer to the hardware). In addition to this the JVM utilizes better garbage collection (which cleans up memory or unused objects no longer running). Instead of shutting down all threads (like other operating systems) on a Server to run garbage collection, iSeries shuts down one thread at a time picking up a double digit performance boost.

And what about TIMI? The Technology Independent Machine Interface (some call it "Firmware"), which allows a company to change the hardware without affecting the software and change the software without concern for the hardware. This is unheard of on most operating systems.

Also - I remember Over 65,000 virus threats to other operating systems - none to IBM i operating system or data. DB2 for IBM i data is particularly difficult to penetrate. Check Symantec's Site - it is likely there are still zero threats to iSeries or IBM i data...even today.

These are a very small number of the long list that makes IBM i so different... but each makes IBM i boxes less expensive to own. So I suggest businesses look at the longer term cost of a server or operating system... instead of just the acquisition cost. Acquisition of other servers may be inexpensive...but they often bite you over the long haul. It CAN be much more (or much less) to OWN a system ...versus what looks like the low cost of ACQUIRING a system. "caveat emptor." "

Paul Harkins, Harkins Audit Software, Inc

"The Best Corporate Computer there ever was

The IBM System/38 and its follow-on computers, the AS/400, the iSeries, and now the IBM Power System with IBM i are the very best combination of brilliantly conceived and revolutionary computer hardware and software that I have experienced in my 43 years in corporate programming.

In fact, the introduction of the System/38 in 1980 prompted me to abruptly leave the IBM Data Processing Division (DPD), where I was a systems engineer supporting the

System/370 mainframe computers, and switch to the competing General Systems Division (GSD) which developed and announced this fantastic computer.

I was about to accept a great three-year assignment with IBM World Trade Corporation, in the IBM Process Industry Center in Düsseldorf Germany, to develop an IBM apparel product for the unannounced IBM 4300 (code named E series) replacement computer for the System/370 when I was stunned by the elegance and power and the simplicity of the IBM System/38 announcement.

The reason for my giving up skiing in Switzerland and living abroad at an IBM headquarters location for IBM was selfish. The development of the IBM ERP apparel system on the System/38 would clearly be many times more productive, and be much simpler and more satisfying, and produce a better product in less time than developing with the aging and difficult software available on the System/370 or its follow-on IBM 4300. I actually told my furious Germany born wife Gisela and our children that they would be skiing in Switzerland while I was trying to finish my ERP product by the required announcement date.

With the System/38, IBM Rochester had made what was difficult very easy and transparent to programmers. For instance, in the System/370 doing online screens required working with the IBM online product known as the Customer Information Control System. CICS required very small program modules called Transaction Processing Programs (TPPs), which were a maximum of four thousands bytes each, and complex Assembler or COBOL, processing of these online processing programs.

The System/38 totally simplified both batch and interactive programming by **integrating and simplifying** the online screen processing in a conversational programming approach within the OS/400 operating system. This allowed System/38 application programs to be programmed, in a natural way, in a powerful, but easy, Report Program Generator (RPG) programming language as the programmer implemented the application and in "pleasingly plump" robust application programs that were very easily maintainable.

IBM and particularly Dr. Frank Soltis and the Rochester programming team got it incredibly right with the System/38 by doing all the difficult system hardware and system software things and shielding the corporate programmer from that difficulty while allowing corporate programmers to focus on the creative part of programming corporate business applications. The result was perhaps a ten times increase in corporate programmer productivity with the System/38 and RPG over the System/370.

IBM has multiplied the power of the original System/38 hardware by many thousands of times with the new IBM Power Systems processors running IBM i as the OS, and is poised to multiply the IBM i processing power another *billion* times over the working career of a programmer.

Today, the Power System with IBM i also enjoys the unprecedented capability to completely audit the execution of every source statement and the variable data in real-time as programs execute. This allows programmers and auditors to see everything executing inside the computer and to audit or log everything for later review. This auditing capability uniquely satisfies the Sarbannes-Oxley legislation requirement of "auditing at every level", and provides a quantum jump in program quality and programmer productivity. "

Bob Morici, Former IBM Systems Engineer (SE), iSeries Brand Representative

The Casino System

"The casino industry was not automated in the late 1970s. Legal gaming was limited to Las Vegas. The Las Vegas casinos were largely family owned, with the exception of Howard Hughes' corporation (I can't remember their name, but they owned the Sands, The Dunes and 3 other famous properties). There were some systems running payroll and other back office functions, but the general consensus was that you could not automate the gaming functions. It was a service industry and good service required a high touch environment.

Casino gaming was legalized in Atlantic City in 1977. The State of NJ was determined to keep organized crime out of Atlantic City. As a result, there were many more regulations in Atlantic City than there ever were in Las Vegas, plus the market was quite different. While Las Vegas had vacationers and high rollers, Atlantic City had over 20 million people within a 2 hour drive. This resulted in lots of day trippers, some of them were regular Atlantic City visitors. For example, one large AC casino brought in over 150 busses per day.

The intense regulations along with the millions of fairly small, but regular, day trippers required a level of automation far in excess of what existed in Las Vegas. The IBM sales team in 1978 located a Hotel system from a hotel in Atlanta, Ga. It ran on a System/3 under CCP. This system was brought into Atlantic City to run the hotel side of the business. The local sales team brought a banking terminal, the 3610, into the casino industry and programmed it to be a point of sale device attached to the hotel application. This was the only terminal that the System/3 supported. The last part to be automated was the casino application.

I had been hired into IBM in April 1979. I had been a programmer at several large IBM customer sites. As a result, I was asked to write the first automated casino system on the System/3. I worked closely with Larry Cole, VP of IT at the Sands Hotel & Casino. Larry had worked with the accountants at the Sands to spec out a casino system. We completed the system and went live in August 1980. The Sands also sold the system to the Claridge Hotel/Casino and they went live with the application in April 1981.

The System/3 was outdated and we all knew that it had to be replaced, but it was all we had at that time, plus, having a working hotel system for the System/3 was a big plus. And we were GSD [IBM's small system division at the time], so we had to sell what was on the truck. The System/34 was available, but did not have enough power for these applications.

In early 1982, we started our rewrite to the System/38. Four members of the team wrote the hotel system, which later was called HRGAS (Hotel Reservation Guest Accounting System), another member of our team wrote a point of sale system, based on 3483 cash registers attached to the Series/1. I began work on the casino system. I did receive some assistance from one of the hotel system programmers. No one really does anything by themselves, and we were a tight knit group.

I worked with Larry Cole of the Sands again. We developed the system, but the Sands was in the process of being sold, so we took the application live at Bally's Hotel/Casino, which was across the street from the Sands. The IBM account team was instrumental in working out all of these joint efforts.

We took the application live in early 1984. We actually completed the application in 1983, but at that time the Casino Control Commission was fighting with the property owners for 'unfettered access' to this new system. The industry does not like regulators wandering around their systems. This issue went all the way to the NJ Supreme Court who finally ruled in favor of the Casino owners, and we were able to go live.

Our Branch Manager, Harry Griffiths, had wanted to create a Hospitality Competency Center in the branch office. Las Vegas was changing. Large companies were building casinos, the old time family owners were moving out. Howard Hughes died. Harry knew that our systems would fit in the new Las Vegas and this would allow us to poach in their territory. So we tried to purchase these applications from the Sands (casino) and Harrah's (hotel). We wrote the applications under contract with these customers, so they owned the rights. IBM management did not have the foresight that Harry had; they soundly rejected this idea. IBM did not want to get involved with the casino industry.

Larry Cole at the Sands did not want to be a software vendor, but he owned a valuable asset. He made an agreement with Russ Keil of the Claridge. Russ left the Claridge and formed Logical Solutions Inc. LSI added marketing modules and started the re-write of the point of sale system. Since the POS system was not System/38 based, but Series/1 based, it had to be re-written every few years as technology changed.

Today, the Casino system is owned by one of the casinos. Russ has retired, Larry Cole died in Oct., 2002. It has a market share in excess of 70% worldwide. The Hotel system has a similar market share, but the POS never really achieved the market success of either Hotel or Casino. The People's Republic of China authorized 3 casinos on Macau, which had been returned to China from Portugal. All 3 of them run this casino system.

In 2001, my second daughter, Krista, went to work for Bally's in AC. She used the system that I developed the year she was born. I received quite a bit of free advice as to how I should have done certain interfaces. Krista has since left Bally's and returned to school.

If our AC customers had gone with the darling of the industry, they would have written this on Wang, then rewritten it on a DEC Vax, then Unix (several iterations), perhaps VSE, and someone would have given Windows a try (a couple of iterations there too). As it was, they have never re-written a line of code because of the changes from the System/38 (at release 4.1) through the AS/400, through the iSeries and the i5 to the new IBM Power System running IBM i..

This next piece of the story involves two casinos that were part of industry consolidations and neither exists today so I will just call them Casino 1 and Casino 2.

I was still working in AC in 1991. At that time, one of the casinos where I did some work on behalf of IBM owned 4 other large casinos. With the Casino Software I wrote, they managed it all with only 9 professional systems folks. It was a major operation. There were also secretaries and operators who are not included in this count.

Then, this casino (a. k. a. Casino 1) bought another casino (a. k. a. Casino 2) that was actually bigger than them. Casino 2 had been running on IBM mainframes because the IT management there did not want to use the System/3, when they opened in 1979, and instead chose the IBM 4341 mainframe.

I went over to Casino 2 at the time of the acquisition and was really impressed with the large number of people walking around, the massive size of the IT staff and the huge computer room with lots of blinking lights. Soon, I realized that they were not doing anything more than our AS/400-iSeries-i5-Power System customers, and they weren't doing it as well or Casino 2 would have bought Casino 1 and not the other way around.

As a system that really affects the bottom line, the Casino 1-Casino 2 story, as much as any, demonstrates the value proposition of today's IBM Power System with IBM i and that goes way back to the IBM System/38. With IBM i, as I have found in most instances, less is more (staff, downtime, errors) and you get much more for much less, and that costs a lot less than more. As you might expect, the rigors and exactness of the casino industry could accept nothing less."

Biographies:

Jim Sloan is a retired IBMer (1991) who is now President of Jim Sloan, Inc. Jim was the lead software planner on the System/38 Operating System project in IBM's Rochester Labs until he retired. From the beginning of AS/400 time, through the early stages of development, through completion and to the ultimate success of the System/38, Jim Sloan saw major action with the historic AS/400 product line. He continued in this capacity through the development and the early releases of AS/400 and through his company, Jim Sloan Inc., Jim has worked with the AS/400, the iSeries, the i5 and the Power System with IBM i. While he was still working on System/38, Jim started what is known as the QUSRTOOL library and he wrote all of the "TAA" Tools in the library. Since 1991, Jim Sloan, Inc. has had a license from IBM to include the TAA Tools in his TAA Productivity Tools product. Jim is the developer of this product.

My interview with Jim Sloan was the first time I had the opportunity to be one on one with him, but I had spoken with him as part of small groups at COMMON conferences over the years. He is quite a guy. He is one of my favorite technical speakers of all time. He knows APIs and CL programming like the back of his hand, and he has a masterful presentation technique. As an aside, Jim has spoken at every COMMON Conference since 1979. He is truly an AS/400 and System/38 folk hero. He is a legend for those of us that have been with the product since its early days. It is a pleasure to include Jim Sloan's comments about our favorite system:

Skip Marchesani retired from IBM after 25 years and is now a consultant with Custom Systems Corp, an IBM Business partner. Skip spent much of his IBM career working with the Rochester Development Lab on projects for S/38 and AS/400, and was involved with the development of the AS/400. He was part of the team that taught early AS/400 education to customers and IBM lab sites worldwide. I met Skip in Philadelphia, in 1980. He was my instructor for several weeks of internal IBM System/38 education when we were preparing to initially install System/38 boxes in the local offices. Those were the days.

Skip is recognized as an industry expert on DB2 for i and AS/400 and author of the book DB2/400: The New AS/400 Database. He specializes in providing customized education for any area of the iSeries, AS/400, and IBM i. He does database design and design reviews, and general iSeries and AS/400 and IBM Power System consulting for interested clients. He has been a speaker for user groups, technical conferences, and iSeries and AS/400 audiences around the world. Skip is an award winning COMMON speaker and has received their Distinguished Service Award.

As noted in the comments section, **Al Barsa, Jr., Mr.400** was President of Barsa Consulting Group, LLC and Barsa Systems Distribution, Inc., at the time of his death in April, 2008. His company still specializes in the iSeries - AS/400 - IBM Power System with IBM i. Al was the President of the Long Island Systems User Group and he always covered new hardware and software announcements for iSeries News. Al was very active in the COMMON organization as a frequent speaker at both US COMMON and COMMON Europe, as an Editor of the COMMON technical library and as a member of the Speaker Excellence Committee, and has addressed other user groups throughout the world.

In the past, Al had been voted COMMON's "Best Speaker", won Gold, Silver and Bronze medals, and has received COMMON's highest honor, the COMMON Distinguished Service Award. For the year ending 2002 and in six prior years, Al was named on the 'AS/400 Insider Weekly's' "10 Biggest AS/400 Market Influencers" list, making him the only person in the world ever to be named seven times! Both Barsa Consulting Group and Barsa Systems Distribution are IBM Premier Business Partners. Barsa Consulting Group was the recipient of the IBM Business Partner Mark of Quality Award.

Albert Simon Barsa was only 55 when he died suddenly Thursday, April 3, 2008 while attending the annual COMMON Conference, at which he had always been a staple, a well-known and popular person. As a longtime respected member of the IBM midrange community, Barsa was the recipient of many tributes after his passing and as noted, he was the recipient of many awards during his lifetime. And, Al appreciated them all.

Al Barsa was also one of life's finest speakers to have ever graced a podium and he had been voted COMMON's best speaker numerous times. But, above all, he was one of the best people you would ever want to know. Al was good people! He deserved all of his many honors and accepted them graciously. He was a friend. We'll miss him big time. When the Computer Hall of Fame is finally built, Mr. 400 will have an esteemed position.

Bob Warford is the Director of Information Systems / Computer Services at Labette Community College in Parsons, Kansas.

Doug Hart is a midrange systems consultant for Whitenack Consulting, located in Rochester NY and operating in Upstate New York. He has been in the IT industry for over 30 years, with much of it focusing on the AS/400 family of computer systems. Doug works with systems used in very small "Mom and Pop" companies to the largest Fortune 500 enterprises.

Ken Anderson, Quadrant Software -- A frequent speaker at QUEST, multiple midrange ERP specific conferences, and local user groups, Ken Anderson has spent the past six years of his tenure at Quadrant Software promoting the concept of Electronic Document Distribution (EDD) solutions to iSeries users and IT managers throughout the North America. He has helped over 400 companies including Sara Lee Foods, Phillip Morris, and Office Depot recognize the value of automating document processes. As a speaker, Ken combines the business strategies behind EDD with case study examples for an informative and thought-provoking presentation.

Dave Books. For the last three years prior to retiring (for good), Dave was an AS/400 consultant for Venture System Source, an IBM Business Partner. For the three years prior to that he was an AS/400 services consultant to IBM. Prior to that, he spent 30 years with IBM, mostly as a Systems Engineer. Dave ended his IBM career with the title AS/400 Consulting Services Specialist.

Bob Cancilla has spent 30 years managing large-scale systems development projects and technology for both large insurance companies and independent software development companies, and he has been involved with AS/400 Internet technology since its inception. He was the managing director and founder of the 6,500-member computer user group Ignite/400, before being hired by IBM in its Toronto Application Development Tools Lab..

Paul H. Harkins, President and Chief Technology Officer of Harkins Audit Software, Inc., is still an active corporate programmer.

Mr. Harkins has been working with IBM systems for more than 40 years, including 21 years at IBM, where, as a senior systems engineer, he was involved in hundreds of customer accounts worldwide and where he created the original IBM Apparel Business System, the first on-line IBM software package ever designed for the apparel industry.

Paul has published articles relating to programmer productivity in several information technology magazines, and is the author of the newly published book "How to Become a Highly Paid Corporate Programmer". He also pioneered a software auditing technique to increase programmer productivity, the Real-Time Program Audit (RTPA), an award-winning software utility. In August 2004, Paul was awarded U.S. Patent 6,775,827 B1, for his invention of the Real-Time Program Audit software auditing idea.

Mr. Harkins holds BS and MBA degrees from Drexel University, and is a graduate of the IBM Systems Research Institute (SRI). His email address is paulhark@aol.com.

Bob Morici is a former IBM Systems Engineer (SE) who, at the time of this original writing, worked for the IBM iSeries-i5 Brand. In that position, he focused on IBM's largest iSeries customers worldwide. Bob's IBM career spans 29 years.

As an IBM SE in Atlantic City for 14 years, he took on the major role in developing the Casino System and he assisted in opening most of the Atlantic City casinos. When IBM changed its business model to resellers, Bob left Atlantic City and became a certified AS/400 sales specialist in the Philadelphia area. For a brief period he left IBM and became a business partner and several years ago he rejoined IBM in the position noted above.

Chapter 6   IBM i -- The Unsung Operating System!

IBM Was the Only Game in Town

In the early 1970's, when I worked for the local IBM Branch Office in Scranton, PA as a Systems Engineer, IBM small business computers were the only game in town. Burroughs and NCR were pushing quasi-ledger card machines as computers and Sperry Univac had yet to create a small system solution. If they had one at the time, they did not market it in Northeastern, Pennsylvania. Digital Equipment Corporation (DEC or Digital), Data General, and Wang began to make machines called minicomputers. In their early incarnations, these small, but powerful machines were most often used as special purpose computers to control processes such as traffic signalization for cities. Eventually, they gained some business processing capabilities.

Minicomputers were quite prevalent in academic institutions because they were affordable and because the manufacturers would make deals with the academic institutions, so that the graduates would have an affinity to their products. By the late 1970's, DEC as the company was known then, became the leading minicomputer vendor, though Wang and Data General and Hewlett Packard had a nice piece of the pie.

DEC introduced its very popular VAX system and by the end of the 1970's, all the minicomputer vendors had added business compilers and better data capabilities to their systems. The whole game changed at this time. While IBM's small business systems were far easier to use and far more conducive to a small business that was barely computer literate than the competition, the minicomputers cost less and were far more capable in terms of range of capabilities (also provided analog processing and multiple terminals) than the IBM small business line.

In fact, if IBM read the bid specs, often influenced by a minicomputer vendor, and chose to bid on a new opportunity, the specs would force IBM to bypass the small business line and propose a small mainframe instead of a System/3. Once this happened, the cost of the IBM system was often three to four times the cost of the minicomputer and IBM more often lost the business than gained it.

But, before this happened in the early to mid-1970's, IBM had owned the small business sector of computing. There was no real competition. IBM Systems Engineers were used by the company to increase the number of new computer accounts dramatically from the 1960's, as the cost of computing was coming down and ease of use characteristics were built into the IBM System/3 and then the System/32 line of computers. So, in the early 1970's IBM had the edge on being able to supply hardware and software solutions for small businesses.

Its systems, for the day and age, were remarkably easy to use. A small IBM lab in Rochester, Minnesota helped IBM begin its dominance by introducing a machine called the System/3 in 1969. By the time 1975 came around, a smaller version of the machine had been introduced as the IBM System/32. Chapter 7 provides full details of the System/3 origination and its progression to the IBM Power System with IBM i.

The new system in 1975, the IBM System/32 was unique in its small size for the time. We joke today that it was desk-sized, not desk-top as today's many PCs. This machine was actually bigger than most server racks are today in small businesses. But, it was desk sized. Well, in reality it was big desk sized.

No, it did not use the all-everything operating system that this book is all about but, at the time, IBM's General Systems Division, in which I worked, treated it as the all-everything machine for very small businesses. I must admit that for its day, it was quite a unit. And in historical context, its operating system contributed a number of the notions that are in play today in the all-everything operating system, IBM i.

Application Software Challenge

At the time the System/32 was announced, IBM had a division specifically designed to create and sell small business computer systems. It was the best organization that IBM ever had to address the focused needs of the small business community, many of whom had never seen a computer system before. IBM's General Systems Division had intentions of being the leader in small business systems and they executed their mission very well.

From my perspective, this division was the best place to work in all of IBM. Helping new IBM customers implement their first computer application was always a challenge; yet, it was at the same time a wonderful experience. It gave both the IBMers and the customer a great feeling of accomplishment when it was done and the IBM client was live on their new System/32, enjoying the benefits of "modern" business data processing.

One if the big advantages of the 1975 IBM System/32 was that it was reliable. Like all real computer systems that I have ever worked with at IBM, the System/32 did not break... ever. OK, it did! But when it did, even the IBM repairman was surprised.

To be a leader, GSD had to supply application software solutions to its prospects. Though these packages sold well at the time, the only surviving software package of the many developed at that time by GSD for the System/32 is something called MAPICS (Manufacturing Production and Information Control System). MAPICS is a popular ERP package that exists today as an offering of the Marcam Corporation from Newton, Massachusetts. This package evolved from a System/32 version called MMAS, which stood for the IBM Manufacturing Management Accounting System.

In a way, having just one survivor is a big clue that the System/32 application software effort did not succeed in a historical sense. Over 50 different packages, as I recall, were introduced by IBM's GSD in the mid 1970's and MAPICS is the sole survivor and even MAPICS is no longer an IBM product. That is not to say that the packages were not good or that the customers were unhappy. The packages were good and the customers were mostly happy and the System/32 was an absolute raging success for IBM. Quite frankly, I still do not understand why IBM exited the application software business.

These "Industry Application Packages," or IAPS as they were called, were sold by IBM GSD Reps to first time computer users. The new users typically had been conducting business with pencils, erasers, ledger cards, paper accounting journals, rubber bands, and paper clips. IBM had a staff of trained computer experts at the time called Systems Engineers (SEs) who patiently held the hands of its System/32 customers, sometimes round the clock, until the kinks, and sometimes the attitudes, were ironed out.

Some Customers Got Free Program Code

Though IBM had unbundled on June 23, 1969, and technically software and SE services were billable, most if not all IBM GSD Branch Offices ignored these rules. When our office in Wilkes-Barre / Scranton merged with Reading, PA to form a larger office, we learned that not only were most offices providing free installation and programming services (whatever it took), some were actually giving away software packages that they had either written or had clandestinely acquired.

My peers in Reading called this software "drawer code." I love that term. They had the code on big 8 inch diskettes stored in their desk drawers. When a customer needed software in order to close the deal, the drawer was opened and the big diskettes came out. The code got copied and the IBM SE installed the system along with the free "drawer code" applications.

IBM was making a killing on new accounts because of the innovation of many in its field sales force, who by the way, could have lost their jobs if caught. And, IBM's new customers were very pleased. The drawer code was enduring and helped many businesses get a great head-start.

Lots of System/32 Installations

In the mid 1970's, I can attest that SEs were feeling the strain of working sixty to eighty hours per week to assure the success of branch office sales to its prospects and customers. Though we wanted the office to meet and to exceed quota for sure and we were all motivated to get the job done and leave the client as a happy, repeat IBM customer, the work was long and sometimes even too long.

Moreover, the inefficiencies and the "bugs" in the new IBM application software (not the drawer code) caused the SEs and System/32 customers much angst and many overtime hours. IBM had taken Systems Engineers from Branch Offices and put them in labs in Atlanta during this time to build these "fail-safe" application packages. Unfortunately, the code was so new and so complex that IBM SEs were reluctant to modify it to make it work for their clients -- fearful they would break something else. IBM, like most software companies did not support modified application code.

Worse than that, the labs in Atlanta were very slow to respond when the need for a fix was clearly identified. So, the code was complex. SE's did not understand it as well as drawer code, and the code could not be fixed by the labs expeditiously enough to rapidly install a new System/32 account.

Knowing the state of the software, you can imagine the reaction of IBM's own customer support team when the company launched its best small business advertising campaign ever. I present this for historical purposes. In retrospect it is funny but, it was not funny then.

IBM's Best Advertising Campaign Ever

It is in the light of 60 to 80 hour work weeks with no relief in sight that I reminisce about the best advertising campaign that I can recall for IBM's small business offerings. At the time, this was the IBM System/32 and its Industry Application Programs. It was clear to me when I saw the TV ad for the first time that the IBM Company intended to sell a zillion System/32 boxes and lots of application software. It was brilliant.

I admit that I had two emotions about it at the time. I was first tickled that IBM was aggressively marketing because I knew there would be good results and my job would be well secured. At the same time, I was concerned that there were not enough of us locally to make the installations occur. New customers who received IBM's mass marketing message had their expectations for a quick and smooth, completely painless installation set by the ad, would be less understanding when something went wrong. Being a bit tired of working so much at the time, I can recall my deep fear that they would all decide to buy at the same time.

I can remember the ad almost as if it were yesterday. In fact, I would suspect that most Systems Engineers working with

IBM's System/32 clients still remember it well. The three biggest problems that we had with the television ad were as follows:

1. We felt that customer expectations for a smooth installation would be over-inflated.

2. Since initial expectations would more than likely be unmet, we felt that customer expectations for support above and beyond the call would also not be able to be met.

3. The ad would create a customer who would not trust IBM or its representatives (us) again.

Show Me The Ad!

I will be the first to tell you in retrospect that I feel that the ad was sheer genius. IBM has yet to advertise the Power System with IBM i as it did the lowly System/32 back in the mid 1970's. The GSD Division actually wanted to sell computers and it knew how. If IBM marketed the IBM i based systems in the fashion of this IBM System/32 ad, more people in this universe would have heard of the AS/400, i5, the iSeries, and the new "IBM i" operating system.

The System/32 ad may not have been reality, but neither are most ads. Since that ad, over thirty plus years have passed. The hyperbole used by IBM's competitors in today's ads makes this little ditty from the mid-seventies seem mild in comparison. I wish I could give you a YouTube link. Maybe somebody in the IBM Archives Department will release this baby one day. It was special.

Picture the beauty of this scenario as the camera breaks away from your favorite TV program to an ad with no announcement. You see the loading dock of a company like yours. There is a long haul carrier truck backing in. You see the desk-sized System/32 being wheeled into the factory / warehouse and then very quickly into the office. Whoosh! It is that fast!

You see a short period in which a small amount of packing material is removed and the brave installer from IBM plugs the unit into the wall – all very quickly. (I forgot to note that the machine needed electricity -- in fact, just about all the electricity that one wall outlet could pump out!).

An already trained System/32 operator from the company lucky enough to receive this ready-to-go unit goes ahead and takes control of the machine and quickly types a command. That fast, the camera moves to the printer and already this miracle computer is rapidly producing the company's aged receivables report – just in time. And, you could see it on the printer.

It was using the current customer information and it was just amazing and all of the company personnel were in awe. It was a miracle. And, everybody lived happily ever after. And that miracle was available, for the asking, from IBM.

Being trained to be a nitpicker, I had all kinds of questions of how that could ever be. Where did the data come from and how could the customer person already know everything to do. Selfishly, I saw my workweek increasing even more than it already had – for no additional compensation. None of my peers were thrilled with the ad either. We hoped nobody actually saw it and if they did, we hoped that they did not believe it.

You Gotta Be Kidding!

I am in my fifties today (OK sixties) and perhaps then some. Back then I was in my twenties. I have learned plenty since the 1970's. In retrospect, as noted above, it was a wonderful ad and no rational being expected that this machine would be able to do all that it did in those few seconds in that ad. No company at the time would already have the applications and up-to-the-minute data pre-loaded on the computer at the plant from which to produce the business reports that just kept coming off this obviously phenomenal new machine.

For anybody in IBM who was not working the 60 or 80 hours per week, it was viewed immediately as a great ad. IBM had done the right thing with the ad. It worked. The systems sold as fast as IBM could ship them. People in strange places were talking about an IBM business system. The ad had done the trick. Perhaps, just perhaps, advertising actually can help a marketing organization.

So SEs had to become better friends with their customers to get the extra time needed to make the increased installations a success. We did! Looking back, it was all good. And, IBM customers really appreciated the effort. IBM had a killer machine for the small business community.

As you will learn in the next chapter, the all-everything operating system came from the same roots as the System/32's mini OS. It was intended for the same general audience, though perhaps the specific takers of the newer technology would have somewhat larger wallets and bigger issues to solve.

In 1978, IBM announced to the world its first iteration of the all-everything operating system as an infant in the data processing industry. It had a very humble name back then, Control Program Facility (CPF). There was a huge worldwide series of announcement meetings and a big press conference in October, 1978 when the first all-everything OS was unveiled with the System/38. However, from 1975 to today, even on the IBM Power Systems with IBM i worldwide announcement day, I cannot recall an IBM sponsored TV ad that was so realistic that IBM's own technicians did not know how to limit the customer perspectives and expectations.

Do You Know about the All-Everything Operating System?

So, "Why have you not heard about the all-everything operating system?"

The business answer to that question is that IBM has been successful with small businesses systems for over thirty years from well before the time of the infamous System/32 ad. The IBM Company has not had to advertise in order to achieve its sales or revenue objectives. There are those of us out here though who have a feeling that we may have complained a little too loudly back in the mid 1970's when IBM broke its tradition of not advertising on TV and chose to tell the world about its marvelous "little" System/32. Hey IBM, It's OK to tell the world about the all-everything operating system – even if sales are good.

At any rate, though IBM's systems are still very successful, and they still sell, it is my humble opinion that more and more business people should know about today's all-everything OS. It is a fine alternative to the most hyped systems and operating systems of today coming from Intel and Microsoft and from Unix and Linux vendors.

Windows Reliability = Low Expectations

Let me give you just one general scenario that I hear about all the time. Over the twenty-four years since I retired from IBM, I have had many business friends and even my graduate business students at Marywood University ask me if it is a normal thing to not be able to use their business computer system for days at a time. In almost all cases, they refer me to a Windows Server running on Intel Hardware. They have never heard of IBM i and in most cases think IBM has sold about 500 huge computers to Fortune 500 companies and that is that.

Some try to minimize the time their systems are down by hiring an extra person or perhaps even two people to keep their servers and the software running so that the business can conduct business. I tell them that the systems with which I work don't behave that way but, their own experience often causes them to doubt me. They think that all computers are the same and that perhaps I did not understand that they were merely expressing frustration about the way life is using all computer systems.

The fact is that IBM has the only hardware and software on the planet that actually plays to the crowd for the answer to that question. But, IBM does not advertise its wares so nobody knows or desires its solid, fully functional, never go down solutions. So, I tell those that ask that I use a PC for my own small business because my part-time business cannot afford IBM i but, I regret the choice every time I must do work that otherwise, I would not have to do, when my own desktop PC goes down. And, with Windows, and Intel, that happens quite frequently.

Yes, you may accuse me of being prejudiced in favor of IBM products. But, if you looked at my resume for any length of time, you would see that I have worked on just about all systems. Not to be snippy, but I have been there and I have done that. The IBM i platform is simply the best there ever was and the good news is that it still is.

No other system comes close to stacking up, feature by feature to a system family that has endured and has advanced and has helped many businesses prosper and has now evolved into a system that is truly powered by an immensely capable Power 6 processor and an all-everything operating system.

So, you may be asking, what is it about this all-everything operating system now that you know that it is special? You are about to learn its origins in Chapter 7 and more about it in each of the following chapters. It's a big story. I can't tell it all in one book.

Even the all-everything OS will not be pumping out your A/R reports right off the truck. However, I can tell you that it is a quantum leap in sophistication, elegance, and capability over the ever popular IBM System/32, and all systems and operating systems between then and now. You and I would both be tickled if we had as system running this OS running our respective businesses.

Chapter 7 Brief History of Computers from IBM Rochester

The Rochester Mission

I am about to begin the story about the all-everything operating system as if it is a fairy tale that obviously is too good to be true. Though it is too good to be true, through 23-years at IBM and a number of years afterwards, I have made my living on this system, so I know it is real.

Once upon a time, in a small IBM laboratory in Rochester, Minnesota, there was a team with a big mission. Their job was to build a more modern set of unit record equipment. The Rochester team was blessed with the electrical and mechanical engineering know-how that could make the project a success; but, they realized that because it was the 1960s, electromechanical machines would soon not be in demand. After all, the first IBM System/360, the first solid state chip-based computer had already been shipped; it was already a huge success; and computers were really catching on in the marketplace. Oh, and by the way, Rochester did not have a mission to build a computer system.

> Note: Unit record equipment is a term used to describe the family of machines that would read or punch out IBM cards prior to the advent of bona fide computers. This gear was also called punched card processing equipment. Even after computers came to town these machines continued to provide accounting reports, sorted and/or merged card decks, duplicate card decks, and interpreted card decks, as well as calculated punched card decks for countless businesses. It was always impressive to see and hear all of this 80-column card gear in action. For a better understanding of unit-record gear and to see pictures of many of these behemoth machines, please read the next section. ...

A Quick Look at Punch Card Gear

In 1969, when I joined the IBM Company, the Company trained me to wire the panel boards that controlled the myriad of punch card machines that had been the mainstay of the company for decades. Back then, IBM customers could get themselves a keypunch, a sorter, and an accounting machine for just over $500.00 per month. Before the Rochester mission was accomplished, to get a jump on automated data processing, many chose to do exactly that.

I hope you enjoy this quick tour of a number of the machine models that were necessary in the pre-computer 80-column card processing world. If you do not want to take the tour, feel free to move to the heading announcing the end of the tour.

Over time, the machines you are about to see and learn about were collectively and methodically replaced by the Rochester mission. Therefore, this is the right place to view this equipment, as the history of the IBM Lab in Rochester, Minnesota and its all-everything operating system continues to unfold.

The Punch Card Equipment Tour Begins

Let's start the tour with a look at the IBM 129 Keypunch as shown in Figure 7-1. This is a machine that data entry personnel would use to type in data. The process of typing data into a card was called keypunching. For each of these unit records (cards) that were typed, the keypunch machine would "punch out" a card to represent the information record that had been keyed.

Figure 7-1 IBM 129 Keypunch Circa 1970

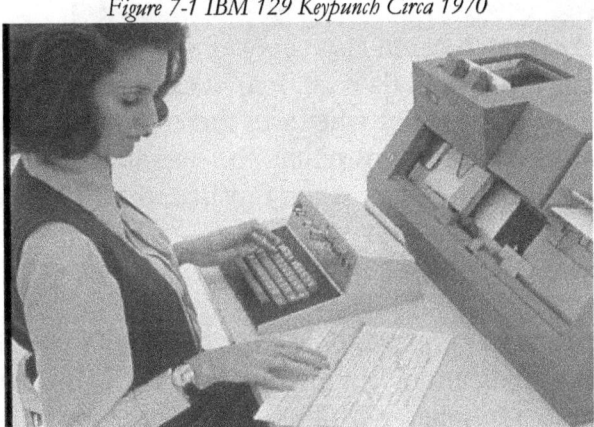

Early keypunches had no memory. When the typist typed an "A," for example, the unit immediately punched the holes in the card to represent the letter A. The codes had been determined earlier by one of the founders of early IBM whose name was Dr. Herman Hollerith. Thus, these holes punched in the card columns were said to use Hollerith encoding.

Back then, to assure that the input process would not discover errors, immediately after a stack of cards was punched, the original source documents containing the information as well as the keypunched cards were sent to the verifier station. Using a machine that looked very much like a keypunch, the verifier would read the holes column by column as the key-verifier retyped the important card columns, thereby assuring their accuracy. So, before any cards were processed, they were key-punched by one operator and key verified by another. Yes, if you are counting, the data was typed twice.

The IBM 129 keypunch was a later model unit with memory. Just like a memory typewriter, the card would not be punched until it was complete and the keypuncher said it was OK to punch the holes. Thus, if an operator made a mistake, they could tab backwards to the column to correct the error before the card was destroyed by the punching process.

The 129 keypunch could also serve as a verifier. It read the card into memory and then compared each keystroke, signaling the key-verifier whenever there was a mismatch in a column. If there was a mismatch, the operator would type in the correct code and then, when finished, the 129 would punch out a new card that was perfect and the operator would throw the old one away.

Once cards were punched, they were arranged in batches for the various applications and filed temporarily. From the file they went to a number of different machines that could perform operations on the stacks of cards. The machines that we show below are capable of operations such as sorting, merging, collating, matching, reproducing, interpreting, calculating, gang punching, printing, and more. Let's look at these units now.

An IBM 082 Sorter is shown on the left of Figure 7-2. Compared to other electromechanical card processing units, Sorters were reasonably small electromechanical machines, typically with one input hopper and eleven stackers. There were ten stackers for the digits 0 through 9 and an eleventh stacker for cards that could not be read (rejects).

Figure 7-2 IBM 082 Sorter circa 1965 and IBM 085 Collator

The operator would place cards in the sorter and the machine would read the value in the selected column and place the cards in the proper stacker after one pass. The operator would carefully place the results from all the stackers one on top of the other and the card deck would be in sequence (sorted) on that column. The operator would then again place the partially sorted cards into the hopper and repeat the process for as many additional passes as there were columns remaining to be sorted.

An IBM 085 Collator can be seen on the right side of Figure 7-2. I operated one of these when I was a student aide in the King's College Computing Center, in my sophomore year. This was a larger electromechanical machine than a Sorter. It typically had two card hoppers and four stackers. In normal operation, the operator would use the Collator to merge cards together.

However, the unit was programmable through wired panels so the operator could use a different panel board and use the Collator to match cards instead of merge them. This process would help assure that there was a master card, for example, for every transaction card. The extra stackers would be used to select the unmatched masters and the unmatched transaction cards, respectively.

The IBM 519 Reproducing Punch is shown on the left side of Figure 7-3. Like a collator, this was a large electromechanical machine that would read in a deck of punched cards and punch out an identical deck. In addition to duplicating cards, it could also be hooked up to an accounting machine via a big cable and be used to gang punch summary data produced by the accounting machine into blank cards.

Figure 7-3 IBM 519 Reproducing Punch and the IBM 548 Interpreter

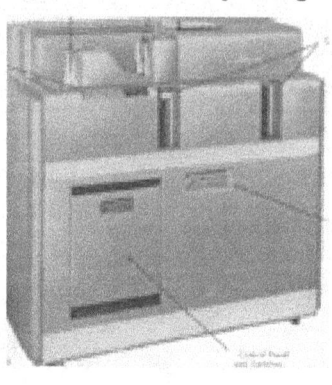 

When the cards were punched by the IBM 519 or another automated high speed punch -- such as a card punch connected to a computer system, the cards came out with no printing on top. As a next step in the process, the decks of just punched cards were placed into the hopper of something like the IBM 548 Interpreter as shown in Figure 7-3 on the right side.

This was another large electromechanical machine that would read in the cards that had been reproduced without printing, interpret the holes mechanically then, it would print their meaning in the form of letters and numbers on the top print line of the 80-column card.

When unit record gear was used for big operations that required calculations, it was time for the operator to use a device known as the Calculator, such as the IBM 604 Calculator shown on the left side of Figure 7-4. This huge machine was capable of performing computer-like mathematical functions using electromechanical circuitry. A technician would wire a panel describing the work to be done, for example to read in values from distinct columns of an input card and the calculator would produce a result, such as a price extension. To show the results of the calculations, the machine would punch the result into a set of columns that were different from the input columns on the same or the machine could punch out a new & different 80-column card.

Figure 7-4 IBM 604 Calculating Punch (Calculator) and IBM 407 Accounting Machine

The old sage of all the electromechanical behemoths was the Accounting Machine, as shown on the right side of Figure 7-4. This circa 1969 Accounting Machine, as shown, is an IBM 407, which was a very capable and very large unit for its day. This unit would read in pre-arranged decks of cards -- after all the sorting and manipulating -- and it would produce accounting / business reports. So, in many ways, it was a big card reader with a big printer. "Programmers" would wire a panel board to tell the machine which card columns to read and which print columns to print the various data elements on the card. Additionally, the machine itself could be used to perform light calculations and print the results on a report.

The Punch Card Equipment Tour Ends

The purpose of this tour was not just to show you the magnificent machines of early IBM fame. Many of these very machine models shown in the figures above were made in Rochester, Minnesota. Now, you see the reason why IBM Rochester was chosen as the place to build the newest punch card units. IBM was hoping to get a set of smaller 80-column units that were less expensive to build and, perhaps, a bit faster and more capable. As you are about to see, IBM got lots more than what it had asked for.

Rochester Moves on with Its Mission

The Rochester team was well aware that the mission to build real computers rested elsewhere in IBM, yet they earnestly believed that they should use computer technology in addition to electromechanical circuitry, in the new set of machines. Though there may always have been a desire in Rochester to produce the all-everything operating system, before 1969, when they completed this mission, they knew that if they called this new machine a computer in its internal project stage, they would not gain IBM's approval to build it. The small mainframe lab in Endicott, NY more than likely would have been selected.

However, Rochester was approved and it got the budget to build the next generation of "card processing machines." Officially, that's what they began to develop. Unofficially, however, the team knew they were designing and building a new computer system based on unit-record storage. The machine that flowed from this work would be called the IBM System/3. It would change IBM forever, offering ease-of-use computing to small businesses for the very first time.

Once the IBM System/3 was introduced in the fall 1969, the Rochester team: was no longer able to hide the fact that it had built a bona fide computer system. The first System/3 Model 10 Card System would be recognized in the industry and in IBM as a computer system, albeit one with limited capabilities.

Lots of Time to Think

Some say Rochester, Minnesota is a land where all there is to do is think. The opportunity to think in the cold while enjoying more than 250 days of sunshine each year made Rochester the perfect site for the conception of a new generation of computing. Though the System/3 was simple, it was very capable and innovative. A picture of the announced System/3 Model 10 card-only system is shown in Figure 7-5.

One-Third Size, 20% More Data

The first innovation at Rochester was the introduction of the 96-column card (see Figure 7-6). It was one-third the size of the 80-column punched card forms, in which many people over the years had received their paychecks and income tax return checks. By using a smaller card, all of the card processing equipment would be smaller and therefore, less costly to build. After cards were processed, as you can see on the left side of the unit, the System/3 had its own printer, the IBM 5203 which could be used for report production.

The main input unit for this card size on the System/3 was a device called the 5424 multi-function card unit (MFCU). It is located on the right side of the picture in Figure 7-5. This name is a derivative from IBM's System/360 Model 20, which had a similar, but much larger, multi-function card machine (MFCM) that processed 80-column cards.

Figure 7-5 IBM System/3 Model 10 with MFCU (Right) and Printer (Left)

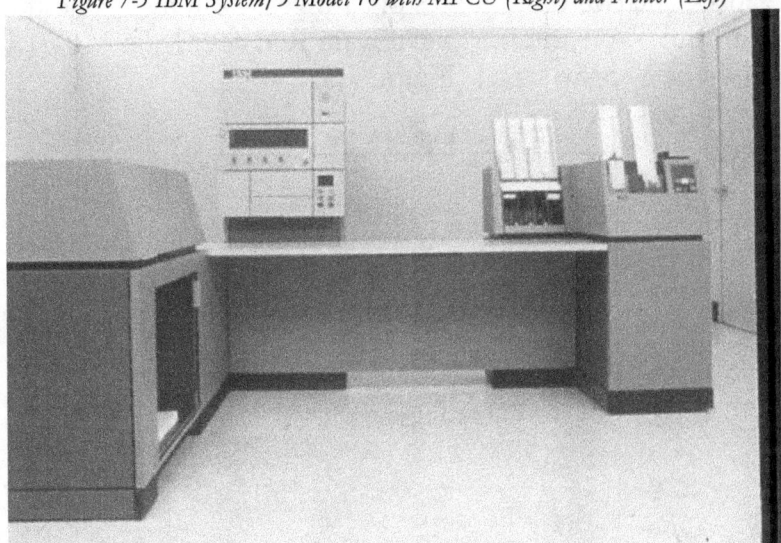

Figure 7-6 No Holes, 96-Column, System/3 Punched Card

The 96-Column Card Processing Gear

In addition to the System/3 itself with its magical MFCU, Rochester actually did build a new set of unit-record equipment. Along with the MFCU, this gear could do all of the work for 96-column cards that IBM's 80-column workhorses had been doing for 80-column cards since the 1930's. The two other pieces of card gear built by Rochester at this time were the IBM 5496 Data Recorder (Figure 7-7) and the IBM 5486 sorter (Figure 7-8).

Figure 7-7 IBM 5496 Data Recorder

Figure 7-8 IBM 5486 96-Column Table Top Card Sorter

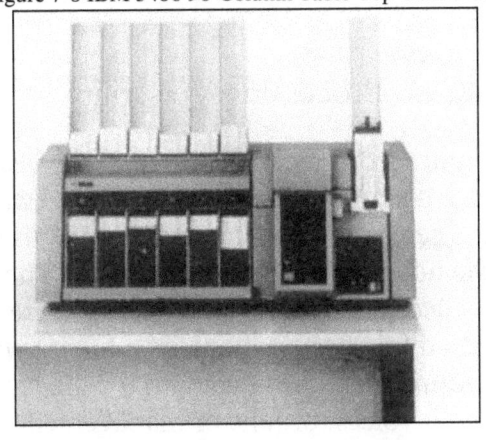

The IBM 5496 "keypunch" was very much like the 129 keypunch described earlier in this chapter, and it had all its attributes, but it was lots less expensive. The IBM 5486 had the same functionality of the IBM 082 sorter, but it had less stackers and thus required more sort passes. Compared to the four stacker MFCU shown in Figure 7-5; however, the 5486 was quite effective, plus it did not tie the main system unit up while it was sorting.

By any other name, the 5496 data recorder, just like the 80-column IBM 129 Keypunch would be an intelligent keypunch machine. It was the source of original entry. Its purpose was to permit an operator to create 96-column punched cards that represented either master records or transaction records for the business. Combinations of holes in the three-tiered card represented numbers and letters. Together, these were the data elements that provided input for the system.

Before being processed in the MFCU, the data often would be sorted using the IBM 5486 sorter. This was a two-tiered desktop device and was necessary in order to re-sequence cards for processing. IBM also provided a sort program for the System/3 to companies that believed that they could not afford a 5486. This permitted them to sort their cards using the two hoppers and four stackers of the MFCU attached to the System/3.

96-Column Card Processing Versatility

Unlike other unit record incarnations over the years, there was no separate collator unit needed to merge two decks of sorted cards. There was no interpreter needed to print the meaning of the holes on the top of the cards. There was no reproducer needed to duplicate card decks. There was no big calculator needed for computations. And there was no 96-column accounting machine needed to list the cards and provide printed invoices, orders, or management reports. As shown in Figure 7-5, the System/3 could provide all of these unit-record-like 96-column card functions by itself. It had its own printer and the MFCU which was truly multi-function

For example, the MFCU, instead of a collator, could be used for merging card decks. Special card programs were provided that enabled two columns of cards to be merged into one. The 5496 data recorder served double duty as it could interpret already punched cards in the same fashion as the big IBM 548 80-column unit. Thus, the IBM 5496, shown in Figure 7-1 served as a keypunch, a verifier and as an inexpensive interpreter to print on the cards punched by the MFCU.

Another special card program permitted the System/3 MFCU to reproduce cards by reading one deck on the left side and punching out a duplicate deck on the other side of the MFCU. The central processing unit (CPU) of the System/3 provided any calculations and report formatting. The CPU frame can be seen as the highboy column in the middle of the picture in Figure 7-5. Finally, the System/3 hardware complex included a choice of printers. The 5203 Printer (shown on the left side of Figure 7-5) printed reports at several hundred lines per minute. Faster printers, such as IBM's 1403 eternal workhorse, became available as the product matured.

There was no disk on the original System/3 computer system. Cards were the only storage medium. The system came with just 8k of memory as standard. That's a mere 8,096 memory positions. The System/3 card system did have a mini no-name operating system. It was provided in a stack of cards less than an inch high. This deck of cards was called the System Initialization Program (SIP), and its job was to simply "boot" the system. After powering up the unit, an operator would place the SIP deck in MFCU1 (the first hopper of the MFCU) and press the Start button. The system was hard wired to begin reading cards at power-on. When the SIP deck was read, the System/3 was ready for business.

Powerful Business Language for New S/3

Another major innovation for IBM at the time was the perfection of the RPG (Report Program Generator) programming language in the form of RPG II. This language was originally built for very old IBM computers in the late 1950s, such as the IBM 1401. As innovative as it was, it was never quite perfected for the IBM 1401, and prior to its use on System/3, it had a questionable reputation. The newly named RPG II language for the System/3 included many improvements.

To sum it up, RPG II had all the characteristics of a real programming language. Additionally, it was rich in business functions including decimal math, and thus it made the System/3 a real business computer. The language was instrumental in making the System/3 an instant success in small businesses. It was simple. It was somewhat English-like, and, unlike COBOL, it was not verbose or intimidating for new programmers. Most of all, it was easy to learn.

Since there were not many for-hire programmers back then, the lucky folks tapped to learn RPG in the 1970s with System/3 were often young, bright, and trustworthy. They held other positions in their companies and seemed like the right candidates. Most of these programmers have grown up to become the gray-haired IBM i professionals who are now approaching retirement age.

Disk Drives for the System/3

In late 1969, IBM saw the need to make the System/3 an even more capable computer by adding disk storage. As shown in Figure 7-5 and in 7-9 below, in the area directly under the MFCU, Rochester provided space for four disk drives. These drives were known as 5444s, and they were stacked two in each of two drawers. In each drawer, one drive was fixed and the other drive permitted removable cartridges to be mounted / dismounted, thereby providing additional removable storage. Each drive, fixed or removable, could hold 2.45 million characters of storage. That was it. But back then it was so much that for disk based System/3's, the second drawer was optional. The Photo in Figure 5-3 shows the optional second drawer open and a friendly IT person is inserting a removable disk cartridge.

Figure 7-9 System/3 5444 Disk -- Open Bottom Removable Drawer (R2)

New Disks Form Basis of New System/3

In 1970, IBM created a new model of the System/3 with a keyboard console and a dot matrix printer as part of the basic setup. The System/3 Model 6 also used the new IBM 5444 Disk Drives. The keyboard was its only input device. No card reader / punch would ever be attached to a Model 6 so, disk was its only storage.

Later as CCP (See CCP later) became successful on the large System/3 models, IBM re-introduced the System/3 Model 6 with a name change. It had substantially more standard memory, along with local terminal capability. The System/3 Model 4, announced in 1975, looked almost exactly the same as the Model 6 since it used the same frame. The one noticeable difference was that a model 4 had a 480 character CRT as its communications console. A picture of a System/3 Model 4 is shown in Figure 7-10. Take the CRT from the picture and you have a Model 6.

Figure 7-10 IBM System/3 Model 4

More Storage, Please

As the demands for more storage on the System/3 model 10 increased, the 5444s did not hold back the masses for too long. So, IBM attached its more capable mainframe heritage 2319 drives to the System/3, re-christening them as the 5445 Disk System. (See Figure 7-11.) Each of these drives could hold 20.48 million characters of storage. No, I did not say gigabytes, it was megabytes. A few million bytes was about all you could get back then, as disk drives were in their infancy. Look how physically large each unit is! And, that young lady in the picture is tall.

Figure 7-11 IBM 5445 Disk Drives

As the System/3 product matured, the 5445 drives were no longer adequate to satisfy the storage requirements of larger System/3 customers. In the mid 1970's, IBM announced that four of the mainframe developed, innovative 3340 disk drives using the 70 MB IBM data module were able to attach to the System/3 model 15D, the largest System/3 ever built. Four IBM 3340 drives are shown in Figure 7-12, along with an IBM 70 MB data module sitting on top of the third drive.

The BattleStar Galactica

Quite often, I would have to accompany my computer clients from Wilkes-Barre / Scranton to large datacenters in Philadelphia, New York, or Syracuse to convert their data to the IBM data module shown on the top of the cabinet in Figure 7-12. I never drove very new vehicles as I always wanted to look poor to IBM management. That way they would not skip me on the next raise cycle. Hah! Just kidding -- but not by much!

The best explanation for the quality of the vehicles I drove at the time came from a co-worker, David Smith, who has since passed on. David referred to my huge two-tone teal and light blue Buick LeSabre as the "BattleStar." I do not think that at the time, teal had even been formally introduced as a real color. When he first called my vehicle the BattleStar, his eyes lit up and I knew that he thought that the color combo and the aging never-waxed look made my car look like a large piece of space junk. So, rather than call my car "Space Junk," he upgraded me to the "Battlestar." For years until that vehicle's retirement, I relished in the fact that I was driving one of the few land-based BattleStars in the universe.

The data modules shown in Figure 7-12 retailed from IBM at about $2,500.00 each. I am not kidding. IBM offered no discounts on "disk packs." For 70MB, about 1/10 the storage of today's CD ROM, the price was $2,500.00. Often, I would pack as many as four of these in my car and take the customer to a remote data center for a data conversion. During these trips, my car was always worth about four times its normal value.

Figure 7-12 IBM 3340 Disk Subsystem with Data Module

Tape Drives and Faster Printers

For backup, all of the models of the System/3, except the Model 4 and Model 6, were able to attach the IBM 3410/3411 Tape subsystem as shown in Figure 7-13. Some companies had big enough budgets at the time to choose to back up on removable data modules. Backups were much faster and no tape drive had to be purchased.

Figure 7-13 IBM 3410/3411 Tape Subsystem

Eventually, faster printers, such as the legendary IBM 1403 (1100 lines per minute), as shown in Figure 7-14, were added and the System/3 line became a very popular small business computer capable of large computer print jobs. All models of the System/3 were very successful and profitable for IBM, and the machine was well-loved by its users.

Figure 7-14 IBM 1403 Printer

IBM rewarded the Rochester Lab for its accomplishments by permitting the lab to continue making these computers. The biggest and most powerful System/3 was introduced in 1973. It was known as the Model 15D. Other System/3 models included Models 4, 6, 8, 10, and 12.

System/3 Models

The System/3 model 15 is shown in Figure 7-15. The System/3 Model 12 is shown in Figure 7-16. The System/3 Models 4, 8, and 12, were introduced later than the Model 15 in the System/3 product life cycle.

Figure 7-15 IBM System/3 Model 15

Figure 7-16 IBM System/3 Model 12

During this period, IBM moved from card-oriented processing to floppy disks in eight-inch packages. The later System/3s all used this technology and were shipped as "cardless." (See Figure 7-17 for a picture of a System/3 model 8 cardless computer with its direct attached IBM 3741 Data Station / diskette reader. Note also that the Model 12 in Figure 7-16 is also "cardless."). Without card systems being built anymore, the unit record façade for Rochester soon came to an end; yet, the plant continued to make

System/3 machines, which everybody referred to as "computers."

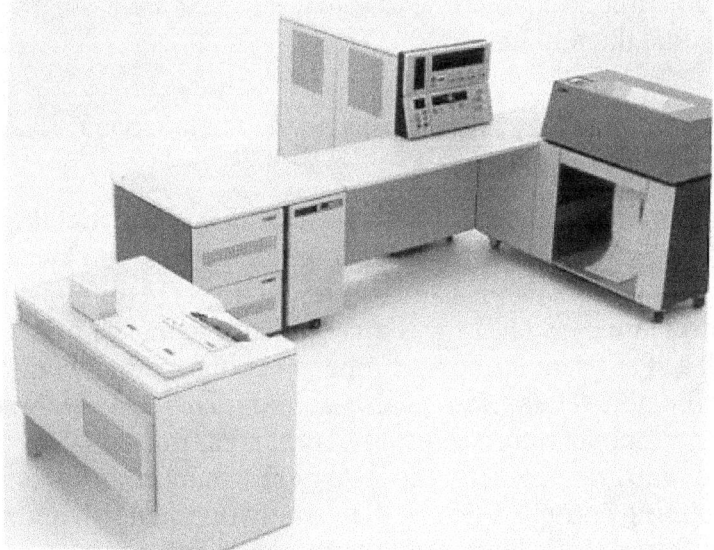

Figure 7-17 System/3 Model 8 "Cardless" Computer with attached IBM 3741

Made for Humans, Not Machines

In addition to RPG, one of the factors that made the System/3 easy to use was its control language, known as the Operator Control Language (OCL). All computers preceding the System/3 required humans to learn cryptic languages, such as AutoCoder, Symbolic Programming System (SPS), or Job Control Language (JCL), in order to communicate with the machine. Rochester intuitively knew the old way was not going to fly with a machine destined for small businesses and run by non-IT professionals. Programmers, at the time, who got their first look at OCL for the System/3, especially those who were mainframe-trained, were amazed by its simplicity.

IBM made the System/3 control language easier for the programmer and user in the business environment, rather than for the software engineer in IBM who had to write the complicated routines that would scan the cards and interpret their meaning for the machine. Before the System/3 existed, the control language used on IBM's and others' machines was very cryptic and quite difficult for a normal human to read, and even more difficult to write. A control language statement for a mainframe disk drive, for example, might look like the following:

```
// DLBL,,,3,,42,,sys011,,39,payroll,,,,99999,,,en
```

There was nothing easy about writing this type of mainframe statement. If you are an old mainframe person, you know that this is not exact but, it is representative. Mainframe job control language (JCL) was quite difficult to master and it took a significant amount of time to get this stuff to work. For the non-veteran, it was almost impossible to know how many commas were needed in-between parameters. If you were off by one comma, the statement would mean something entirely different than what you intended, and the mainframe machine was very unforgiving and not very helpful in debugging. System/3 OCL was much different. It was English-like, keyword-driven, very forgiving and instructive. A sample statement might look as follows:

```
// File Name-Payroll,Unit-F1, etc.
```

The purpose of showing these statements, of course, is not to teach about old computers, but to give a perspective as to how much simpler the new System/3 made computing at the time. Because the new OCL was keyword-oriented instead of positional, programmers no longer had to worry about how many commas to leave in between parameters. The "Unit=F1" part of the S/3 statement above was needed because the system back then had more than one disk drive. Just like a PC with multiple disk drives uses one-character symbols, the letters A through Z, to distinguish the drives, the System/3 used two-character symbols. Instead of A, B, C, or D drives; the System/3 drive names were F1, F2, R1, and R2. The F's were for the two fixed drives, and the R's were for the two removable drives. Today, other than diskette, CD, and DVD drives; disks are "fixed" in all computers and are non-removable. They are fixed in place. The day of the removable hard disk passed when System/3 technology made its exit from the marketplace.

Terminals for System/3

During the mid-1970s, IBM developed a program on mainframes called the Customer Information Control System (CICS). This program ran in one part (or partition) of a mainframe and permitted many terminals to be used simultaneously with the machine. CICS was in a phrase, "difficult to use." The IBM 3270 terminal (Figure 7-18) was the terminal of choice at the time for CICS and other IBM terminal oriented operating systems.

Figure 7-18 IBM 3270 Terminal as Used on System/3

So that System/3s could also support terminals, after disk drives were introduced and accepted, Rochester built a program called the Communication Control Program (CCP) between 1971 and 1972. The System/3 model 10 was too small to support CCP well, so IBM built and introduced the

System 3 Model 15. This box came with three partitions so that CCP would be able to have its own partition while the rest of the machine could do normal batch processing.

I can remember learning CCP in Syracuse NY at the IBM Education Center and then bringing back the "foils," to teach my peers in the IBM office in Scranton, Pennsylvania. CCP was very similar in function to CICS. Along with the new capabilities, however, CCP added a higher degree of complexity to the System/3 environment for terminal processing, but it was nothing close to the degree of difficulty brought forth by CICS in the mainframe environment. Nonetheless, CCP was not for the casual System/3 programmer.

The IBM System/32 Is Introduced

With all of this innovation, the System/3 became a big hit in businesses all across the world, and Rochester became a big hit within IBM because it was making money for the corporation. In 1975, IBM Rochester was at it again. The lab introduced a System/3-like machine that was desk-sized. Notice I did not say desktop. Desk-sized is about as small as it got back then. This unit had a keyboard and a small monitor, and it had a printer attached to its back. It was an all-in-one computer called the System/32 (see Figure 7-19). In Chapter 6, as you may recall we discussed a TV commercial, which IBM ran during the System/32 era?

Chapter 7 Brief History of Computers from IBM Rochester

Figure 7-19 System/32 – Circa 1975

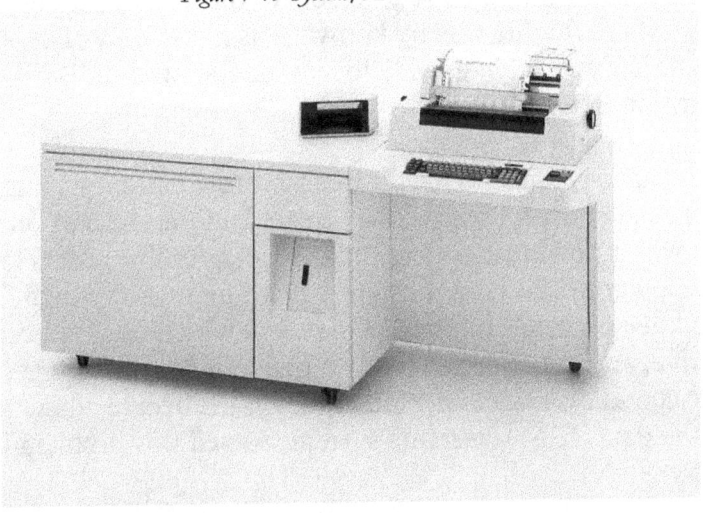

The System/32 used the same notion of OCL, as did the System/3 disk systems—shown in Figure 7-19. However, since there was just one big disk drive on the left side of the unit, the OCL was even simpler than that of the System/3. There was no need for the R1, F1, R2, and F2 designations in OCL since there was only one disk. So, for System/32 OCL, IBM removed the Unit parameter and it was never to return. Note below the two OCL statements. The first is System/3 format with the Unit parameter and the second is System/32 format where it is not needed.

```
// File Name-Payroll,Unit-F1, etc.
// File Name-Payroll, etc.
```

Though System/32 had just one drive, all IBM small systems that followed the System/32 took advantage of the big change in OCL brought forth with the System/32. There was no unit keyword needed since there was only one disk. This change may not seem revolutionary but subsequent systems had multiple disk drives and yet the OCL did not require the unit parameter. IBM Rochester had begun to make their systems more intelligent and more self-managing. The operating systems, the predecessors to the all-everything OS, knew where the file was by knowing its name only. The system had internal tables to locate the files and the programmer was spared the work.

IBM small systems no longer had to care about how many disks existed on a system. They treated all the disks as one. This was a powerful notion and current Windows users know how powerful this is as they struggle to figure out which files Windows manages on the C Drive and which ones are on the D drive, and the E drive etc... When Windows shops get that second disk, all of a sudden they must decide where to put the data. IBM operating systems solved this problem in 1975.

The IBM System/32 came with one major disadvantage -- even for its time. Like a modern PC, it had just one input keyboard attached to the top part of its frame. Though key to diskette units, such as the IBM 3741, could be used to help with the keypunch (date entry) load, and the System/32 did have a diskette reader that could read the standard fare 8" diskettes of the day, the one keyboard proved to be the major disadvantage of the box. As such, the System/32 lasted for just two years before IBM improved the design and changed multi-user computing forever...

In 1977, IBM announced the new and improved System/32. It had everything but the name and the limitations. It was a big, boxy computer (not desk sized at all) called the System/34 (see Figure 7-20). It used Operator Control Language, just as the System/32 and the System/3 before it. Therefore, the System/34 was also easy to work with. IBM's invention of OCL was a big reason.

With the System/34, IBM shipped up to two disk drives. Unlike the System/3, whose OCL had to tell the system which drive a file was on, as a predecessor to Single Level Store (Chapter 13), IBM had improved its ability to treat all disk drives on a small business system as if they were part of one mass storage unit.

> Note: This was in 1977. Windows and Intel and Unix and Linux have still not achieved this major ease of use characteristic.

By using as many as sixteen terminals instead of a built-in console keyboard, the System/34 solved the "one keyboard" problem of the System/32. It had no console keyboard whatsoever. Up to sixteen separate terminals could be attached to just one System/34, providing fifteen more online input devices to the system than the System/32. Try typing that fast! The computer console could be any of those 16 terminals and when it was not in console mode, it was a regular terminal.

Thus, the big difference between the System/32 and the System/34 was that the new System/34 was a multi-station, multi-user system. Its multiple keyboards were provided by PC-like independent stations that were dumb (unlike PCs) and they communicated directly to the System/34 processor in very similar fashion to how the PC keyboard talks to the PC. Just one difference, the terminal waited until the user hit the "ENTER" key to send all the data to be processed.

By introducing the notion of multi-user and multi-programming / multi-tasking with the System/34, IBM enabled each user to have a piece of this one computer system as if it were his or her own machine. At the time, it was as if each user had their own PC.

Figure 7-20 IBM System/34 Multi-Station Computer

Though the System/34 used terminals, it did not need the complexities of IBM's System/3 CCP or anything like IBM's CICS or even BEA's Tuxedo. (See Chapter 19, Integrated Transaction Processing.) Terminal management was built-into the S/34's System Support Program (SSP) operating system and the system's hardware. It was an industry first.

> **Note: Tuxedo is BEA's terminal monitor program, introduced in the 1980's with similar function and purpose to CICS and CCP.**

For the first time on any computer system anywhere, the compilers were written to recognize a terminal as a real device thus making programming the S/34 for interactive work far easier than any computer vendor has even yet to achieve. Moreover, you could attach these semi-intelligent, high-speed terminals to the system over a local high speed wiring type called twinaxial cable, without the need for modems. Because data communication over the Internet today is so fast, many of us have forgotten how slow getting data to the main computer once was.

Programmers even had it easier as IBM provided a link to RPG and COBOL so that programmers could directly control one or all terminals from one program rather than requiring a program for each terminal. The all-everything operating system design notions were in play with the IBM System/34, but there was a lot more function to come.

Hardware was important back then because smart terminals were not really the notion of the day. Most actually were pretty dumb. The new terminal that IBM invented was also a major innovation for its day. Though it was big and square, built by Rochester, it was ahead of its time. IBM called it the IBM 5250. See Figure 7-21.

Each of these terminals, at the time, could be purchased for about $4,000. Though 5250s are no longer sold, the green-screen 5250 legacy continues today through PC products that emulate the 5250 terminal's data stream. The System/38 machine and the AS/400 historical line including the IBM i5, and now the IBM Power System with IBM i, use the 5250 display station protocol as their native terminal discipline.

Figure 7-21 IBM 5250 Type Terminal

The 5250 terminal had actually been built for the Rochester designed and developed System/38 computer system, which was to be the follow-on computer to the System/3 Model 15D and the entire System/3 line. The System/3 had used the IBM 3270-type terminal (Figure 7-18) that had been the normal device for mainframes. The 3270 line continues to be popular on mainframes today and is an often-emulated terminal device.

In 1977, when the in-process System/38 was taking much longer to complete than IBM originally anticipated, Rochester decided to announce the System/34 product line as an upgrade to the System/32 and as a stop-gap while the System/38 was being perfected. The 5250 terminals and printers that were designed for the System/38 were thus first used on the IBM System/34.

The First Version All-Everything Operating System

The very first all everything operating system was something called Control Program Facility or CPF. It was the brains for the most advanced commercial computer system ever built, the System/38. As we have learned in previous chapters, this was the direct predecessor of the AS/400, on down to the current line IBM Power System with IBM i.

To say the System/38 was unique is an understatement. It was a well-designed system for sure and being part of IBM, it used the best notions in computer science. It represented what the entire IBM Company knew about computers. Rochester, Minnesota had never really built a sophisticated computer before and so there was a longer learning curve than there would have been if the mainframe division were to have built the System/38.

Having said that, I would bet that Rochester engineers and developers would argue that I am wrong. They would probably be right but we'll never know.

It was almost impossible for any group of engineers and scientists, mainframe or otherwise, to anticipate the difficulty in achieving the groundbreaking technical advances brought forth with the System/38. As good as the 48-bit hardware proved to be in the System/38 unit itself, the biggest part of the accomplishment was the first commercial shipment of CPF, which, as noted above, was the first iteration of the all-everything operating system.

Unexpected Delays

When IBM announced the System/38, in October 1978, IBM Rochester knew that the machine was not working well enough for prime time. However, based on experience with other systems, the Lab felt that the machine would be ready in 1979, in time for the first customer shipment.

System/3 Model 15D customers, as well as many others, who were using minicomputers or the small computers produced by the BUNCH (Burroughs, Univac, NCR, Control Data, and Honeywell), were enamored by the outstanding specifications of the System/38. They signed up in droves on the day it was announced in 1978 for an early shipment of this new box. They actually expected to receive one soon after they ordered the machine. IBM had not missed a shipment since its 1964 introduction of System/360 and the executives were not about to start missing shipments with a small system built in Rochester, Minnesota.

For IBM's System/38, there would be no early shipments. The Rochester plant seemed to take forever to give customers a ship date, and when they finally got one, it was over two years out. I saw the reaction to the implicit, unannounced delay. My customers were outraged. There were big technical problems with the box. There were so many new computer science attributes built into the System/38 that for a time it seemed almost improbable that the system would ever be completed, no matter how hard IBM tried.

Yet, IBM did not compromise on the underlying advanced architecture of the System/38. The company just dug in and made it work. It is no wonder why even today there is not any system in existence that has yet to catch up, technology-wise, to the System/38 machine that IBM announced way back in 1978.

Of course not being able to get a system out the door as promised created a big public relations problem for the IBM Company. It is ironic that Microsoft, a company competing for IBM's all-everything OS customers today has never seemed to have a problem announcing new worlds and delivering often less than a city block in need of immediate repair. At IBM, however, the inability to bring out a system on time was looked upon as shameful.

In 1979, to call off the dogs, Frank Cary, Chairman of IBM at the time, appeared before IBM's customers and the world, and asked for forgiveness for delaying the System/38 for 11 additional months so that it would be ready for business use when it was first shipped.

Make It Work, Please!

IBM called upon many employees in the corporation to help bring this box out so that it could work well in a customer shop. I was one of those who got the call. I had the pleasure of spending time in Rochester in January 1980 in the freezing cold, months after the first shipment was missed. My job was to test the first conversion package built to move System/3 shops to System/38. Understandably, IBM considered this critical for the product launch so that it could have immediate successful implementations.

Not only was the product that I was working on inadequate, it was buggy and would fail in the middle of long runs and it could not be restarted. Our group recommended that it not be announced and that a better way be found. At the same time an SE in Atlanta, a folk hero now to many of us, Gerson Arnett, wrote a much more simple conversion tool that saved the day.

While in Rochester, in addition to the problems with the package, I recall the instability of the OS pre-releases at the time. You could set your watch once an hour as our test machine would fail like clockwork. The new term for a software failure introduced with System/38 was "Function Check." We saw lots of these and often they required an IPL, or as Microsoft would call it, a reboot. The IPLs were a real pain as they took at least a half hour. There was clearly plenty of work needed to be done on the all-everything operating system before it would be perfected.

Another one of the problems that I discovered was that the messages would often not give a reasonable clue as to what caused the problem. Sometimes there was no clue at all. In the brief time that I was in Rochester, a number of new versions (builds as they called them) of the OS were installed on our test machine.

By the time I left Rochester, the function checks were fewer and farther between and I saw hope that this machine and its operating system would eventually be completed. It was like no other OS that I had ever worked on. Its design was right on and, at that time, in very early 1980, the only thing separating the IBM System/38 from its future greatness were the bugs. As I personally observed, the software developers had huge swatters and they were on a mission to eliminate all the bugs to create a stable system. Eventually they did just that.

1980: First Year System/38s Were Spotted

Clearly, to build this all-everything operating system, IBM Rochester had bitten off lots more than it was able to handle without help. When IBM is embarrassed about anything, it does have the horses to solve the problem. Frank Cary made sure those horses were available to help Rochester. In retrospect, from what I heard after the fact, a good number of the many horses often just got in the way. I got the sense that Rochester engineers, scientists, and developers for the most part solved their own problems. They just needed more time.

The System/38 finally arrived in mid to late 1980 to a mostly welcoming customer set (see Figure 7-22). It was the best system that IBM had ever built. It used the all-everything operating system principles that are described fully in Chapter 10. Its underpinnings were so advanced that no machine, besides its direct descendants, the AS/400, iSeries, i5, and now the Power System with IBM i, has ever reached the same level of hardware and software technology and integration.

Figure 7-22 IBM System/38, Announced in 1978

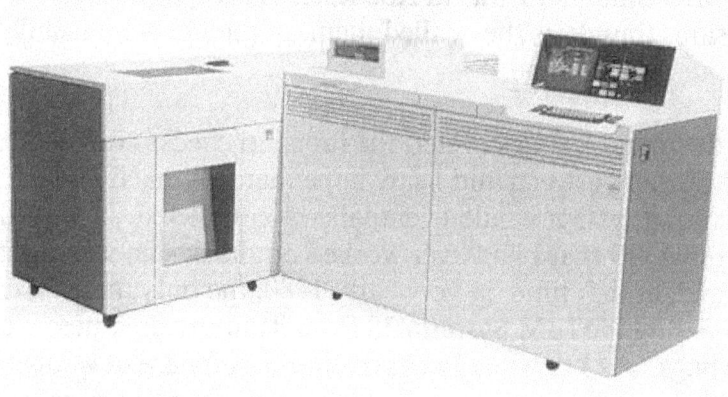

System/34 Was Available

Because of the delays, as well as the remarkable popularity of the 1977 introduction of the IBM System/34, total sales for the System/38 never surpassed 50,000 units. There are unofficial estimates that the total of System/38 shipments was even as low as 20,000 units. Yet the System/34, with its 5250 workstations, caught on like gangbusters and shipped well over 100,000 units. These would have been lots and lots of System/38s had it not been for the delay.

The System/34 became so popular, it had its own user "cult." IBM expanded the capabilities of the System/34 and announced new hardware to permit the box to handle expanded workloads. IBM's 1983 introduction of the System/36, for example, expanded the number of locally attached devices (no LANS then) to over 70 from just 16 on the System/34. The System/36 was very much like the System/34 but it was much stronger.

Mainframe: Who Are those Guys in Rochester?

In the early 1980s, the mainframe division of IBM became concerned that there were too many IBM systems aimed at the same customer. Mainframe executives were never particularly happy that Rochester built computers, and felt that job should be done in a mainframe plant, such as Endicott or Poughkeepsie. As Jim Sloan noted in his remarks in Chapter 5, IBM's mainframe executives tried to eliminate the System/38 from the product line a number of times in the 1980's.

Looking at the architecture of the System/38, IBM mainframe executives knew that its all-everything operating system, and its overall architecture, was built better than anything the mainframe had available. They feared that one day it would compete in IBM for the same customers that were in the mainframe purview. Considering that today's IBM Power System with IBM i is more powerful than IBM's largest mainframe, perhaps their fear was well founded.

The First Big Consolidation Project

Ostensibly to assess the feasibility of a product line consolidation and to get a jump start on that effort, IBM commissioned a big project called Fort Knox, and spent hundreds of millions of dollars trying to come up with a new system that, among other things, would do everything that the System/34 and the System/38 could do. Many of us in the trenches knew that this was a mainframe division attempt to eliminate the advanced all-everything OS from ever becoming an integral part of IBM.

The team in Rochester knew very well that IBM did not want them to be building a better mainframe than the mainframe and they certainly did not want Rochester to be building anything that Corporate IBM and its customer set could not do without. The problem, as those familiar with corporate politics can easily recognize, was that this highly advanced but small business oriented machine had been developed in Rochester and not Poughkeepsie where all the smart people in IBM worked.

Before this new Fort Knox product design, which the mainframe chiefs in IBM anticipated would herald Corporate IBM's all-everything operating system, to replace the all-everything OS built by Rochester, had born any fruit, it was canceled for failing to come close to accomplishing its mission. The project did bear some fruit. So, if I were IBM at the time, after paying for a forest and receiving just a tree, I would not have been pleased either.

While Fort Knox was underway in the early 1980's, the IBM Rochester Lab designed a new system to replace its aging System/34 line. It was a snappy little box called the System/36. See Figure 7-23. Even while Fort Knox was underway, Rochester could not stand still with its small system line as customers were demanding more horsepower and unlike the mainframe division, they paid with cash. The

System/36 was in many ways a chubbed-up System/34 so it was not a really large effort to create as was the System/38.

By 1985, it did not matter anymore that Rochester's work with the new System/36 might have been redundant to the Fort Knox effort as the systems consolidation project had failed. IBM lost millions of dollars trying to eliminate System/36 and System/38. When Fort Knox was cancelled, CPF (S/38 OS) was the only contender in IBM, and in the world to be a successor to the System/36 with an advanced enough OS architecture, even more advanced than the mainframe, ready to live on as the all-everything operating system.

You Can't Handle the Truth

Jack Nicholson would have a fine comeback to the mainframe division who kept thinking they had the one true system. You know he would have said, "You can't handle the truth." The fact is that the mainframe division did not have to handle the truth since their benefactors ruled the IBM Corporation.

Looking back, even the mainframe component of IBM with access to all of the secrets of the System/38 advanced machine, could not launch an affordable product that would include all of its design points. There is no question that IBM was "mighty" during this time period. If the mighty IBM itself, with all its resources, could not re-build the System/38 as part of the Fort Knox consolidation project, it is no wonder that nobody else has yet to be able to do so. Regrets to Intel and Microsoft and Sun and HP and many others. It'll never happen.

Even after twenty plus years, other formidable 1980 era computer companies from DEC (DIGITAL) to Microsoft to Intel to HP to Sun have not been able to introduce a system as architecturally powerful as the old System/38. I mean even today nobody has yet done this. Considering that the underpinnings of the System/38 are well over thirty years old, IBM's competitors clearly had the time to catch up. The fact is that they could not and still can't. Even IBM couldn't do it again, as it once tried with its Fort Knox project.

The fact is that if IBM had known, when it launched the System/38 project in the early 1970's, exactly how much effort and internal cost the System/38 was going to require, most analysts would bet that the machine, no matter how good, never would have seen the light of day. That's why the Rochester team kept it a secret, even from mother IBM.

A naïve new IBM computer lab in Rochester, Minnesota literally did not know it could not build a system as powerful as the System/38, and so they went ahead and ultimately did it. Without this naiveté, and mother IBM's big pockets, when Rochester failed in its prescribed time frame, the company would not be in the position that it is today of reaping the benefits of all this effort with its very own all-everything operating system. .

Figure 7-23 IBM System/36, Announced in 1983

Finally, the AS/400

After Fort Knox had failed, a project called Silverlake was initiated at Rochester in the mid-1980s to create one replacement box for both the System/38 and the System/36. Many books have chronicled the Silverlake Project for its many triumphs in an IBM environment that would have been just as happy if it had failed.

IBM had wasted a ton of money and precious time on Fort Knox and nothing came from it; so, the company had missed the normal replacement cycle for the System/38 and System/36 units. It was time to catch up. After just a little more than two years, and one of the most heralded efforts of all time, in June 1988, IBM announced the results of its secret Silverlake project as the Application System/400, or AS/400 (see Figure 7-24). Those who tell only the truth will tell you that Silverlake was such a non-secret that by the time it came out, it had been re-code-named Olympic. How about that?

Figure 7-24 AS/400 Model B60 Circa 1988

In many ways the AS/400 emergence from the Silverlake Project was a repackaging of the System/38, but it also ran System/36 programs untouched. It also ran untouched System/38 applications in its own separate environment. Besides all that and with a far superior processor than the System/38, it also ran specific mainframe programs using a facility called the Cross System Product (CSP).

After quite a few incarnations, including CISC technology to RISC technology, explained in many parts of this book, in May, 2004, the AS/400 was reincarnated again as the eServer i5, or what I called it at the time, the all-everything machine, running the all-everything operating system. The hardware is shown in Figure 7-25. In 2006, IBM subtly rechristened the system with the introduction of Power 5+ technology as the System i.

Bringing us back to the present and the future, in 2008, IBM changed the whole notion of 64-bit RISC based computing with its introduction of new hardware that used the most powerful IBM chip, the Power 6. This new chip along with the final touches to the former System i frame, and IBM was able to create a box that could run the System i operating system known as I5/OS. Unix and / or Linux also ran on this box and IBM i was not necessary to accommodate this.

The IBM Company also changed the name of the all-everything OS to IBM i, with the "i" meaning integrated. So, today's platform is known as the IBM Power System with IBM i, and it is the best system ever made by IBM. The IBM Power System Family is shown in Figure 7-26

Figure 7-25 The IBM eServer i5, the New All-Everything Machine.

Figure 7-26 IBM Power Systems Announce April, 2008

The Best System Ever - The Best Operating System Ever

It was way back in 1978 with CPF and then again in 1988 with OS/400 that the AS/400 became the great ... grandfather and the basis of the all-everything operating system that now drives the best versions of the IBM Power System. If you start adding them up, the AS/400 machine in 1988 was equipped with the following four major facilities:

- Native AS/400 Processing
- System/36 Environment
- System/38 Environment
- Mainframe Environment with CSP

Note: The AS/400 is the immediate successor and a derivative of the revolutionary System/38 that was introduced by IBM in 1978. In October 2000, IBM renamed the AS/400 as the iSeries. In 2004, IBM renamed the iSeries as the eServer i5, a.k.a. IBM i5. In 2006, the box became the System i. Then again, in 2008, IBM renamed the AS/400 hardware as the IBM Power System and it began to market the all-everything operating system separately under the name IBM i.

System/36 Shops Had Reservations

The 1988 AS/400 was a resounding success by all measurements, but one. System/36 shops were not too happy about it. It was much different from the System/3, System.32, and System/34 heritage machines. It appeared to those looking for the same look, but on a faster machine, as a more complex unit because of the many new features in the all-everything operating system.

Computing was far simpler in those days, in the IBM small business world, and few were looking to complicate their lives with advanced computing notions, no matter how easily they could be achieved. Moreover, and perhaps more importantly, when the AS/400 came to market, its emulated System/36 environment did not initially perform as well as System/36 customers had expected. In fact, from my experience, the AS/400 running the System/36 OS in an emulated environment in 1988 was functionally complete but it ran like a dog.

As another bugaboo for System/36 users, IBM did not hide the look and feel of the AS/400 from its S/36 users. Thus, many were intimidated at the lack of the same simple interface as provided by System/36.

While the AS/400 was a resounding market success, it was not because System/36 customers liked it. The System/36 crowd expressed their displeasure by keeping their old System/36 boxes as long as they could, and when they upgraded, they would buy either a second used System/36 (same size) or a bigger used System/36. It took a long time for IBM's System/36 customers to warm up to the AS/400. However, there was enough new AS/400 business at the time for IBM, from the former minicomputer vendors, such as DEC and Data General. So, at the time, it was OK with IBM that the System/36 installed base stayed where they were, in their existing, "happy-with-their-old-system-state," for many more years.

AS/400 Evolution

In 1994, IBM was in the process of changing its AS/400 hardware to 64-bit RISC from 48-bit CISC, yet the company chose not to rename the system. Other than being bigger and faster, when the AS/400 replaced the System/38 it was mostly a change to bring more powerful but similar hardware on board. Customers had been clamoring for more capacity, more memory, and more CPU power. AS/400 addressed all that big-time. It was so big that IBM changed the name. Yet, the fundamental system hardware stayed at 48-bits and the architecture stayed in the Complex Instruction Set

Computing (CISC) realm. There was no hardware bit-change and no move to Reduced Instruction Set Computing (RISC).

Moving from 48-bits to 64-bits was unprecedented in 1994. Moving from a CISC architecture to a RISC architecture without forcing a recompile had never been done in the history of computing. Yet, the name remained as the "AS/400" because IBM believed that there was a good market sense about the name. But, the changes actually made the hardware completely different. The all-everything operating system basically stayed the same, requiring a relatively small amount of effort to ride on the new RISC 64-bit hardware. See High Level Machine Interface in Chapter 12 for a more complete explanation of how IBM achieved the OS migration to 64-bit RISC.

A Gift for the System/36 Community

At the same time, IBM made some additional changes to the box, and the new chips (early stage Power processors) permitted the former System/36 operating system called System Support Program (SSP) to run natively on a pre-release version of the new RISC chip. IBM announced their work-in-process RISC chip in 1994 in a small frame AS/400-type box that it called the AS/400 Advanced/36. The AS/400 version of the chip would not be ready for another year.

In other words, after six years from the time the AS/400 was introduced until it moved to RISC technology, many System/36 users stayed on their old hardware. Why? Because they liked it and they perceived the AS/400 world as too complex.

This new RISC based AS/400 style hardware machine performed exceptionally well, and it ran IBM's SSP operating system with an updated set of code called Release 7, right from the Power chip. System/36 users were quite pleased that their OS was in full control of AS/400 hardware. IBM gave them exactly what they wanted in this new RISC

AS/400 known as the Advanced 36 model. While IBM was perfecting the RISC chip for use with the new line of AS/400 boxes to come in 1995, they were able to etch the more simple System/36 instruction set onto the Power chip. Since this worked so well, IBM was able to release the AS/400 Advanced 36 RISC machine about a year before the RISC-based full AS/400 line.

1995 -- IBM Announces 64-bit RISC Processors

IBM's System/36 customers rewarded IBM for giving them what they wanted by purchasing lots of these new boxes with the partially implemented RISC chip. Eventually, IBM was able to place the entire System/36 instruction set, as well as the AS/400 instruction set, and other instruction sets on the newer and better 64-bit Power chip.

After just a few years, IBM did so well that it was able to withdraw the Advanced System/36 from marketing since the AS/400 actually was able to run the System/36 applications in the same fashion as the System/36 had previously. Today, the AS/400, the iSeries, the i5, and the IBM Power System with IBM i can all perform System/36, System/38 and AS/400 operations from instructions built within the same Power 6 chip.

Continual Improvements in Power

Since 1995, with the introduction of the 64-bit RISC processors, IBM has boosted the power and the number of processors that are available on the AS/400-iSeries-i5-Power System with IBM i product line. In 2004, for example, with the POWER5 series of microprocessors, the company doubled the number of processors that could be packaged in one IBM i5 machine from 32 to 64 and increased the performance of each processor by well over 200%. In addition to changing the system name to the eServer i5, IBM also changed the name of the operating system from OS/400 to i5/OS.

The Power 5 chip brought with it the capability of having sixty-four phenomenally high-speed computers operating simultaneously in one i5 machine. That sounds a lot like a mainframe because it is. The eServer i5 running the all-everything OS was recognized as a mainframe-class machine. Industry watchers, who expected function and power to be extended with the introduction of the Power 6 chips, were not disappointed. IBM has hinted that perhaps the mainframe will be using the Power 7 chip when it hits the market in a year or so.

With all of the enhancements over its 20 + years, the AS/400 heritage machine, now embodied in the IBM Power System with IBM i, clearly uses the most architecturally elegant and capable machine configuration in the industry. From the ground-up, it is built as an integrated machine with the all-everything operating system as the go-to component.

When you add this internal elegance to the powerful engines (64-way Power 5, Power 6, and soon to be Power 7) now available with the IBM i advanced OS technology, the Power hardware and the all-everything OS together are clearly the best and most powerful computer system of all time. With all this going for it, the Power System with IBM i is the machine that is recognized as giving the most value to businesses for the least cost.

Is It Really That Nice? Yes!

If the all-everything OS were as easy to explain as it is to use, the public would already be aware of its nuances and ramifications. Knowing about the systems that came before the IBM Power System from the Rochester Lab, and recognizing that the hardware and the all-everything OS is the follow-on to all those technologies, it is easy to surmise that with IBM i at the heart of your computing infrastructure, life could not be much easier or more productive. It is a fact that IBM i adds more business value and that value goes right to the bottom line, exponentially more than any other operating system running on any other system or server.

Enhancements & AS/400 Marketability

As you can see in this little history of the IBM Power System with IBM i product line, the company has enhanced the machine to make it a technology leader in many areas. However, until May 4, 2004, IBM had priced iSeries hardware substantially higher than the same hardware in other systems. As an integrated machine that shipped with a complete operating system, integrated database, integrated transaction processing, etc..., customers always saw great value in the machine and its all-everything OS; so, sales were not affected by what some thought was a higher price. Most of IBM's AS/400 heritage customers believe that the most advanced operating system in the world ships with the system, and so the extra value is worth the extra charge.

When the company announced the new IBM Power System with IBM i, IBM signaled that a big part of the additional hardware cost for acquiring a new iSeries family machine was being eliminated. With the April, 2008 jump in power and capability, coupled with a substantially lower price, the IBM Power System with IBM i is now an even more affordable machine for many small businesses.

There sure is no reason for complaining, especially if you examine the cost of Windows server software and Microsoft SQL Server software. Microsoft licensing makes today's IBM Power System running the all-everything operating system an even better value than the popular AS/400 heritage systems of the past.

Chapter 8   IBM Power System with IBM i

The Best Operating System Ever

The historical IBM i5 (now known as the IBM Power System with IBM i) is the best and the most special computer ever built. It's IBM-built all-everything operating system is now known as IBM i and as you well know by Chapter 8, it is the premise of this book. It is also the vehicle that drives the hardware platform to its many accomplishments.

That is why it is inconceivable that the company that owns the rights to this operating system does not seem to try hard to earn even bigger revenues from it. For you music lovers out there, it may help to know that the IBM Power System with IBM i is to computers as what Bose is to great sound. Bring on the music.

As the direct descendent of the System/38's CPF, IBM i is even more functional and more powerful. The older System/38 line was not as well-endowed performance-wise. In fact, because it was intended for smaller businesses, in its infancy it suffered from capacity constraints imposed by the culture of IBM's mainframe division. Just as you would run your company, IBM management found no value in the idea that Rochester machines would compete with traditional mainframes while the mainframes were bringing in the bucks.

So, in the beginning, IBM gave the engineers in Rochester specific constraints to assure that this all-everything operating system was being built to support small businesses. IBM was very careful in its cautions that the Rochester systems were not to be used for big businesses. For these, IBM targeted its mainframe line of computers. The resulting first iteration system was known as the System/38 and IBM introduced it in 1978. It was well underpowered for all of its inherent advanced capabilities. However, it was a heck of a machine for small businesses, most of which had no idea the box was so underpowered for its architecture. It just happened to work well for them because the all-everything operating system is so spectacular.

As underpowered as it may have been, the System/38 was built with the same advanced architecture, and thus, by design, it was the same high tech machine as the AS/400 and now, the IBM Power System with IBM i. Therefore, one could argue that the historical IBM Power System and the System/38 are singularly the finest computers that any company has ever made.

AS/400 Becomes eServer iSeries

In the fall of 2000, IBM changed the name of the AS/400 to the eServer iSeries 400. While IBM had no problem changing the name of the machine in 2000, the Company left well-enough alone with the all-everything OS and it remained as OS/400. However, in 2004, with the i5, the Company chose to rename the operating system as i5/OS to match the Power 5 chip.

Before rechristening the OS as IBM i in 2008, and changing the name of the box to the IBM Power System, in 2006, IBM subtly renamed the AS/400 yet another time. This time the name reflected the new religion in IBM that its machines were systems and not servers. So, Big Blue renamed the i5 as System i and the p5 as System p, and that brings us to today.

IBM's customers see the new IBM Power System with IBM i as a logical extension of the finest computer system ever built, the System/38. When the Application System/400 (AS/400) was introduced in 1988, it was so different looking and had such better hardware specifications that System/38 and System/36 aficionados accepted the AS/400 name with no complaints. It was clearly a different hardware machine inside and outside; however, the base attributes of the operating system and the underlying chip architecture had remained the same.

Regardless of what you call it, the all-everything operating system is still a computer science phenomenon and the finest OS and computer hardware combo that any company anywhere has ever developed and marketed.

Anyone who takes the time to look deeply into the full system package would see a machine and an OS that is the embodiment of all that IBM knows about computers, implemented with elegance unparalleled in the computing era. Perhaps now that the Unix and IBM i systems are consolidated there will be no more need for big name changes and IBM can pack away that hot branding iron for the long haul.

Only IBM Could Create an All-Everything OS

Besides the all-everything operating system, the IBM Power System hardware is also quite special in that it incorporates all the advances in chip technology that make IBM Power chips the best in the industry. Additionally, because the chip and the hardware components and the OS are built together, the operating system is chip aware as many software instructions are imbedded in the silicon to help the system's function and performance. Additionally, while IBM i runs at 64-bits, along the way to 64-bit Unix, IBM added instructions to assure that both 32-bit and 64-bit Unix could run on the same hardware using native chip instructions.

The pundits in the know suggest that within a year or so, when IBM ships its Power 7 processor, the Company will add the mainframe instruction set to the chip along with the mainframe optimization instructions that have been buried in the mainframe chips for years. Now, how's that for a special hardware platform? For all that to happen, the hardware really did need to be separated from all the operating systems yet be fully cooperative with them all, not just IBM i.

Experts in the industry who regularly study all computing platforms know the value of the mainframe and IBM i computing. Surely Microsoft and Intel, and Sun and HP fear the day that IBM realizes this also. On that day, IBM will announce that IBM i for Business is its best all-around business OS and its proprietary mainframe line is the best large enterprise system bar none. On that day, IBM's system competition will have plenty of reason to fear. For now, for its own reasons, IBM chooses to let its customers choose the type of system they wish to deploy.

Only a big company with such huge resources as IBM could have ever conceived, designed, and built such a superior OS and machine model. For this, I regularly thank the IBM Corporation. IBM spent billions of dollars to develop and billions to improve the advanced integration features of the IBM Power System with IBM i. None of the company's current competitors are in a position to even consider making such a technological investment.

If IBM i were IBM's only operating system product, Big Blue would choose a different course of action regarding its public face on the power of IBM i. It would no longer have to protect the less capable platforms that bring in the most revenue. So, IBM would be in a position to raise the technology standard and up the ante for prerequisite features in an advanced operating system. If Microsoft or Sun or others could not meet the technology standard, then their offerings would be inferior by comparison. IBM could have a field day educating the masses about the power inherent in its all-everything operating system, simply by highlighting the unique features that have been part of the IBM i base function for thirty years.

As you will see beginning in Chapter 10, the capabilities built into IBM i are superior to any operating system that was available before the System/38. CPF on System/38 changed IBM computing paradigm forever -- and yes, for better. Ironically, the approach used internally for the operating systems that claim to be modern, namely, Windows, Unix, and Linux on Intel hardware, uses the same architecture as the systems that predated the revolutionary IBM System/38.

A less than savvy marketing manager could go to town on the facts in that statement. In other words, all other operating systems than IBM i are legacy-ware design brought forth to the future. Yet, for all the truth is worth, the industry press continues to hail the majesty of Windows et al. wares for technical accomplishments and it consistently refers to these wares as modern. It is IBM; however, that has the most modern architecture ever developed for any computer system. It sits in the attractive frame of an IBM Power System and it runs the all-everything operating system. Any questions?

Yet, again, for all the truth is worth, the press has no problem calling IBM's compelling operating system and machine combination, a legacy system. Hah!

IBM Has the System Bases Covered

What a blessing the IBM Corporation has in terms of advanced technology in its stable of products. It has all the computing bases covered. IBM is the only operating system and hardware vendor that can sell anything from first base to a grand slam home run. If you are IBM, that is a blessing. If you are an IBM i shop hoping that one day your wife or husband or significant other will hear about the platform that you use, the fact that IBM can do fine without IBM i is somewhat of a curse. When you consider that Microsoft has just a piece (though a reasonably large piece) of just one base,

PC software, you can readily conclude that IBM has the armaments that should power it to victory in today's computer marketplace. There really should be no prisoners.

First Base – PC Servers

In the personal/micro/X86/X64 space, just a few years ago, IBM had first base well covered with its industry-heralded ThinkPad, its appealing and inexpensive ThinkCentre, and its NetVista line. Now, IBM markets none of these personal machines but, all are offered by IBM partner Lenovo.

The IBM company also has its high-function, high-speed Netfinity Servers (now the xSeries). The mainframe-enriched xSeries servers compete head on with all PC Network servers running Windows NT, Linux, Netware, and OS/2 LAN Server. Most of IBM's success in this space is shared with Microsoft and Intel, who provide the bulk of the software and processor hardware in this system area. However, today, there is no question that IBM has very formidable offerings in this area.

Second Base – The Unix / Linux Box

In the multi-user and advanced workstation Unix spot, IBM is well positioned at second base with a rugged "taken no prisoners" submission. The Company had developed a mature offering with its RS/6000 hardware which migrated to the eServer pSeries, then p5, and recently to the IBM Power System. The other part of the equation is IBM's high-powered and stable Unix offering under the name of Advanced Interactive Executive. Dubbed AIX by IBM, this is the company's Unix operating system offering. If you want to buy Unix from IBM, you would buy its AIX offering.

Along with Unix as AIX, IBM also runs the Linux operating system on the IBM Power Systems and this has only strengthened the product line in the overall Unix marketing space. The IBM Power System offers top tier hardware facilities to system customers who prefer the personality and the unique applications of a Unix or Linux machine. IBM i can run along with Unix and Linux on the same processor if the customer so desires. There's no question you can get to second base with today's IBM Power System as it has extended the capabilities of Linux and AIX even further.

Third Base -- Mainframe

In the traditional mainframe system arena, IBM's leadership in commercial hardware technology is unquestioned. Mainframes are the types of computers that Exxon, Boeing, AT&T, Metropolitan Life, and other Fortune 500 companies use as their main processors to run their billion dollar businesses. IBM's System/390 product set (now called the System z) competes against relatively few. The players in the large mainframe and supercomputer marketplace include Fujitsu, Hitachi, Cray, and not many others. In this period of resurgence for the power of mainframe computing, IBM is doing very well for itself. For sure, you can get to third base with a System z. And, there's not much wrong with a triple!

Home Run – IBM i (for Business)

In the business solutions sweet spot, IBM has hit a home run with the IBM Power System with IBM i product line as it stands on home base as the obvious winner. If there are any runners on base when IBM i gets its chance, you can expect a grand slam.

The biggest recognition problem here is that since the work that IBM i does so nicely can also be performed on the other three bases, though with far greater difficulty, IBM has a real marketing dilemma in knowing exactly how to position its IBM i box to capitalize on its inherent market strengths. The company also has a dilemma in making its purpose for the IBM i box crystal clear to its IBM computer prospect list. Unless you already know about the compelling business case for IBM i, or you are reading this book to learn, it would be hard to tell the circumstances in which the IBM i box would be the overriding system choice over IBM's other fine servers.

Regardless of where it is positioned however, IBM has invested tons of money into the IBM i platform and has in fact created this all-everything operating system on top of the finest processor chip and the finest hardware packaging in the industry. Some analysts predict we will one day soon be able to run applications from all of the popular operating systems on the IBM Power System with IBM i platform. This includes Microsoft Windows and the many IBM mainframe operating system flavors including z/OS. We'll see.

Though Windows and z/OS are not yet on the list to run natively on the Power Systems box or the Power Chip itself, in 2008, both Linux and AIX (IBM's Unix) made the run and now all three of these operating systems run on the upgraded System i server now known as the IBM Power System. Additionally, these operating systems can still run in partitions under IBM i so that even a small IBM i machine can run all of these operating systems at the same time with just one processor engaged.

Other than some confusion in product positioning as IBM works out the details of releasing the full bodied all-everything operating system, the Company is well positioned with the new IBM Power System with IBM i on home plate for the big home-run score of the millennium.

Even More Environments

In Chapter 7, we discussed the base capabilities of IBM i in terms of computing environments supported within the one operating system. Running four different environments plus running Unix and Linux under IBM i is surely the makings of an all-everything operating system. To refresh your memory, the four IBM i environments are as follows:

1. Native AS/400 and i5 Processing
2. System/36 Environment
3. System/38 Environment
4. Mainframe Environment with CSP

With the availability of running multiple operating systems as noted above and with about fifteen years of work perfecting a native Java Virtual Machine (JVM), the all-everything operating system can now do even more, as shown in the following add-on list in addition to the four items above:

5. Java Processing through an integrated Java Virtual Machine
6. Unix Processing through AIX and IBM i partitioning
7. Linux Processing through standard distributions and IBM i partitioning

Considering that there are only two operating systems / environments that the IBM i OS does not support today on POWER processors, (1) Windows and (2) IBM mainframe OS flavors such as z/OS, from a hardware and operating system standpoint, the future IBM Power System is the future all-everything machine running the all-everything operating system. This combo is certainly well on its way to realizing its full future. In case you were wondering, no other machine in the industry, from IBM, from HP, from Sun, or from Dell can do anything close.

Mainframe Future on Power 7 up to 2017 (Power 9)?

As we keep telling you, if you can believe the industry prognosticators, both of these missing capabilities will be added to the Power chip hardware when IBM changes the microprocessor base from the Power 6 platform to the Power 7—at least when it comes out with Power 9 in 2017..

It makes sense that IBM will stop making expensive CISC (complex instruction set computing) processors that are unique to the mainframe and begin to migrate mainframe OS ware to run on the Power 7 processor line. The newest chip in the mainframe line, the z6 does have a lot of Power 6 chip features but, it is still its own proprietary mainframe baby for sure in lots of other ways.

The fastest AS/400 heritage machine today is the IBM Power System model 595 with 64 integrated Power 6 processors. Such an IBM Power System rivals the mainframe for best commercial performance. With even greater CPU power available in the IBM Power 7 processor expected in 2010, it would be imprudent for IBM to continue investing billions in unnecessary mainframe-only technology. Those billions would clearly be better spent making the mainframe OS run seamlessly on the next generation Power processor. That's what I see happening; but, it won't be without the mainframers getting a lot more mainframe-only stuff on the Power chip than currently exists.

Windows on Power 7 or Power 9 Anyone?

Then, there is Windows. In many ways, knowing the haphazard methods that Microsoft has historically deployed in its OS construction over the years, as characterized in the book, Barbarians Led by Bill Gates, and in other media, IBM is understandably skeptical about running an error-prone operating system on such a solid hardware machine. The book, Barbarians Led by Bill Gates, was a joint effort by Microsoft insiders, Jennifer Edstrom (daughter of Gates long time PR chief, Pam Edstrom) and Marlin Geller, a 13-year veteran developer who worked on DOS, Windows, and the Pen operating system. This book is so revealing about Microsoft's lack of discipline in its OS development efforts that there is no longer a mystery for me as to why I must reboot my PC so frequently.

IBM is not looking for unique ways to have to bring down its steady as a rock all-everything operating system or it would have embraced Windows already, as an IBM guest on the Power Platform. One can bet that the IBM Company is concerned about machine stability and that surely is one of the impediments to having any Windows type operating system run on Power.

Having said that, it is a fact that Windows NT is the grandfather of Windows XP and Version 4 of Windows NT once ran on POWER technology. We know that Windows 7 will be coming soon as Vista has run into its own Microsoft adoption issues.

In 1999, Microsoft decided that Windows NT would no longer be updated for any processors other than Intel and the DEC Alpha and it stopped development for the IBM PowerPC chip. The DEC alpha was taken over by COMPAQ in 1998, which merged with HP in 2002. So, one would conclude that the IBM Power System is a "never again" for Windows. Yet, the Microsoft X-Box 360 runs on IBM Power chips. How'd that happen? Did Microsoft dust off some of that old Power processor code from the NT days?

Knowing this history, it is clear that there are no technical reasons why the Windows Server operating systems could not be up-tuned to run again on Power technology. In fact, many speculate that Microsoft already has XP, Vista, 7, et al. running on Power and is just waiting for its negotiations with IBM to complete. There would be no reason at all why Microsoft would not like to enjoy the benefit of the solid, reliable hardware base in the IBM Power System platform so that Windows would be able to scale substantially better than in the Intel line and run right along with the all-everything operating system.

Of course, once the mainframe z/OS and Windows next version runs on the IBM Power System, IBM can change its hardware name to the all-everything machine for indeed it will have become exactly that. Add these two to the list above and you have a machine with just about all the needed capabilities to have it all:

8. Windows XP Native Processing
9. Mainframe z/OS Native Processing

Now, that's an all-everything machine from a hardware and OS perspective if I have ever seen one. At this point of the game, the IBM Power System with IBM i would be able to run all applications from all operating systems. Moreover, since the applications would be from four different environments, it would be proper to conclude that the Power platform would be providing four times the business value of one machine. That sure is a lot of everything for one machine to handle by itself. Having the all-everything operating system as one of those pillars means that many more companies will be able to take advantage of all-everything computing on the IBM Power System.

Chapter 9   Autonomic Computing from the Start

Automatic Transmissions 'R' Us

From the very beginning, the IBM i operating system was designed to be simpler and more capable than all others. To this day, no other platform has such a good balance between "easy-to-use" and "powerful." Unlike Mainframes, Windows, and Unix/Linux, IBM i comes without a clutch. It's got a fully functional automatic transmission. In fact, when you drive one, you find that for the most part, you are not needed as the system drives itself--it's like cruise control! You can know enough to run an IBM i-driven Power System machine when you know less than a few percentages of what there is to know.

With IBM i, the all-everything OS, for example, much of what you want to do is already set up with default values, and thus, you do not have to think out each piece of a command. You just run it. With a minimal amount of training, one person can in fact know enough to run an entire company using IBM i. It's done all the time. That's why once people have worked with IBM i, they become spoiled and resent working again with other machines.

In basic no-frills form, IBM i is hard to beat for a new install of a reliable system at any new customer location. PCs are still for fluff things such as e-mail clients, drawings, messaging, chats, and things requiring really cheap connectivity. You may not yet want to surf the net with an IBM i as a client, but you surely would not want to trust a fully audited, transaction-controlled, mission-critical invoicing application running on behalf of 100 users if it were written in a PC-oriented kids' language, and if it were running on a farm of Windows PC servers with multiple label printers in multiple plants. For this, you need a nice sized professional staff--- yes and then some--- even for a PC-based system. I ask myself all the time, "Why would anybody do this with a PC-based system?" If the system were an IBM i, just one person would be able to handle the mission, and the person would also be able to take lunch. And, the box would not go down.

Part of how IBM i is able to get lots done in a reliable fashion is that it is much easier to use, and its rules are stricter than any other environment. Hackers don't like rules, so for the most part; they stay clear of IBM i. On other platforms, for example, you can write a program that destroys the operating system and leaves you to reload it. You can do it intentionally as a hacker, or you can do it by error, unintentionally, because you did something wrong.

Most of us have seen the ease with which viruses can be created on Windows systems and how hackers break into Windows and Unix boxes all the time. IBM i prevents this within its architecture. It prevents users from killing themselves. It is not unimportant that the techno-geeks don't like it as much as they like Unix or Windows. They get stopped at the door like a wolf and a brick house. They can't hack IBM i and bring it down successfully--and they really don't like that one bit!

Ease of Use for Technical Staff

AS/400-iSeries professionals love the ease with which they can manage the IBM i system and its integrated DB2 for i relational database facility. On mainframe computers and Unix boxes, and even Windows boxes, it is not quite so simple. For example, on all three of the non-IBM i flavors, the database is not integrated. That means that you get to buy it, install it, apply the patches, and ensure that it is fully functional before you ever get to use it.

For the record, Oracle database administrators, which are needed in heavy database environments, get paid a ton of money. Oh, they are worth it all right! Without them, your Oracle database would be crashing as often as a Windows client PC. See Skip Marchesani's comments on Oracle in Chapter 5.

With this environment, you get to make sure all the pieces work. You get to integrate it with everything else on your machine. It is shipped as piece parts. Moreover, as noted above with Oracle and SQL Server, in order to have a database, you have to hire an expensive extra person to your staff. This new person is called a database administrator (DBA) and he or she comes with a price tag of more than $80,000 per year. Whatever business value a system with a database provides, the extra care and feeding and the extra staff quickly chip away at that value.

A DBA is definitely needed in a mainframe shop, but that's not the only environment in which one is needed. When A PC (X64) server is used for real business applications, a DBA is required on this inexpensive platform as well. Moreover, on the PC platform, you always install servers in pairs, in case one goes down. Of course you have to buy the backup server first and then install its software and install the synchronization software before you get to deploy it. So you get to do the OS and the DB installation work twice.

If you know of any advanced PC shops with database products that do not have a DBA, you also know they are not doing too well, operationally. Though the IBM i OS makes the IBM Power System a database machine, you need no DBA because the database is built into the OS. The OS and the database and all the other advanced componentry is already installed when you get the machine from the plant. It is somewhat humorous in new installations that often users and even programmers discover that they have been connected to a database long after their applications have been using it successfully with the IBM i family for years.

IBM i Power Systems Keep on Ticking

Internet and IBM i-oriented magazines have many wonderful stories about how the machines just go ahead and get their work done, regardless of the level of attention the systems get. The newest IBM i units and even the older ones are very much like good old Timex watches. Sometimes, however, IBM i units keep on ticking long after they are forgotten. For example, this story relayed by Mark Villa of Charleston, South Carolina, is one that brings the ease of AS/400 operations picture well into focus.

> "There was an AS/400 in a plant that was doing its thing on a regular basis, and it was basically unnoticed out in the plant. Unknowingly, the company built a wall in the area during some construction, and someone went hunting for the AS/400 months later, and found it was enclosed in brick."

That quickly gives us an idea of how much constant care an IBM i database requires. Not too much!

Runs Many Applications At Once

Unlike Windows Servers, IBM i based machines run many applications at the same time on behalf of as many as thousands of users- all that on just one physical system. Even Microsoft Certified Professionals admit that Windows servers do not do well when used for more than one function on the same machine at the same time. That's why a single-server PC grows into a small farm of PC servers almost overnight. Today's IBM i machine can be a Web server, a Domino Notes server, a Java Virtual Machine, a firewall, an invoice machine, an accounts receivable machine, and so on -- all on the same single-processor box, without even having to partition the unit.

With partitioning, of course, your IBM i unit can also be a Unix Tuxedo Application Server, or a Linux application server. More industry analysts are noticing this facility and giving IBM i very high marks in their total-cost-of-computing analyses. There is a high cost to run a server farm as each machine needs attention. Additionally, the more machines you have in the 'farm,' the more likely one of them is down right now.

An IBM i unit can actually be a server farm under its one set of covers in just the one system box. It can also provide the same facility for Windows servers as a storage area network (SAN). Because IBM i is so many machines in one, sometimes it gets no credit from the industry press for being any, when it is actually closer to all than none. From its inception, IBM highlighted the IBM i family as its workhorse of midrange servers for business.

IBM called the early AS/400, for example, its midrange business system. It still is IBM's finest business system in its newest form, IBM Power Systems running IBM i (for Business). If it sounds impressive, that is because it is impressive. When IBM's next Power chip iteration comes out and all the pieces (mainframe and Windows) come together on the one chip, the IBM i platform will be even more impressive.

> Technical Note: A SAN is short for Storage Area Network. This is a modern notion involving the separation of the data storage elements from single computers and the centralization of that data on a central disk server, the role of which is storage management. A topology would show many servers all accessing data from the same set of disk drives managed by the Storage Server in the Storage Area Network. Because many Intel servers can be installed as blades in an IBM i Power System chassis, the box itself already serves as a SAN for Windows Server blades at 10% to 15% of the cost of a typical SAN approach. Considering that reduced cost is one of the most typical and most quantifiable categories of business value, one can see the impact that an IBM i based SAN, instead of the "farm," can have on the bottom line.

Today IBM i on the IBM Power System is alive and kicking, with an installed base of more than 400,000 and, perhaps as many as 750,000 systems, in about 250,000 businesses around the world. Between 30,000 and 90,000 new IBM i systems are sold each year, according to industry analysts. The IBM i platform continues to be successful because many of its customers buy a new one every four or five years, and because IBM continues to enhance the product line to levels far exceeding all other machines on the market.

Old Reliable

The most cited reason behind the continuing popularity of the IBM i heritage line is its reliability. The unprecedented ease of programming, ease of use and the low cost of management follow right behind. The IBM Power System models continue to be out-of-the-box products with bundled applications, communications software, and an integrated database. No commercial system requires the small amount of care of an IBM i box- and, when you try to sign on, the machine lets you in because it is not unexpectedly down.

Ease of Migration

The system provides the ability to integrate new technologies with very little disruption to business operations. IBM i heritage users have been benefiting for many years. For instance, Pagnotti Enterprises of Wilkes-Barre, Pennsylvania, a holding company for some mining and insurance businesses, replaced its old AS/400 CISC architecture system with a 64-bit RISC system in 1999. Two years ago, the company's older RISC machine was taxed enough from the Company's growth that management chose to replace it. Each time they had ever replaced an IBM i heritage machine, the new box had cost less than the old. The last go round to the i5, they saved money again. In retrospect, despite the magnitude of the 1999 shift from CISC to RISC, resulting in a major performance increase, no changes were required to the application code or logic, according to Betty Carpenter, IT Director, at the time, for the company.

"The conversion to 64-bits was as simple as restoring the objects on the new system," said Carpenter, who had worked on AS/400s for more than a decade. That's why IBM i customers do not want to switch. Betty retired several years back and her protege, David Dakin, along with yours truly, masterminded the recent Power System upgrade.

In 1988, IBM launched the AS/400 to replace its aging System/38. It renamed its all-everything OS from CPF to OS/400. Over the years, IBM has kept many of the original features but adapted the overall system to the technology changes needed for the times. Over these 30 years, counting the System/38 years, IBM also has succeeded in making the platform far more open than anyone ever would have expected. For instance, the IBM i OS today offers native support for mail and messaging technologies, such as SMTP, POP, IMAP, PHP, MySQL, as well as Lotus Domino, and ERP from companies such as SAP, PeopleSoft, and Baan.

Logical Partitioning Can be Logical

The IBM Power System with IBM i has grown to become a mainframe in size at the large end, and a mainframe in capability on all models. Super mainframe capability can be seen in a concept called *logical partitioning* using IBM i. This feature was borrowed directly from the mainframe. Using this capability, an implementer can define one processor as if it were many processors running IBM i or other operating system flavors. Each part of a processor (partition) can behave as a separate machine. Moreover, one unit may be running IBM i OS, Linux, or IBM's AIX at the same time. The future is wide open. In private meetings, IBM has announced that Bill Gates would like Windows to run on an IBM i type unit, and IBM has not ruled it out.

How Popular Is the All-Everything Machine?

Besides my little cadre of IBM i customers in Northeastern Pennsylvania, there are several hundred thousand others. Of course, I think they all should be my consulting customers, but I am happy with what I have got. A few national and world-class IBM i heritage customers, last time I checked, include the following:

Enterprise Rent A Car,
with over 40 AS/400s, 20 of which are dedicated to handling an application with 1.3 million transactions each hour.

Ball-Foster Glass Container Co.
in Muncie, Indiana.

J&L Fiber Service
in Waukesha, Wisconsin, a materials supplier for the paper industry.

Cornerstone Retail Solutions
in Austin, Texas.

Bergen Brunswig Corp., a pharmaceutical distributor in Orange, California.

Saab Cars USA,
Inc., in Norcross, Georgia (U.S. headquarters).

AppsMall
(AppsMall.com) in Rochester, Minnesota.

CoreMark
One of the largest candy and tobacco wholesalers in Canada and in the United States.

Nintendo of America
Seattle, Washington, Nintendo's major distribution arm in the U.S.

Costco
Seattle, Washington. Running several of IBM's largest IBM i boxes and controlling their distribution and retail network across the World. IBM i does such a good job of running their business their growth is more limited by electric power than their Power Systems.

Marywood University,
Liberal Arts higher education institution in Scranton, Pennsylvania. Once used multiple IBM i Power Systems for Academic and Administrative functions.

Better than half of all IBM i heritage machines are installed in countries outside the United States.

Users and Consultants Who Check It Out, Like IBM i

You'd have to pry an IBM i box away from its users with the biggest crowbar ever invented in order to create some separation. Check out this comment from a leading IBM i news company, NewsWire/400, of Penton Media:

> "We've been running our Web site on Domino on the AS/400, and we're not even running on the latest and greatest platform. We're running on a [model] 50S. The beauty of it is, the thing never goes down. Our maintenance on it is almost nil. We don't do anything with it; it just runs."
>
> --Terry Bird, principal, Appsmall.com

It's not just the IBM i-biased media that pump the IBM i line from time to time. In an *InfoWorld* article on July 31, 2000, just before the rebranding of the AS/400 to the iSeries, Maggie Biggs, writing for the "Enterprise Toolbox" section of *InfoWorld*'s e-magazine, noted that the industry perception of the AS/400 heritage family seemed to be changing.

In her article, Biggs discussed the changing perceptions as the traditional AS/400 heritage box morphs into what she calls a powerful, dynamic e-business server. The article was published a few years after IBM had stuck the little "e" on the back of the AS/400, making it the AS/400e. While writing the article, as a matter of course, Ms. Biggs felt compelled to suggest that IBM start marketing the box more aggressively.

> "Actually, the AS/400 has been e-business-ready for several years, but it's nice to see the marketing folks at IBM finally catching up with the platform's technological advances."

Biggs continues:

"Our experts from the Test Center and Info-World Review Board (made up of our free-lance writers) examined the newest release of the AS/400 and its operating system, OS/400 [now IBM i]...

"After more than 10 years of advances and a metamorphosis into a beefy e-business server, the majority of people still view the AS/400 [IBM i] as a legacy platform. This is a shame because the AS/400 [IBM i] is a multifaceted server capable of fulfilling a myriad of business needs regardless of the size of the enterprise or the tasks that are thrown at it. And the AS/400 [IBM i] continues to be one of few platforms that can simultaneously support legacy, client/server, and Web-based computing.

"...what kind of ROI you might expect to gain by adopting the AS/400 [IBM i]... found the costs low when compared to the software and hardware capabilities of the platform, which stand out favorably in many ways when measured against competing servers...

"These servers can be configured to meet the requirements and budgets of businesses both large and small. IBM has enabled technologies that let you run both Unix-based applications and Windows NT and Windows 2000 applications within your AS/400 [IBM i] environment. You might use these technologies to consolidate servers, reduce expenditures, or to improve business process integration...

"From what we experienced during our testing and analysis, the AS/400 [IBM i] appears ready to provide some stiff competition for its server rivals. You may not hear about the AS/400 [IBM i] as often as you might hear about other platforms, but just ask any of your colleagues who have worked with the platform and I think you'll hear a positive response."

Amen!

As the client/server revolution went sour and Windows server farms began proving to be more and more difficult and expensive to manage, there has been a resurgence of interest in the IBM i platform, fueled mostly by word of mouth. Businesses are fed up with their systems being down on a scheduled basis and especially with unscheduled outages. It is a Microsoft / Intel way of life.

It does not have to be that way, though most non-IBM i shops think that I am kidding. Businesses seeking a reliable, scalable platform are starting to notice that out of all the technology that is inside the IBM Power System with IBM i, the bottom line is that it works well and it does not go down.

Though it would be good for IBM to let the word out, most IBM Power System shops are not complaining about the tenth generation, 64-bit architecture of the box. The IBM i platform continues to benefit from Big Blue's ongoing, annual multi-billion-dollar investment in technology. There would be no IBM Power Systems today running IBM i without IBM's support and heavy investment.

IBM i Waiting to Be Successful

IBM i is poised to become the flagship for IBM once again, as Big Blue completes its transition to the all-everything operating system and chooses to hoist the flag. Besides having the most elegant packaging of computer basics, its features include enterprise e-commerce applications, and a free "integrated" version of IBM's WebSphere server.

Not to be outdone by the big jobs, the IBM Power System running IBM i also boasts support for Windows NT, Windows 2000, Windows XP, Windows 2003, and even Microsoft's newest operating systems as application servers through special bolt-on Intel processor logic cards (like blades) that are installed inside the Power System chassis.

A little farm of diskless Intel boxes can also be managed externally from the IBM i box, and in these cases, the IBM i management of the Windows environment actually helps Windows stay up with less crashes.

A Reliable Team on Duty

The free IBM i operating system shipped with the first processor of every IBM i machine is on duty from the moment you turn it on. The Windows process of installing the base operating system and then adding all the Windows fix packs is not necessary. The IBM i operating system, originally known as Operating System/400, or OS/400, then i5/OS and now IBM i is pre-installed at the factory, and is tested for hours before shipping.

As you would expect, like the Spaghetti ad, as you list features that an operating system should have, when you talk about the IBM i all-everything operating system, you'll find yourself saying, "It's in there!"

Before I close this chapter, I would like to present a quick laundry list (Figure 9-1) of some of the advanced facilities that you will find in your average IBM i system. If you are not technical at heart, it may not be too meaningful.

However, the list at least gives an idea of the Power System running IBM i and its full capabilities to solve business problems and its ability to provide solutions in many areas that might not at first be obvious

Figure 9-1 Some Major IBM i Capabilities

- Up to 64, 64-bit Power 6 RISC-based architecture – IBM's most powerful RISC processors.
- 128-bit software architecture.
- Spooling and job management for multiple users/separate queues.
- Performance management for allocating resources.
- Single level store (IBM i unique).
- Technology-independent machine interface (IBM i unique).
- Integrated DB2 for i Database (IBM i unique).
- Capability-based addressing for integrated security (IBM i unique).
- Object based (IBM i unique).
- Clustering--integrated.
- Consistent, intuitive command language
- Apache Web Server (HTTP) Server--integrated within system.
- Web search engine.
- Enhanced TCP/IP stack and utility--integrated within system.
- Native encryption for communications and backup media.
- File serving and client/server integrated features.
- Logical partitioning--advanced system facility.
- GUI application development tools for client/server and Web.
- Intel integration--Windows under the covers.
- PHP / MySQL packaged with IBM i
- Etc..., etc..., etc...

It's simply the all-everything operating system running on the industry's best hardware with the fastest processor chip ever developed. That's all it is.

Chapter 10   Advanced Computer Science Concepts in the All-Everything Operating System

IBM i Has What It Takes!

From traditional code crunching to Web services support to Linux, Unix, Windows, and even autonomic computing, the often-underestimated IBM i platform can match any IT environment. This truly all-everything operating system literally can do it all.

If you strip from the newest IBM i platform all of the fancy stuff the press seems to be excited about, such as client/server, ODBC, Linux, Windows, logical partitioning, AIX, PASE, QSHELL (Unix KORN Shell), and Java, you are still left with the most elegant, most functional, and most powerful operating system in the world. It is just waiting to be loved by the masses.

Along with a number of other graying IBM i lifers who worked with the advanced technology of the System/38 after its announcement in 1978, and saw it become the AS/400 and now the IBM i box, I know that there is no computer that can top IBM i for pure architectural elegance.

After this chapter you will know the principles of advanced computing of which I speak. After Chapters 11 through 19, you will have a more detailed perspective.

In Chapters 1 to 3, as you may recall, I briefly introduced the architectural elegance and advanced computer science facilities that are built into all models of the all-everything machine. In just a partial list, as you may recall, I identified 39 high profile business value factors for executives along with 60 some major technical factors that demonstrate the efficiency and effectiveness of this killer technical system to the IT department.

I am now compelled to ask the question: "why shouldn't an organization be able to have no-sweat, low cost, highly functioning IT facility, while providing the IT department with tools that make the whole thing easier than it has ever been?" The answer to that question is simple: "There are no reasons to not want an IBM Power System with IBM i."

In Chapters 1 to 3, we identified a number of features that affect the bottom line in terms of benefits, costs, and organizational productivity.

In this chapter we introduce nine advanced factors that separate the IBM i from all other computing environments and, in the next nine chapters, we put substantial meat on the bones of these features. The objective is to help the most doubting of the Thomas' to understand how this all-everything operating system provides so much benefit for so little cost.

To Know the IBM i box is to Love the IBM i box

There is no reason not to love IBM i if you really know it. So I might be so bold as to suggest that the Teddy Bears, a musical group from the 1950s, would have taken notice of the AS/400 in 1988, if the non-IT world were in on IBM's secret weapon. They would have been able to capitalize on a great theme to reenergize their group for a new hit tune to meet the times. Yes, the Teddy Bears could have taken the now defamed Phil Spector's hit tune and adapted it to the computer world back then and again today by changing just a few of the lyrics: "To know, know, know IBM i is to love,

love, love IBM i!" "And I do!" As silly as it may sound, I know I do as do many others who use it every day and, our reasons are not silly. They are big and compelling. It's how we feel and we have good reason.

Twenty some years after the 1958 song, starting in 1978, with the introduction of the System/38, followed by the AS/400 in 1988, the iSeries, and IBM i in 2008, this not-so-well-known IBM platform parlayed **advanced system architecture** while never abandoning the notion of **small system ease-of-use**. That's another way of saying you get the error-free, function rich, highly secure computing model that the big companies get with mainframes, but you get it with a personality that is a perfect fit for a small business. Moreover, it comes at a cost that a small business can readily afford.

If you are still not impressed, please think of this fact. It has been over thirty years and it is still the newest idea in town. No other platform comes close and I will prove that to you in this chapter.

The purpose for this duopoly of advanced architecture with ease-of use is to enable powerful customer-oriented applications to be built that will last long into the future, without having to be scrapped or reengineered. If there is any legacy that the IBM Power System with IBM i possesses, this is it. However, because software code runs forever and yes, for better, on this platform, competitors and the Windows-dominated press have chosen to call the IBM Power System with IBM i itself a legacy (meaning old) system. I don't think so. .

Yet, if called to task, no industry expert could deny that IBM i is an "all-everything operating system." Combined with the IBM Power System it provides a compelling information technology platform that is the best in IBM and in the industry. It is by far, the most advanced, the most unique, the best, the most productive, and the least cost all-around commercial system that has ever been conceived, designed, and built. That does not sound much like legacy to me.

All Everything OS: Six Advanced Principles

IBM i is the only operating system you can buy that offers nine major advanced architecture facilities as part of its standard, integrated offering. Six of these are in the computer science realm. The fact that many of the OS functions are implemented right in the Power chip itself makes the notion of tight integration even more compelling.

The purpose of this book is not to teach about IBM i per se. However, in order to gain an appreciation of this computer system platform, some things are helpful to know. There is no other commercial system or server that has been able to deliver even one of the below advanced architectural properties.

Let me repeat that please: *There is no other commercial system or server that has been able to deliver even one of the below advanced architectural properties*. At the core of the IBM i platform's machine and software architecture are the following six advanced computer science principles:

1. Integrated system functions
2. High level machine
3. Single-level store
4. Object-based architecture
5. Integrated security / capability-based addressing
6. Integrated relational database

Because IBM itself did not announce a seventh or eighth or ninth principle, I chose not to include these next items in the above list, but, from my perspective these three items belong there because they are part of just about every IBM i box and together, they help make IBM i serve as every programmer's dream machine.

No other operating system has any of these facilities integrated into the operating system / machine. The add-ons that are used on other platforms to provide this function are at best less functional and at worst, difficult to program and use.

These principles are explained in Chapters 17, 18, and 19 after all of the six advanced principles are fully explained in the next six chapters. I would call them principles 7, 8, and 9 as follows:

7. Integrated business language compilers
8. Consistent, intuitive command language
9. Integrated transaction processing

These nine features provide a platform that is renowned for flexibility, large system function, ease of use, and non-disruptive growth. To help you get a better appreciation for what these mean, without hurting the non-technical brain along the way, let's take a nice peak at each of these nine principles in turn, one chapter at a time.

Chapter 11   Advanced Computer Science Concepts: Integrated System Functions

Integration Beats Add-On Any Day

The traditional approach to gaining computer function has always been to use add-on software. IBM i uses a different paradigm. Everything is included or "integrated" from the beginning so there is little or nothing to add. IBM calls this the integrated approach and the little i in IBM i means integration. The other approach is called a piece parts approach or an a la carte approach as parts are pieced together as the need for them is discovered. In the piece parts approach, for example, if you need a database, you buy one. If you need a transaction processor, you buy one. If you need language compilers, you buy them. Keep your wallet out because there are lots of pieces.

Getting more specific about piece parts, you may have heard of Tuxedo as a transaction processor facility for Unix and Windows and CICS for mainframes. You may have heard of Oracle or Microsoft SQL Server or even MySQL in the database area. Moreover, you may know that Bill Gates' company from Redmond, Washington got started making language compilers and that Microsoft makes a lot of money in these areas even today. These are all piece parts.

For example, you may have heard of Microsoft C Language, Microsoft Visual Basic, and Microsoft COBOL. All of these are separate products that IT professionals get to install and make them operational on various computer systems in IT shops. To get those from Bill Gates, you just have to write Microsoft a check for each one you want.

Traditional A la Carte Approach

This traditional approach to computing thus is an a la carte approach. You never get a full dinner. In fact, as you read the above paragraph you get the idea that the parts of the dinner are coming from different restaurants. And, they are. So, there is no guarantee that they will always fit nicely on your one plate or all be ready at the same time at the same temperature.

I like to call this traditional approach to computing *legacy computing* since its style dates back to the 1950's. Most vendors in this legacy software space work with the Unix and Windows operating systems. They have found it easier over the years just to add software function as patches and sell them as new products. They make patches to their products seem like exciting new products to get you to buy them but they are nonetheless patches for pieces they forgot to include when the designed the operating system.

Moreover, they have found this a far more cost effective approach than ripping the guts out of their operating systems and adding the function where it belongs. Thus, no operating system vendor has ever started over and designed an operating system the right way from scratch. Well, nobody but IBM.

OK, Microsoft tried a few times, but each time had to revert back to their standard code as the basis for the "new function." Is Windows 2000, a lot different from XP, and Vista and 7, 10, or the Windows operating system du jour?

I can think of no time in the history of the IBM i operating system, and the several renames along the way, which any customer said, "no thanks, we like your older version better." Has anybody ever said that to Microsoft? IBM i has proven you do not need go to Vista or Windows 7, take it or leave it. Actually, with IBM i, it would be OK if you left all your

Windows behind, unless you like unplanned outages and lack of function.

If you have followed Microsoft's history, you may recall that Microsoft has asked its software vendors to deep-six their wares and start over as the Microsoft Company changed critical OS interfaces with their new named operating system versions--and not just once.

They do not just add things, they deprecate the old method so you must use the new. Then, when they are done, the user community gets to buy the new version of the old product as if it were a new product. Additionally, in some cases, you get to buy your software again, such as your office ware, or your programming tools. You see what I mean? It is good for Microsoft revenue streams, but not too good for a stable computing environment.

Way back in 1978, the first predecessor of IBM i was introduced as the System/38. IBM in Rochester, Minnesota, took its list of best computer science features that its mainframe division had collected from its customers and started building an operating system from scratch. The mainframe division also gave Rochester the benefit of the current thinking at the time as to how to achieve the customer objectives.

It took a lot of years to get it right and it cost IBM a pretty penny to make it happen. IBM i is an integrated platform and that just does not happen. Nobody else has even attempted it because no other vendor has the resources or the hardware / software lineup to get it done.

Unix, Linux, Windows: Legacy at its Best

As you may have concluded, Unix and Windows still have not abandoned their legacy a la carte tradition, and Linux models itself after Unix. Even IBM's mainframe systems never went back and did it completely right. Actually they couldn't, and really nobody who expects to support its customers on its new iron can ever go ahead and just start from scratch. Thus, all other operating systems, other than the IBM i (for Business), are full of patches and add-ons, since their architectures were never fully redone to accommodate the future.

New ideas require new thinking

At the time that the System/38 was being scoped out, among other things, the library of programs in IBM System/3 accounts was not substantial. It had been just nine years since the System/3 was originally made available. Moreover, the System/3 did not support many users concurrently and it was tough to write terminal programs. Consequently there were few terminal oriented programs written for System/3 and CCP (Interactive). Moreover, there was no database on System/3 so there was no database "conversion" per se.

The migration path for System/3 customers to migrate their RPG or COBOL code to the new System/38 was well thought out. An interactive aide was not necessary. Even without a CCP aide, 75% of interactive programs were usable and with just a bit more effort, they ran fine on System/38.

IBM in Scranton PA, where I plugged away as a Systems Engineer during this time, got pretty good at the interactive conversions as did most offices. It wasn't long after the methodology was in place that many System/3 clients were enjoying the benefits of the System/38. When the word got out, the rest came quickly. Batch programs moved to the new compilers quite easily with no real work.

Admittedly, the fact that System/3 customers at the time used terminals for very few functions made conversions lots easier. I know this for a fact because as a Branch Office Systems Engineer, my job was to assist IBM clients in making the transition. Once System/3 clients made the transition to the System/38, they never looked back. Their programmer productivity factors went through the roof and they became IBM loyalists from that moment on. I know of no IBM System/38, AS/400, or IBM i professional who voluntarily switched platforms. If the business chose to move from the IBM i historical platform, the IT people either grimaced and stayed or quickly changed jobs to an IBM i shop.

No Systems Programming

Systems programming is something that is not required in the typical IBM i shop because of integrated system functions. Since Systems programmers are very well paid, this is a value factor for those keeping score about the business value of an IBM i system.

To put the patchwork quilt puzzle into perspective, because of piece parts and a la carte software on other platforms, there still exists a function in IT called systems programming. In many ways, systems programmers finish the computer vendor's work in the IT shop. When as many as 40 or 50 essential software products must be installed, tailored, configured, and continually monitored, you can bet there is a high-paying job opportunity available for a highly technical person. The function name of this person is "systems programmer." To be frank, in many ways, it's like hiring a mechanic to drive with you, wherever you go.

The systems programmer position, which was introduced in the 1960's in IBM mainframe shops is now required in many Windows and Unix shops to assure that all of their heterogeneous piece parts fit together well enough to run the data center. Of course they don't call it that, especially in Windows shops. Instead you have a Microsoft Certified Engineer (MCE) or a team of them assuring that all goes well on your server(s). You can bet the "farm" on that! Next time you hear MCE, think "Systems Programmer."

The fact is that these Windows Certified Engineers, in some shops, are nothing more than systems programmers, a throwback to the old legacy computing days. They don't write programs or add value in any way to the IT shop, yet they are essential because they take piece parts and build and maintain operating systems and software applications on the IT shop floor. Without their efforts, of course, there would be no completely installed servers with which to work. So, they are very necessary. Such a position does not exist in an IBM i shop because the system is designed to manage itself.

Well, for full disclosure, there are some IBM i shops that need systems programmers. But there are very few and these are so big that they have hundreds of processors in their enterprise data centers running on several of the largest IBM Power Systems.

Companies like Costco and Nintendo USA, and other mega-companies need so many systems to run their complex operations that they need several people with systems expertise on staff. Most of the time, however their "systems programmers" are like Maytag repairmen. Now, if they chose to use Windows or Unix, they would need more people and they would be on their feet most of the time.

So, only in the most complex, multi-system environments is such a position required in an IBM Power System with IBM i shop. I know of no small businesses that are using IBM i that need a systems programmer. IBM ships the system complete and already assembled so that its customers can use it immediately, instead of first having to finish building it on site. That's what we mean by integrated system functions.

For those paying the bills, this can be thought of as a huge cost savings and it also increases the productivity of the organization because the system is already built when it arrives. Just consider at least $100,000 per year for a systems programmer over the three to five year life of the system. You can buy an awful lot of hardware for that... perhaps even an actual farm.

Unlike the Windows and Unix piece parts approach, one of the major design criteria for the 1978 System/38 was to ship a complete product to IBM's customers. The System/38 was designed not to need additional time, effort, or skill for its completion. That's system integration, as in the "i" in IBM i. The great grandson of the System/38, IBM i uses the same integration paradigm.

The Best of the Future

In the early 1970's, IBM had a major project underway for their large customers that would permit them to use the most advanced technology that IBM or any computer company could produce. After millions and millions of dollars spent on analyzing customer needs and after consulting the brightest minds in computer science at the time, along with the consultation and leadership of a phenomenal cast of engineers and scientists within IBM, the result was a definition for the finest computer that could ever possibly built. Not only was it spectacular in its immediate capabilities, but it was so inclusive of advanced technology that the IBM team believed it covered so many advanced notions that it would last as much as 30 years into the future.

When I tell you what happened next, depending on who you are, and how much you know about the internals of IBM, you may not believe me. Please note that it was not a bunch of clowns in the corner trying to rick mother IBM. This was IBM's finest scientists and engineers coming together with a solid recommendation for the future.

To be exact, and to be a bit facetious at the same time, it handled everything, or at least everything that these big brainiacs could conceive would be important in the future. The bad news for most brainiacs is that eventually they must meet the business people and convince them that their recommended approach is best for the company.

IBM at the time had this thing called the Corporate Management Committee. If you had something to say, no matter how much had been invested in it by the very people to whom you were presenting, you had better be prepared to make a great case for your idea. No idea stood by itself.

I think you know where I am heading. IBM was run by mainframe chieftains who were already realizing a major cash flow from the mainframe software and hardware the company was producing. There was no business crisis that needed fixing. Things were already good! Every other new system that IBM had introduced, from the 650 to the 1400 to the 360 had caused its customers major disruption in order to gain its benefits.

IBM business analysts saw this as an impediment for an ordinary business to move to newer IBM technology. Perhaps more importantly, IBM had promised its customers with System/360 that those days of year-long conversions were over.

Consequently, with the advice of the IBM business analysts, the CMC rejected the notion of what by then was called "Future System" or "FS" for short. There would be no future for "Future System." The business analysts and the executives in IBM's mainframe division believed sincerely that it would cause too much disruption for their large customers to make a major conversion to this phenomenal technology idea.

At the end of the project, IBM had built a model for a system that would be the best for the times and would be a 30-year blueprint for all future computing. Corporate IBM felt compelled to scrap the project to save its customers from the anguish of another major conversion.

Did FS Hurt IBM?

Bad news for some is sometimes good news for others. While IBM was protecting its System/360 and System/370 large system customers, some places in IBM did not have the same constraints. The Rochester IBM team, who had built the System/3 and who had the System/34 in its cross-hairs, were looking for a machine to capture the small to medium sized market once and for all for IBM.

IBM was really doing well with billions of cash reserves and a future that looked like it went to infinity. The corporate chieftains, especially Frank Cary, IBM's Chairman for a good part of the 1970's was often concerned about the US Justice Department's anti-trust suit than conducting normal business. Cary wanted Uncle Sam off his back. One of Cary's pet notions was that if the Uncle Sam axe were to fall on IBM, it would be better for IBM to decide how the company was to be split than to have Uncle Sam do it.

This was not lost on the Rochester team, who knew that if IBM split, they were the first to go... and maybe that would be enough. Frank Cary positioned Rochester and in fact all of IBM's General Systems Division to be an easy spinoff. It was no secret. So, in addition to looking for a machine that would be a winner for the System/3 client set, Rochester was looking to create something that could grow very big, if need be, to compete against mainframe IBM if it ever had to do so. Yet, the system, while Rochester was part of IBM, would have to be small in horsepower, yet large in potential. .

Nobody, including mainframe IBM, cared how big it was in architecture. Having bright people on the team, some of whom were also on the FS team, gave Rochester access to the full content of the FS report as well as the "back and forth." Moreover, Rochester's scientists and engineers had enough self confidence that they knew that they did not have to take a back seat to any of the other great minds in the corporation.

Ostensibly looking for a follow-on design for its System/3 product, IBM's Lab in Rochester, Minnesota spent most of the 1970s designing the architecture and then building the hardware and the software for the revolutionary System/38. The big blueprint was FS, but there were lots of additional innovations, from IBM scientists such as Dr. Frank Soltis, Roy Hoffman, and the most recently deceased Dick Bains.

Soltis, who wrote the Foreword for this book, is credited with being the Father of the IBM System/38, but he would be the first to tell you about Hoffman and Bains. If you ever have a chance, you owe it to yourself to hear Dr. Frank talk about "this baby."

The System/38 itself therefore is the product of the IBM Corporation's finest minds. To keep its mainframe computer systems running faster, better, and more reliably than its competitors, IBM performed advanced research in both hardware and software architectures.

Being a successful computer corporation and wanting to maintain its success, IBM had a division called the Advanced Systems Development Division, whose mission it was to identify the technology that was to be used ten years hence. Consequently, IBM owns a lot of patents and many other companies have licensed its technology over the years. On top of all this, the focused FS project realized major dividends.

Pass the Jigger

The Future System project was not run by a bunch of lightweights in a bar having a few martinis. IBM commissioned a group of its best scientists, engineers, and software architects to study the best possible architectures and the best ingredients for a new system replacement for its mainframe processor line.

After being designed for the mainframe division, this superior design became the foundation for the most advanced computer system that would ever be built. Internally, as noted above, IBM called it the Future System.

Though it would never be a mainframe division product, the work lives on in IBM i. It is no longer a secret that the first system in IBM designed with these Future System (FS) specifications was the 1978 vintage IBM System/38.

Integration was at the forefront of this advanced design notion. If announced today, the 1978 System/38 would undoubtedly be the sixth most-advanced computer ever built. It would follow the AS/400, the iSeries, the i5, the System i, and the IBM i platform.

When you build a computer system in which the hardware, the operating system, and all of the support for program development and operations are all built together, you can build a system in which function is distributed to the proper layers and components. You can achieve integration. This means smaller code paths, better performance, better stability, more productivity, and less functional redundancy. Everything a developer needs in order to be productive can be built together. Each important piece knows about every other important piece.

Systems like Windows and Unix and Linux built from multiple add-ons and patches and after-thoughts and other bits and pieces cannot achieve this. And, so, they never suggest that their operating systems are integrated with anything, because they simply are not.

IBM announced and made available the most advanced system of its time with the introduction of the System/38 and you can acquire this technology today under the name IBM i. There still is nothing close to it architecturally, performance-wise, or functionally.

No longer do system programmers have to spend hours determining which versions of which products could be built together in a complex on-site system generation process. For the first time, every system model in a computer product line had (and still has) all of the functions. From top to bottom, every System/38 could be used to build and to run the same application programs. It was in there! It still is with the AS/400, the iSeries, the i5, the System i, and now, the IBM Power System with IBM i.

What A La Carte Can Mean (On a Good Day)

In Chapter 10 we used the analogy of a full dinner vs. a la carte to differentiate IBM i from its competitors. Another worthwhile analogy is the notion of a house in which the pieces are all designed and built separately by different companies. What if BEA Systems (Tuxedo) built the bedrooms, and Microsoft (Windows) built the bathrooms [OK the Windows], and Oracle (Database) built the living room, and Intel (Xeon) built the basement. And, what if they never compared notes before they sent the guys to do the work... what would you expect?

Building Airbus 380 Analogous to Building your System in your Data Center

What you would get would be something like the Airbus 380. You may already know that when the European Airbus partners sent their large pieces to Germany for final assembly, they found, the first time, that it did not quite work as it did on the separate drawing boards. This is very similar to how all computers are made. Giving France, Spain, and the UK, different pieces of the plane to manufacture was a great way of splitting the load; but, not having the Airbus 380 built in one place created major engineering snafus that delayed the plane's initial flight by two years.

Many of you may have heard this story of how there was no real coordination of the engineering effort. Thus, even the tools and the measuring mechanisms that were used were different. Hey, they were similar but different enough to cause big issues. Their results were marginally different; but, they were different enough that when the huge piece parts came together in Germany, the plane simply did not work-- because it simply could not work. That was a very costly engineering mistake. I bet you're glad it didn't happen in your data center.

The different engineering groups in the huge Airbus project had their missions outlined fine, but nobody prescribed the specific tools those engineers needed to use to build their pieces. Consequently, the autopsy of what went wrong found that the different labs had used different versions of CAD/CAM and CATIA, etc. ... that were incompatible. The incompatible output of the 3D software created big issues. The results were close, but no cigar!

Additionally, as we know in any software project, change management is very important. Having four separate groups with poor communication caused issues in change control. There was little in the way of rigorous change and management procedures deployed. There were major wiring issues and other engineering defects unveiled during the battery of tests conducted. Even the landing gears had problems and the initial assembly had some weight issues that lead to other delays.

There is no question that such a design / engineering effort put forth by separate labs was bound to create big issues. Thankfully, they were not discovered in flight and have now all been corrected. Like the original System/38 and its production delays, the Airbus is literally a huge continual monument to what mankind can accomplish, when properly motivated -- even if there were major initial issues.

When you have a chance, take a look at the Airbus 380. It is as physically impressive as I see the internals of the IBM System/38 and on to IBM i. The big difference is that IBM i was built by the same labs with the same tools and so there was no real final assembly issue. Integration was part of the design all-along. If integration is not the foremost factor in design, you get an Airbus 380 with parts that do not fit together. Sorry! It is a great notion and now that the Airbus issues "c'est fini;" [are behind us], it is recognized as a great machine and a monument to coordinated technology.

Each corporate datacenter, with its farms of various servers and software from various companies, is a unique, continual project. Unlike the Airbus 380 or the System/38 that can have its kinks ironed out eventually and be good for the next round, the current datacenter paradigm, with heterogeneous servers, engineered in your datacenter, is sheer madness. Only an integrated system can help management avoid such issues. Only the IBM i can help management avoid such issues.

Piece Parts Assembly - By Design

Let's look at a bank and its need for perfection. Why would a bank want a team of software engineers, continually on site to keep an ongoing Windows farm properly seeded? This has been a puzzle for me for many years. I have not solved it. How does that help a bank or any company to require piece parts experts and expert assembly personnel to live in the datacenter along with the machines? I don't think it does.

When IBM i does not get selected by a company, it creates data center chaos. IBM doesn't forecast the chaos since it is not in IBM's interest to do so. Yet, the client knows there will be chaos because there always is. For IBM's part when IBM i is left on the table and it does not win the day, the Company makes a lot more money.

Think about this and it gives some clues as to why you don't see IBM i advertised on National TV. IBM cannot take sides and it does not. IBM wins either way but it wins more when IBM i is not selected. So, as a stockholder, I have no motivation to ask IBM to solve this "problem." Having all those IBM guys on site must prove a reassurance factor to a bank or a big business that even and integrated system cannot replace. Even if the IBM service people were not need in many cases, the large bank would not feel right unless they were there.

Often, the onsite engineers, the software company supporting the bank and even the wireless phone company all may work for the IBM Company's Service Division, directly or indirectly. Feel free to substitute HP or another front-line computer service company to make the story more generic, but the fact is IBM makes lots more money in its service business than HP.

If IBM is involved, many of the people at all levels are paid directly by IBM. Thus, these people, working directly as employees of IBM or as contractors for IBM bring in a lot of service revenue to IBM. In all fairness, they do the same for HP if HP is the contractor.

Why should IBM or HP suggest an integrated solution, such as IBM i when it will decrease their revenue potential? If IBM i wins and IBM loses, that makes no sense. The moral of the story is that built-in integration is great but it won't necessarily be IBM that points that out to you.

Piece Parts Assembly Is Done by Your People

Back to the house analogy, the problems exist in full assembly because the separate companies do not share one design for a house; but, instead, use their standard room functions and components. Just like the Airbus 380, no matter how good the people or the tools are by themselves, without integration from the start, when it all comes together on your lot, there will be some anomalies. Since piece parts computer vendors merely rearrange their standard offerings for different housing needs, it is understandable that the rooms can't all blend well when they eventually come together for the first time. Heck, lets' face it, if there is a way to get into any one of the rooms in this scenario, the home builder and the home buyer are lucky. Plan on having a few hammers and saws available to get it right.

Surely in this type of "build it from standard parts design" with no customization of the parts ahead of time, you can expect to need a highly paid contractor / builder to get the electricity and plumbing working right, cut doors where there are none, steal pieces of rooms for hallways, line up the steps to open spaces, ad infinitum.

Piece Part Design Does Not Work Well

The same inefficiencies that you see in having home parts built by separate contractors unaware of the total design of your house are prevalent when computer vendors try putting their disparate piece parts together in your computer room. You actually pay for the assembly and when it finally is all assembled, before it provides one little benefit, there is often a sense of elation once the big tool has finally been built. The irony is that after piece parts assembly, despite all the money and all the hassle, not one business benefit has been accrued. If you are adding benefits to IBM i for integration, for determining its proper business value, don't forget to add the cost of continual datacenter assembly.

Other than that they all eat the same electricity, there is no other real standard in today's computer systems, especially the most popular using Intel and Windows. In the piece parts approach, two important puzzle pieces come from Intel and Microsoft, two companies who really do not even like each other. They don't trust each other but somehow when their pieces come together, many datacenter managers trust that they will work. (BTW, to see more about the Intel - Microsoft relationship, type in "Does Intel hate Microsoft?")

In computer shops where vendors actually do install their wares, in most cases, the contractor/ builder works for your company, not any of the companies whose products you are using. This contractor/ builder person is your systems programmer (Microsoft Certified Engineer) and the system is not complete until he or she finishes his or her work, at your expense.

There is just too much irony in this scenario and there is more here. If your company is substantially larger than the mom and pop variety then it is highly likely that the Microsoft Certified Engineer who works for your company, in this effort, receives his or her paycheck from IBM. IBM has lots of Microsoft Certified Engineers working for its services division because IBM gets lots more service business from Microsoft shops than from IBM i shops. That alone says something, doesn't it?

A La Carte Software Is a Negative Annuity

Unlike a house, however, the engineers in your datacenter do not go away when the project is completed (when the piece parts software is all assembled and configured and made operational). They're on the payroll or the A/P system as contractors for the long haul.

Because piece parts that fit together well one day in a non-integrated computer shop may not operate well with tomorrow's updates, the systems programmer role is essential to making the system work after it crashes, gets whacked with a virus, or simply hangs. Has this ever happened in your shop?

Thus, these guys get hired and they stay on and are part of the ongoing expense until you choose a different paradigm for computing, such as an integrated, custom built once-and-for-all approach--like perhaps an all-everything operating system.

I am ready to leave the house analogy but it keeps fitting. Think about this scenario: Would you hire an in-house plumber for your home because you expect your cheap plumbing to go down, all the time, or would you consider getting better pipes?

Besides the indisputable fact that it is so much more productive and cost effective, it just makes common sense to have the whole house or the whole system built together. You just don't want the construction done in your datacenter. You don't want the plumber living under your sink. The new paradigm is integrated computing and it is available today with an IBM Power System with IBM i. It's like having the whole house built together. What's wrong with that?

A PC is a PC is a PC

If this sounds like a commercial, it's more than likely because many businesses have come to think that crashes and downtime are part of normal computing. They don't believe it can ever be any different than it is. The Microsoft Certified Engineers are not going to tell the company to get an integrated IBM i box because they have never heard about it. Moreover, they would no longer have a job. All the problems we discussed so far emanate from the Microsoft and Intel "unholy partnership," which took a small-time PV architecture that IBM created in 1981 for desktop PCs and tried to stretch it into the corporate datacenter. The problem is that the rubber bands do not always hold. PC Server shops learn this every day.

PCs were designed for desktops and light computing, not for datacenters. That is the problem. The word "Personal" is the "P" in PC. Like all good things with stretch marks, a PC being can be used to run a business. But once stretched too far, the rubber band snaps, and, chaos is the order of the day.

Problem # 1 is trying to figure out which company warrants which of the piece parts.

Wouldn't it be nice to be able to use a system without rubber bands as a major design component? Wouldn't it be nice to have a well-built tubeless tire, instead of a tube with a million patches plus a tire? You see what I mean?

Having it the way you want it is having an integrated system. There are not that many integrated systems out there. IBM i is the only one that comes to mind. If you find strange people building things in your datacenter, you don't have an integrated system. On the other hand, if you don't even know that your new system has arrived and is operational, it is more than likely because it is an integrated IBM i system, whose mission it is to quietly do your job while you wonder whether or not your company is even automated.

Chapter 12   Advanced Computer Science Concepts: High Level Machine Interface

Pleasing Users--Never Having to Say You Are Sorry

Quite simply, a high-level machine implementation works in favor of the user, rather than the computer guru. Low-level machines, such as Unix, mainframe, and Windows boxes operate with languages and interfaces that are machine-oriented, not people-oriented. If you like talking in ones and zeros, you'd like the lowest level language -- machine language. Most people use a real language like English, and ones and zeroes makes no sense to them.

A high-level machine is another way of saying that user functions are built into the machine without the user having to worry about the machine itself. To simplify this notion, it means that you speak English and the machine hears ones and zeroes. If this were an international notion, you would be able to speak Swahili and the machine in question would hear it in machine language and yes, that would be ones and zeroes. Now, that's a novel idea, isn't it? Yet, for a system that has been out since 1978, you have not heard the IT press doing much ballyhooing about it.

A high-level machine, as implemented in IBM i, is like a high-level language, in that you talk to it in all ways and at all times at a level far away from the ones and zeros and the bits and bytes. Thus, this advanced notion brings with it a tremendous increase in operational and system productivity. There's lots more to this advanced notion. Only companies who must get their work done even care. Only IT staffs that are challenged to address the issues of the day, care. Those companies rich enough to permit the IT expense to be many times what it need be are so well-endowed that they do not even need to check out IBM i. Yet, it's worth a look.

The Technology Independent Machine Interface (TIMI)

Though, many do not care because they see computing as inherently flawed, it would not matter if they knew that access to the vast array of advanced system functions on IBM i is provided by a powerful, consistent interface that computer scientists would label as a **high-level machine interface**. IBM chooses to call this interface the **Technology Independent Machine Interface (TIMI)**.

Would the students of computer science approve of this high level notion? Computer scientists would carry this notion even further and would suggest that the high-level machine interface on IBM i is really a full **abstract machine**, since the architecture of the "machine" and its instruction set are basically invisible. The actual low-level hardware looks substantially different than "English."

Moreover, the user or programmer never needs to interact at the lower levels with the machine. This is known as user and developer productivity. Ones and zeroes are not the way when the interface is at a high level.

If you happened to be an outsider looking in during the late 1970's, in Rochester Minnesota, you would have seen a computing model being built more on the theoretical than the practical. The practical, after all, was the architecture of the IBM System/360 carried forward to the IBM System/370 and on to the subsequent mainframe platforms. The "practical" was ones and zeroes and not much else. There was no reason to surmise that the IBM System/38, in 1978 was more technically advanced than anything IBM had ever produced.

So, would the theoretical win or the practical? Only engineers and computer scientists knew for sure that the inherent architecture of the Rochester produced System/38 was really something to rave about or not. They were right. It is the best idea in computing that any vendor has ever brought to market.

The High Level Machine Interface was one of those things that separated IBM's System/38 and now IBM i from all other systems. The System/38 was built better architecturally than the best of IBM's best mainframes. All system administration and programming functionality were included in the operating system – compilers, database management systems, and backup/recovery utilities.

In addition to the integration and high level machine interface, there were a ton of other things that made the System/38 IBM's finest computer for the 1980's. It was an object-based system, designed around an abstract machine interface. This abstract machine interface or, as we call it, high level machine interface, allowed IBM to upgrade processor hardware, at will, without affecting application performance or stability.

Eventually, in 1988, IBM decided to use the first derivative of the System/38, the AS/400 to kill its major minicomputer competition. Microsoft was still selling desktop operating systems - not servers so, IBM paid little attention to the future Microsoft juggernaut. When it came time to creating an AS/400 from the System/38 and the IBM System/36 lines, both systems made some contributions in different ways.

The System/36 contributed its more advanced communications capabilities, such as LAN communications, as well as its more user-friendly menu interface. The System/38 provided the AS/400's overall architecture –

object-based, imbedded database, relationship with hardware mediated by the high level "abstract" machine interface, and many operating system utilities all of which were object and database aware.

Though all System/36 customers were far from enamored with the AS/400, the System/36 brand contributed much of its large installed base and large community of software vendors to the success of the AS/400. The combined platform, named the AS/400, was released in 1988. Over the years it has undergone major changes in underlying processor hardware, peripheral support, and operating system functionality, without compromising the six underlying design principles upon which it was built. The TIMI was the reason this was able to occur without creating a user burden.

Comparing Traditional Architectures to High Level Machines

Figure 12-1 gives a snapshot of a machine with a TIMI, compared with a traditional architecture machine such as the mainframe, Unix, Linux and Windows. Instead of the IT shop buying the traditional add-on software functions such as those listed on the left in Figure 12-1, access to the system function is provided by a powerful, consistent interface - CL - the visible part of the high-level machine interface as shown on the right side of Figure 12-1.

Figure 12-1 Technology Independent Machine Interface

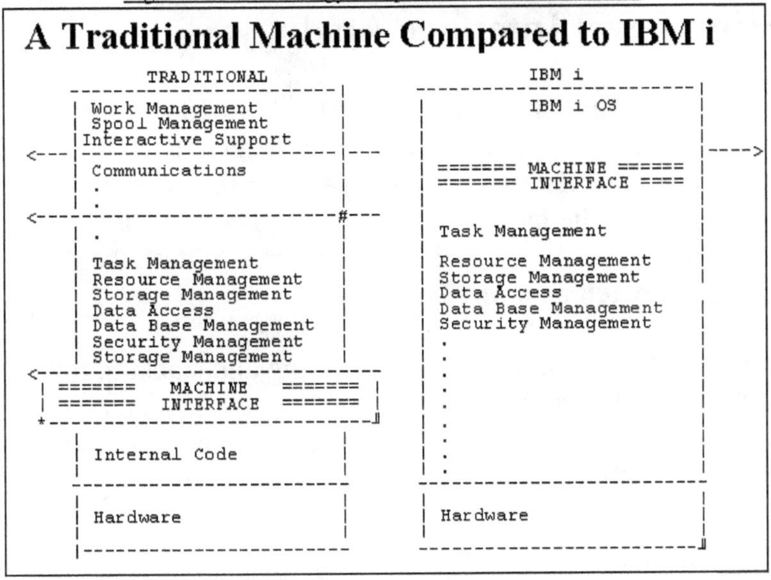

```
A Traditional Machine Compared to IBM i
         TRADITIONAL                            IBM i
 ----------------------------|     ----------------------------
 | Work Management          |     |        IBM i OS           |
 | Spool Management         |     |                           |
 | Interactive Support      |     |                           |
<---|----------------------------|---|                           |--->
 | Communications           |     |  ======= MACHINE =======  |
 | .                        |     |  ======= INTERFACE ====   |
 | .                        |     |                           |
<-----------------------------#---|                           |
 | .                        |     | Task Management           |
 | Task Management          |     | Resource Management       |
 | Resource Management      |     | Storage Management        |
 | Storage Management       |     | Data Access               |
 | Data Access              |     | Data Base Management      |
 | Data Base Management     |     | Security Management       |
 | Security Management      |     | .                         |
 | Storage Management       |     | .                         |
<-----------------------------    | .                         |
 | ======= MACHINE =======  |     | .                         |
 | ======= INTERFACE ====== |     | .                         |
 +--------------------------+     | .                         |
 |                          |     |                           |
 | Internal Code            |     | .                         |
 |                          |     |                           |
 ----------------------------     ----------------------------
 |                          |     |                           |
 | Hardware                 |     | Hardware                  |
 |                          |     |                           |
 ----------------------------     ----------------------------
```

Functions that had traditionally existed above the machine interface were brought below the interface, making it much higher than any other machine ever created. IBM i is shown above the interface and thus IBM i presents a consistent interface to all developer programming, so that when the machine and low level functions change, the user and the programmer's code library are protected and do not have to be re-done.

At the interface point, at a high level, neither programmers nor users have to learn cryptic machine code for normal functions, since the high level instructions are more English-like. For example, at the high level machine interface, one instruction can be used to get a data base record, perform multiprogramming, handle storage management, and query a data base file. In traditional systems, such functions are handled by multiple software programs. The IBM i all-everything operating system is much "smarter" than traditional systems because of the TIMI. For example, it can be told to query a data base with just one above the TIMI instruction.

High Level Interface Analogy:

Unlike a picture, an analogy is worth about 100 words, since it uses words to make the analogy. Nonetheless, an analogy is often far more effective in making a point than a mere description of the facts. So, here we go. There is a good analogy that IBM has used for a long time to describe the high level machine interface.

Suppose that we built two wood-cutting and stacking robots. Let's say we build our first robot with a high-level machine interface. At a "high level," we should then be able to operate the robot with instructions such as the following:

1. Go get some logs
2. Clear out a spot for the cut wood
3. Cut the logs into firewood pieces
4. Stack it over there.
5. etc...

Now, suppose we build our second robot with a lower level interface. With this robot, we will have to give more and more detailed instructions. To minimize the writing for this book, let's just use high level interface operation 3 above as an example:

1. Position a log on the block
2. Find the ax
3. Raise the ax
4. Whack the wood
5. Check the log
6. Check the drop zone.
7. Set the ax down
8. etc...

So, now let's say you need to write programs for both robots. Programs for the high-level robot are less complex, since there are fewer instructions. But both robots perform their required tasks well. It just takes a lot more programming to get the lower level interface robot working; but, once it works, it will work forever, right?

Suppose the Chainsaw is Invented?

Now suppose the chainsaw is invented. What impact does this have on your programs? If you have become a low-level interface fan, you are about to be disappointed. To incorporate chainsaw technology at the low level interface, the low-level log-cutting robot programs must be completely rewritten since they are bound to the specific tool... the ax.

As you can see the reason is quite simple, the second robot operates at the "raise the ax" level which is a low level of instructions. These low-level programs know nothing about starting chainsaws, adding gasoline, or anything to do with the new technology that has replaced the ax. In other words, the old software is tied to an old technology and when the technology is changed, the old programs will fail.

Now, let's look at the high level interface to see where we can incorporate chainsaw technology. Since the program instructions exist at a high level, the high level robot's programs can remain untouched. Specifically, the chainsaw technology is affected by only one of the high level statements, as shown in instruction # 3, "Cut the logs into firewood pieces."

Notice that this instruction says nothing about how to get the job done. In other words, the instruction at the high level does not care if it's an axe or a chainsaw or a Bowie knife or a stick of dynamite or something else. The program for Robot 1 is written to not care about the underlying "how." It is concerned only about the "what." Thus, this robot program, at the high level, is independent of any particular hardware implementation. Thus it does not have to be rewritten to accommodate a chainsaw.

How Does This Relate to Business Computers?

Let's ask ourselves, what if disk technology changes? What if the system begins to use 30,000 RPM technology and there are ten read/write heads per disk platter. The interface question du jour becomes, "Do our programs have to be re-written to use the new disks? How about the following questions?

- What if you get another disk drive?
- Should it be the "D" drive a la PC?
- Should all of your programs change to reference the new D drive?
- What files / programs should you now put on the fancy new "D" drive?
- What if CPU technology changes... like 48bit CISC to 64 bit RISC?
- Should the Operating System be re-written to handle it - like Windows-95?
- Should programs be re-written to use it -- like WordPerfect for Windows-95?
- What if you get a new printer?
- What if you get a high capacity tape drive?

The question really is, do you want to change your software in order to use advanced technology so you can grow - every time? Of course the answer is no. And, with the exclusive TIMI, found only with IBM i systems, you don't have to rewrite one line of code.

For those who are technically savvy, who have been using PCs since the 1990's, you know that each time Microsoft, for example, changed its operating system with an "advanced technology" milestone release, such as Win 3.11 to Win 95 to 98 to 2000, even they had to rewrite their dependent software. For Microsoft, it was MS Office components like Word and PowerPoint and Excel etc...

I bet Microsoft would have liked to have its software written at something other than a "raise the ax," level. Wouldn't Microsoft like to have a TIMI! If Microsoft operating systems were built at a high level, Bill Gates's bank account would be even larger, and there would be less employees needed in Redmond, Washington upgrading Microsoft applications to the new operating system du jour. It's really that simple.

Obviously, with IBM i, and its high level interface, there are no do-agains because of technology. The application software has no idea what the hardware really looks like and that is a big advantage.

Dr. Frank Soltis was the IBM i Chief Scientist before retiring at the end of 2008. He often talks how the TIMI came about in his many speeches and in his published works. The TIMI was an early design decision.

The original System/38 architects decided that the hardware would not interpretively execute the TIMI architecture so, not only was the notion of abstraction part of the original plan but, making it operate natively was a big design decision. In this way, code did not have to be interpreted against the TIMI every time it ran.

Considering that processors were substantially slower in the 1970's when these decisions were made, it was clear that using hardware to interpret such a high-level instruction set architecture (ISA), a.k.a., hardware/software interface, would not provide the level of performance needed for a commercial server.

Moreover, since most commercial applications are executed over and over again, the translation cost would have to be paid too many times for the notion to be efficient. As programmers know, interpretation as a method, is most useful when a program is to be executed once or only a small number of times. The biggest example of this is the CL or control language for the system. Unlike all other control languages, such as OCL or JCL, CL from the System/38 to the IBM i systems is compiled.

As Dr. Soltis explains, because the TIMI would not be directly executed, the architects had to design another lower-level ISA that the programmers above the MI would know nothing about. This "second" ISA had to be created so the hardware could execute. Programs at the Machine interface level would be translated into this lower-level ISA before they were executed. For performance purposes, this translation would occur only once. The translated machine code, along with the original MI version of the program in its template form, would then be stored within a program type object for future use. Thus, when low-level hardware changes occur, without going to source, the template in the object could be re-encapsulated at first-use to immediately use the new hardware--with no human intervention.

Before the grandfather of the all-everything machine (IBM Power System with IBM i) was re-oriented to 64-bits and RISC (reduced instruction set computing) hardware in 1995, the pre-1995 AS/400 used a CISC (complex instruction set computing) instruction set architecture as its executable interface. So did its immediate predecessor, the System/38.

When IBM revamped its 1988 AS/400 line of computers to use a new Power RISC chip as its processor engine, the underlying hardware changed from 48-bit CISC to 64-bit RISC. This new processor was nothing like the 1994 version and thus, this was a major hardware modification to the AS/400 model line.

The older CISC ISA itself was not typical of the ISAs of the 1970s and 1980s. In fact, from 1978 to 1995, the CISC processors that had been used to drive the system were far more advanced than even IBM's mainframes in their virtualization. For example, at a hardware level, these machines worked with 48-bits, whereas the mainframes of the same era used 24 to 31 bits.

As noted, IBM totally changed the hardware and the executable interface on the AS/400 to a 64-bit modified Power processor in 1995. The operating system above the machine interface (MI) thus continued to work, as it had previously, as the materialized OS called the same APIs as before; but, now the code in those objects called were built for the 64-bit RISC chip, not the 48-bit CISC chip.

> Note: API is short for application programming interface. It is the point in which the application code meets the operating system. There is also the notion of an ABI, or application binary interface where the operating system meets the low-level ISA. For this book and this discussion, there is no need to differentiate API and ABI any more than in the last sentence. So, consider an API / ABI as a set of routines, data structures, object classes and rules provided by operating systems in order to support the building of applications. An API itself is largely abstract in that it specifies an interface and controls the behavior of the objects specified in that interface. There's more but for us, if we think of it as the point of contact, we have enough to get the point of the value of the TIMI.

Because the change was at a level lower than the high-level interface, all functions above the MI, such as all the compilers and yes, their by-products, business application programs, continued to work once they were re-linked to the lower levels.

When most technical personnel hear something like "once they were re-linked to the new lower levels," they see themselves running linkage software against the programming library to make this happen. This was not necessary to move from AS/400 48-bit CISC to AS/400 64-bit RISC even though the processors were completely different. They thanked the high level machine interface for that.

For example, in the post 1995 timeframe, when an organization upgraded its older CISC 48-bit AS/400 hardware models to the newer RISC, 64-bit models, as the object programs were reconstituted from tape onto the new system, they were automatically joined to the new hardware. No source code was needed because none had to be changed.

The reconstitution process involved the new system reading the old programs and their high level template, and writing them back out with the proper linkage. This could not have been done without a high level machine interface.

From a programmer perspective, it was that simple. No programming was necessary. Programmers did not even have to know where their source libraries were located. In fact, the source never had to be migrated. The new code and the new interfaces to the new hardware were created on the fly with no developer work at all.

When the system woke up after all the libraries were loaded and it began to execute the business applications, those old 48-bit CISC apps were now 64-bit and they were running on RISC architecture immediately. They were not emulating 48-bit CISC on RISC, they were running 64-bit RISC and they were running very fast.

IBM Won the 64-Bit Technology Race

This is significant technologically because once Intel conquered 64-bit computing, thanks to AMD, and once Windows was able to use the 64-bit-ness of the new Intel / AMD machines, six to eight years or more had passed. That's how far ahead IBM's unknown AS/400, now, the IBM i platform, was in 1995. The Windows servers are still not totally comfortable in this big-bit environment and many Windows applications still run at 32-bits. An IBM ad, at the time, talked about the AS/400 as being "64-bits with no buts," as all programs ran at the 64-bit level from day one. The Intel and Microsoft world, even today, is filled with lots of buts.

Today's IBM Power 6 processors in the IBM Power System with IBM i implement this same 64-bit, RISC notion as the 1995 versions. They are just much faster. The benefit of this overall virtual machine design is that the hardware can change dramatically, as it did in 1995, with no changes required for operating system or application programs.

It is worthy to note that no other commercially available system in history has ever been able to accomplish this feat. That includes the ever popular Intel, Windows, Linux, and Unix flavored machines that dot the computing landscape of today. Though the Unix and Linux operating systems run well on the IBM Power System hardware, they provide none of the high level machine functionality provided naturally with IBM i.

Why? Windows and Unix operating systems have been around for ages. The machines upon which they run do not provide for the object-orientation or high level interface or advanced computing notions we are discussing and they never have and never will. They are not object-based and they are not object-oriented. Though Windows NT and its follow-on versions, 2000, and XP, and now Vista and 7, also have a hardware abstraction layer, it is not nearly as comprehensive as the TIMI approach as used in IBM i. If it were built as well as the IBM Power System with IBM i, Microsoft and Intel would not be struggling today to be able to use the full power of the Intel 64-bit chip in Windows.

Change Made Painless

Even as I write this book, years after IBM was able to use 64-bits with no buts on IBM i, in almost all cases, Microsoft operating systems continue to waste half of the capabilities of the chip. Thirty-two of the 64-bits on the new Intel chips remain dark and unused in the most popular x64processors. Whether Windows 7 makes change a bit easier is for future users to gauge, but judging from Vista, some think that expectations should be kept at a minimum.

If the Windows "hardware abstraction layer" was fully implemented, as in the IBM Power System TIMI with IBM i, all 64-bits would be lit up in short order with no programming sweat. But it is not. Moreover, the same goes for Windows applications. Since the OS cannot deliver consistent 64-bit computing, Windows applications run at 32-

bit speed on the 64-bit platform. Eventually they'll catch up but, if you read the trade press, you'd think that they already had.

Note: Here is the skinny on Windows 64-bit support. Enjoy:

Even now, most Windows users are confused about when their machine is running in 64-bit mode or in 32-bit mode?

To know for sure, click on My Computer and select Properties. If it does not tell you that you are running 64-bit Windows, then you are running 32-bit Windows. It is that simple. Please note that the 64-bit version is only available from MSDN or original equipment manufacturers (OEMs) so chances are half of your 64-bits, if you have a new box with x64 architecture, are dark and unused.

Of course 64-bits is better than 32-bits but it is tough to get 64-bit software for Windows, especially when Windows itself often runs at 32-bits. On 64-bit Windows machines, there is some PC software available for 64-bit. Those programs, specifically compiled to run in native 64-bit, are few and far between. Most are open source (such as Firefox) or they are high-end professional products, such as Adobe's image and layout tools.

You can almost bet that your software, including most office suites, productivity applications and games are typically compiled for the lowest-common-denominator, 32-bits and thus, you are not using the 64-bit machine you bought. You see, there are a lot of buts. In most cases, you can't even upgrade to 64-bit since the Microsoft installers don't support that kind of upgrade. If you get the right environment you would first have to back up your files, format your hard disk and do a clean install to get to 64-bit Windows. Still, much of your stuff would continue to with 32-bits dark.

You might ask if it is worth the trip to 64-bits. Well, if your applications are 64-bits, they will run better and faster. It's like getting a faster processor. A 64-bit processor can operate on integers of up to 64-bits in size. Likewise, a 32-bit processor can operate on 32-bit numbers. A 64-bit processor can also access memory using 64-bit addresses and thus the machine can have more memory. Instead of a 4G limitation with 32-bits, memory is virtually unlimited by the address size.

Many credit Microsoft and Intel for the move of PC technology to 64-bit. However, it was actually AMD that introduced 64-bit processing when it introduced the Athlon 64. The Athlon 64 fully supported previous 32-bit programs. AMD added about ten new instructions and did some other major redesign to the Intel chip structure for the extra 64-bit capabilities, which AMD called AMD64 or x64.

Later, Intel finally realized that its over-hyped 64-bit Itanium chip was not going to rule the world in our lifetime. They then decided AMD had an idea worth copying. Yes, Intel cloned the AMD64 / x64 instructions, But, they tricked us out here in Slumberville by calling their implementation EM64T. Today, all of Intel's Core 2 processors support EM64T. Likewise, all current

AMD processors support AMD64 or x64. BTW, Intel now calls their units Intel 64.

The good news about the failure to use all 32-bits is that the AMD64 implementation was so good that it also permits 32-bit programs to run so all of your programs run in this new Windows / AMD64, Intel 64 environment. Every 64-bit version of Windows has what they call a Windows on Windows 64-bit emulation layer, a.k.a. WOW64. This creates an environment in which 32-bit Windows programs can run without modification on 64-bit Windows systems. Unfortunately, though your programs do run, they won't take advantage of some of the performance benefits of 64-bit Windows.

Though you don't get it just by asking or wishing or hoping, 64-bit Windows has advantages if you can get it and if you can make some of your applications run under the 64-bit environment. But, it certainly is not as easy as merely having a TIMI as on IBM i and waking up one day and IBM has done all the work for you and all your programs run using all 64-bits.

The part about Windows servers that bugs businesses is that they are never sure whether they will be available for duty the next minute or not. I had the pleasure of teaching a course in Health Information Technology just last semester and a Doctor, going for his Masters in Health Care Administration noted that his practice has to put up with outages that are unplanned all the time. He is impressed with technology but, would like technology to be more reliable.

I shared with him that in my IBM career and in my consulting career, my clients must be even more spoiled than I thought they were. My clients expect their machine to stay up and be there when they need it at all times. He lamented that this was not how his practice performed and prior to my class he had believed that all computing was fatally flawed.

The fact is that Microsoft computing is fatally flawed. That which is so easy to set up and get going often forgets that it is supposed to perform flawlessly once the configuration is set and the fix packs are on. Sorry Microsoft, it's how it is.

IBM i programmers love the notion of the TIMI, and they don't want to give it up, because they don't want to have to learn cryptic machine code and silly names for normal functions. Anything less is inferior. Even the machine instructions are more like the spoken word, or as we say in the United States, English-like.

The interface is at such a high level (more human than machine) on the AS/400-iSeries and IBM i units that machine instructions, not add-on packaged programs, are used to retrieve and update database records, perform multiprogramming, handle storage management, query database files, and create indices over DB files.

Having said all that, as noted above but worth repeating, one of the biggest benefits from a high-level machine interface comes when you are changing hardware. For example, when IBM changed its AS/400 hardware in 1995 from a technology known as Complex Instruction Set Computing (CISC) to the IBM-invented, industry-leading Reduced Instruction Set Computing (RISC) model, even though the hardware was completely different, using the TIMI, Rochester got the operating system functional without a rewrite for the new hardware. More importantly the IBM i business community could use the full benefits of the new technology without any additional work. Like IBM's ad said, 64-bits, no buts!

No OS Rewrite Necessary

Only the very-low-level microcode (IBM calls this licensed internal code) had to be touched. This represented less that 5 percent of the code and it existed below the TIMI. The microcode portion presented the hardware machine personality to the operating system. IBM had written the original operating system, called Operating System/400, now called IBM i, using the high-level machine interface. Since OS/400 spoke to only the high-level TIMI, it remained virtually unchanged, even though the processor type and the number of bits had changed. If you are a tech guy or gal, let me ask: Isn't that impressive?

Immediate 64-bit RISC Processing

IBM i still knows nothing of the processor architecture. So, when the processor architecture was changed from CISC to RISC in 1995, and the hardware instruction set was redesigned, and the architecture shifted from 48 to 64 bits, the operating system programs did not have to be modified. All programs ran, even programs from the System/38 era that were written and never modified, ran the same after the hardware change in 1995 because they were always shielded from the actual look of the hardware. And, yes, they used all 64-bits.

Programs for IBM i and its precedents were always based on the high-level interface, and, therefore, they continue to run. More importantly, and I repeat, for IBM's AS/400 customer programmer community, the millions of System/38 and AS/400 compiled programs, written by IBM customers and software vendors across the world, were enabled to run, unchanged with the new AS/400 RISC platform. The source code was not needed. Please note as I say again, "The Source Code Was Not Needed." This could not be done on any other system today or any time yesterday or any time tomorrow.

From a business value standpoint, this feature provides for innate investment protection. Program code written for IBM's System/38 computer from the 1978 era runs today on an IBM i box without recompilation. The TIMI uses a self-adaptation scheme with an imbedded program template and the TIMI re-encapsulates the older program using the new interface. Because IBM can change from 48 to 64 to 128 bits and from CISC to RISC and because programs do not have to be rewritten and because packages do not have to be scrapped or reengineered, there is a tremendous cost savings for the firm. Nobody has to go out and find new software and the CEO does not have to disrupt operations in order to permit his or her IT staff to migrate purchased or developed software to the new wares.

While IBM was changing its AS/400 line hardware to RISC in 1995, it did one more thing that is historically significant at the same time. You already know what it is; but, it really is a big deal as every other computer chip vendor, including Intel, did not make the transition in its expected time frame.

The IBM Company introduced 64-bit processors in 1995. Nobody else was close. Suffice it to say these were much bigger than the Windows and Unix and even the mainframe 32-bit processors that existed in 1995. Another point in all of this is that the more bits one instruction can carry in one machine cycle, the faster the machine.

All this change occurred in 1995, going on fifteen years ago, and the technology was immediately available to AS/400 and now IBM i shops, without even having to recompile their programs to use all facets of this powerful hardware and OS architecture combo.

IBM achieved this in a very short time because of the nature of the TIMI. Intel, a company that IBM enhanced to world status in the 1980s by adopting its chip instead of building an IBM proprietary chip, would prefer that you not look at the facts. It took Intel until the year 2000 to create a 64-bit processor.

The first Intel 64-bit processor did not run well. By 2001, Intel got it right but for a while longer could not figure out how to get applications running in 64-bits. It is still sketchy. As noted previously in this chapter, Windows was not even able to use all 64-bits and still has trouble. Windows is still saddled in most instances to using 32 of the 64 bits. Windows 2000 will never be 64-bit; though it is still possible that Microsoft will eventually get its 2003 offering working with 64 bits. By then, it may be Windows 2010 or 2012 or 2014 or maybe Vista, the most unpopular OS ever offered by MS or perhaps Windows 7 or 10. Only Microsoft knows for sure.

As a point of note, IBM's mainframe division finally got its 64-bit processors out in late 2001. So, even IBM's premiere computing division was behind the all-everything operating system by six years.

TIMI Saves Users and IBM Lots of Time

All of the time it took other companies to try to get to 64-bits was saved by IBM in the CISC to RISC conversion because of the TIMI. Though all of the technology changed, the interface to the existing operating system did not have to be rewritten. That is a significant advancement and will be the same as IBM moves toward 128-bit hardware implementations in the future.

The TIMI gives the IBM Power System with IBM i a big, big technological edge. And, though the Unix and Linux environments may not need all that it has to offer, over time, on IBM platforms at least, you can expect that these two OSs will run better because of IBM's work with IBM i and its predecessors.

Therefore, in addition to making everything on the system easier to work with, the high-level machine interface protects the programming investments of software companies and IT shops by enabling existing programs to take advantage of technology and run in full-speed mode on new hardware without having to be rewritten. Try that with Windows or Unix or the next OS du jour!!

Why Should Programmers Like TIMI?

The TIMI means a lot to a programmer. The fact of the matter is that in the TIMI architecture, the language compilers, unlike other machines, do not really generate executable machine code. They generate an intermediate but very efficient pseudo machine code stored as a "template" in the program object. Program objects contain the low level executable code and the high level template.

The first time the program is run, TIMI compiles the template and generates the actual machine code and stores it in the program object. That's really why AS/400 shops did not have to find their source code to switch to RISC and 64-bit technology.

This comes in real handy when the operating system environment or the hardware changes as it often does. The TIMI looks at the object and detects that it is not compatible with the new environment. Rather than punting, as would happen in Windows or Unix environments, the TIMI regenerates the machine code.

This is one of the key points about TIMI that provides programmers a big plus, compared to all other systems. Moreover, investment protection is assured since program code works almost forever in this environment.

It is the template and abstraction between the logical representation of language code and the physical implementation on the machine that enabled IBM to move from 32 bit to 64 bit CISC to RISC without requiring a programmer in an AS/400 shop to have to change a line of code.

Rather than take a shot just at Unix or Windows / Intel, or Linux, though they deserve to get their shots, I will use an IBM mainframe as the focal point for this next example. Please note that much of what I say also applies to the other three OS environments. I happen to be friends with a mainframe guy who had to make a transition in the 1980s from IBM's MVS/ESA OS. At the time, the System/370 hardware architecture was being upgraded from a 16/24-bit architecture to a 31-bit architecture.

At the time, on the old System/370 machines, the addressable space on the system was just 16 megabytes of memory. When IBM moved to a 31-bit architecture they expanded the size of the programs and the address spaces to over 2 gigabytes of memory.

IBM worked very hard to prevent mainframe programmers from having to modify or recompile their programs, but just as with Windows, there was this notion of above the line and below the line. Programs could not access memory "above the line". The 16-bit code would run fine, just as Microsoft's 32-bit code works fine on 64-bit machines.

However, if the programs really needed memory, (memory constrained) programmers had to modify the mainframe code and recompile programs using the 31-bit compilers and linkage editors of the day. This was as much as ten to twenty or even fifty times greater than the effort for an IBM AS/400 customer to move from 48-bit to 64-bit technology and from CISC to RISC. As many already know, among other things, in the Windows world, not having a TIMI was a big reason for the delay in Longhorn (Vista et al.)

Hewlett Packard faced this same situation. They actually shipped a 64 bit machine (DEC Alpha) long before IBM did with the AS/400 and iSeries. To this day most HP customers still cannot leverage 64-bit applications. A huge percentage of their customer base is running old 32 bit applications. Since a majority of the HP code is written in C++, they must manually rewrite the code.

The growth for the iSeries, because of TIMI is virtually unlimited. Let's say that IBM moves to 128-bit hardware and ships the 128 bit beast tomorrow. What needs to happen? Every object program to be migrated to the new 128-bit machine would need its templates automatically regenerated into new executable machine code and the old programs, without rewrite or even a human touch would need to be immediately be usable to leverage the full power of the hardware. And just like the 64-bit RSC conversion in 1995, the conversions of the future will be just as simple, thanks to the TIMI.

This fact alone make IBM i (for Business) a killer platform. But, since we are not looking to kill anything in this book, we continue to call this powerful inanimate animal, merely, an all-everything operating system, or just simply, IBM i.

Chapter 13 Advanced Computer Science Concepts: Single-Level Store

More than Virtual Storage

Many readers may already understand the concept of virtual storage. It has been used in computer systems since the very early 1970s. Virtual storage permits computers to run programs that are far bigger than the memory of the machine itself. It does this by permitting memory to be over-committed, running many different programs. It uses the disks on the system to store pages of programs that are not being used at a particular point in program operation. This has many advantages, including not being shut down when the system has inadequate real memory resources.

What is Single Level Storage?

Single-level store is an advanced computer science notion that is not available on any other commercial system other than IBM i. It takes the idea of virtual storage one big step beyond.

Single-level store, was first introduced with the IBM System/38. With single-level store, a System/38, through the TIMI, believed that all of its objects existed in a 281-trillion-byte memory continuum, based on just a 48-bit hardware address at S/38 time. That's awfully big for 1978, as well as today!

Single-level storage is a revolutionary storage management architecture that not only gives IBM i outstanding disk I/O performance, but greatly reduces the amount of administration required. So, again one of these advanced computer science concepts, single level storage, adds value by reducing the IT workload.

There a number of features that IBM i users gain with single-level storage:

Single Storage Pool

Regardless of whether your system uses a two-level or single-level storage notion, there are still physical disk drives that do the data and program storing. The management of these physical disk drives is implemented in IBM i in its low-level partner called Licensed Internal Code (LIC) LIC is similar in concept to the BIOS on a PC.

By default, the operating system and applications see only a single large pool of virtual storage (called the System Auxiliary Storage Pool or system ASP) rather than the actual physical drives. Therefore, the management of physical storage is hidden from the user.

To increase the size of the storage pool, the remedy is to add disk drives to the IBM i system and the OS automatically recognizes them as part of the System ASP. For very large systems, in one IBM i system, users can create additional storage pools. These are called User ASPs and cane be independent or tied to the system ASP.

Scattering of Data

IBM i stores everything as a type of object. When you create an object with IBM i, Instead of worrying about where it is stored, the system worries about that and handles it for you. When an object is to be stored, IBM i's single-level storage puts parts on one drive and parts on another and it remembers which parts are where. It scatters objects across all physical drives. Users have no idea in which drive their data is stored. And, this is actually a good thing.

IBM i disk management also supports a notion called fully parallel disk I/O. This provides additional benefits. IBM i recognizes that performance is important and so it provides outstanding disk performance because each object on the system is accessible by multiple disk arms concurrently.

Unlike Windows C Drive and D drive and on down the alphabet, there is no need to be concerned about any particular disk drive filling up, or having to move data from one disk to another to improve performance.

All data management is handled by IBM i. Therefore, IBM i does not require a human being with the title Database Administrator nor does it require a Data Management Administrator for file systems. Since not paying salaries adds business value, you can start adding up the savings. IBM i also assures that there is no disk fragmentation so there are no CONDENSE and COMPRESS operations required as in Windows systems and other operating systems.

Single Address Space

Memory and disk on iSeries form a single 64-bit address space. A single address space enables objects to be accessed by name rather than hardware address, which provides additional integrity and reliability.

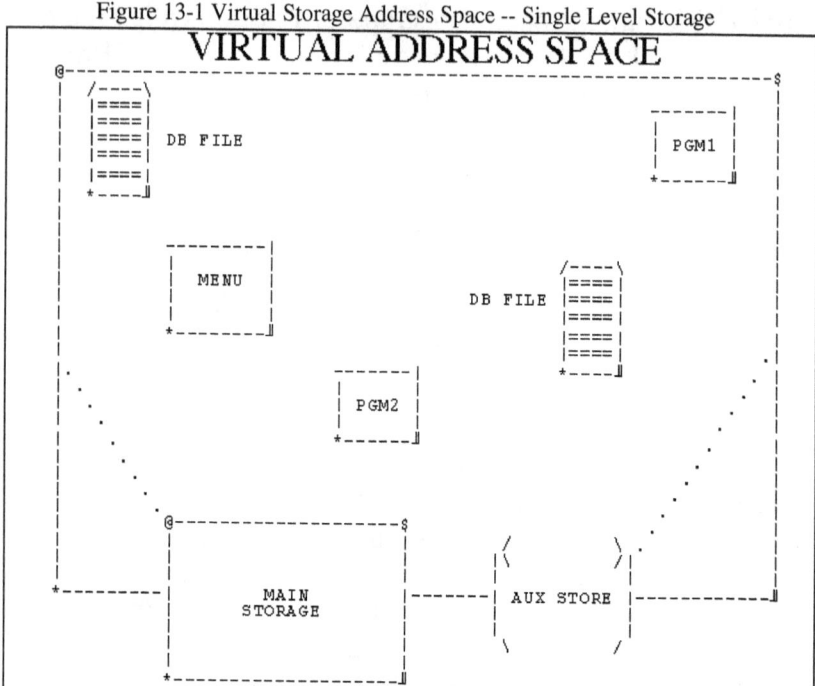
Figure 13-1 Virtual Storage Address Space -- Single Level Storage

Can IBM Actually Have the Best Technology?

There is a lot of irony in IBM actually having the best technology. IBM is the most slammed company of all time for supposedly holding back its innovations, keeping them locked-up tight for marketing purposes. Yet, the IBM i operating system, when unleashed to run on Big Blue's most powerful processor, the Power 6, is actually the most unplugged product of all time.

Adding IBM i to Power takes you to a point unsurpassed in human history. The all-everything operating system is unmatched today and from the rate of advancement activity in competing operating systems, it will probably continue leading for the next 50 years. Once somebody decides to catch up, it will take them a lot of years to produce even a working prototype. Then, come the bugs.

IBM i is so good that if IBM were hiding its best technology, this product would never have been released to its customers. Nonetheless, IBM i does get minimal press. Only a few honest industry reporters have taken the time to suggest that it might be a good deal. It's as if nobody in the press believes that a machine can be built with single level store. Yet, for over thirty years, IBM has sold a commercial product with this capability.

It's not only a good deal, it is phenomenal. Nothing else in the industry, Windows, Unix, Linux, or even any of IBM's mainframe operating systems, have anything close to single level storage and to be fair, IBM's large customers pay for this omission every day in the datacenter.

Single level store provides one big storage space in which all objects reside. It does not matter whether the program objects or the business data actually reside on disk, bubble memory, or bubble gum. It is a fact; however, that today the storage devices continue to be limited to disk technology.

Nevertheless, if bio-storage or chem-storage, or other secondary storage innovations are implemented in the future, single level storage will just go ahead and use this underlying technology with IBM i. Therefore, the programs from 1978 and 2010 and onward will continue to run unchanged.

All the Disk Drives Ever Built

In 1980, I recall giving my first presentation about the System/38 when I was a Systems Engineer with IBM. The presentation guide suggested that the 281 trillion bytes of addressable memory represented the sum total of all of the disk drives that had ever been built at that time. I was impressed, for sure. It took mainframes 20 more years longer to reach this level of addressability, and funding in IBM for mainframe systems has always been generous.

Another Look at Single Level Store

Besides addressability and all of the implementation advantages of virtual storage, IBM achieved even more by taking virtual storage to just one level. This is difficult to fully comprehend without tuning into the natural way that computers handle memory and file systems. The original idea behind virtual storage was to have a big page / swap pool so that programs had to be loaded from disk devices into memory and then the portions of each file when requested needed to be loaded into program memory when requested.

When the program closed the file, the file parts in memory might really be from program buffers or they might be in the virtual swap file. These then had to be copied from the swap file to the file system, in which they were permanently stored.

When the program itself ended / closed, the same thing had to occur for the program's executable code so there was a lot of moving around of data, even on virtual storage systems, just to do normal processing. Though it clearly permitted memory to be overcommitted and in the 1970's memory was very expensive, all of this work took away from the performance of the system.

Having live data in one user's program buffers in memory in the virtual design would not really help data sharing in those applications, such as inventory control and accounts receivable and order entry in which sharing of data records is key to providing the application function.

It was not helpful as, in the time sharing days, to have the memory space of one user fully isolated from the memory space of another user. For sure, time sharing protection kept one user from interfering with another but, it did nothing to enhance data sharing.

When many programs in virtual storage paging files concurrently tried to execute while memory was overcommitted, a phenomenon called thrashing occurred. Intrinsically, you can surmise that thrashing is not good. The term denotes excessive overhead and severe performance degradation or collapse caused by too much paging. That which begins as a shortage of memory turns into a hit on the processor.

Managing pages in thrashed systems takes more processor time than executing the programs themselves. Consequently without thrashing minimization controls, two-level virtual storage also creates performance problems.

Two Level Storage Solves Data Sharing Problem

Systems designers and systems analysts and programmers by design are big-time problem solvers. Because there was a big difference between time sharing systems of yore, in which users had nothing in common, and office systems in which users hope to share the business applications and the data, problem solvers had to solve the memory / data sharing problem. To enable sharing of common data between users, the designers originally chose to keep the file system, where the data was stored, outside of the virtual memory file. In essence, they created two levels of storage, one for data and one for programs. These were known simply as virtual memory and the file system.

So, on System/3's, System/34's, System/36's, big mainframes, Unix systems, Linux systems, and now with Windows systems, this approach allows sharing of the data in the file system. But, as noted previously, the two-level nature of the storage brings with it additional processing and overall system overhead. The other design point in virtual systems is that data and program code can be used and/ or changed only when they are in virtual memory. Since virtual memory is nothing more than a huge file on the system with address pointers keeping track of the page contents, this means that anything in the normal file system must first be moved into virtual memory before it can be used or changed. The performance implications are that disk operations are needed before items can be used in real memory. Think of the word "overhead."

This creates big inefficiencies. Copying programs and data into virtual storage creates overhead and then copying them back when changed creates additional overhead. All of this disk activity is inherent in this design. Though the problem solvers definitely solved the problem of data sharing, they introduced an element of inefficiency that does not exist in non-virtual-memory systems.

However, since memory still is not really cheap, and since multiprogramming systems inherently over commit memory to support an indefinite number of multiple users, virtual memory is an absolutely necessity. But, it comes with a cost. Think about those times when you are sitting at your client desktop PC with a number of tasks open. On the desktop you can hear the disk clicking and on the laptop you can feel it. Part of the price of virtual memory is that systems run at disk speed instead of memory speed.

Two Minus One is One

Enter the notion of single level store in which the machine itself believes that everything exists in a continuum of memory and each object has a memory address whether it is on disk or in memory. With this approach, the entire file system becomes part of virtual memory. The file manager still has its index of where everything is located, but in single level store, the directory relates the file or other object name to the virtual memory location where it is stored. If the object is a file, this location is where the file data is stored.

Unfortunately, once the problem solvers on every other operating system solved the data sharing problem, they were not given the license to go ahead and solve it the best way that it could be solved. When IBM i was originally built, the designers already knew from the frustration of the problem solvers how to create a solution that was best for the system. The problem solvers, unfortunately, were never able to revisit their solution on other platforms and that is another reason why all platforms are less efficient than IBM i in getting real work done.

In the single-level store solution, starting a program no longer involves all the work of creating swap file copies and then updating the file system. Opens and closes no longer copy entire files from their permanent locations on the disk just to use them. Instead, the system provides access to just the records that are needed.

These are copied into memory and their live address pointer in the system tables is automatically changed from disk to memory. Thus, when another user wants to use those records, they can share them while they are in memory as the system has just one set of live address pointers to the object.

Single-level store must use memory and it must use disk. Disk is the only high speed storage technology currently available and memory still is the only place from which code runs and data initially gets updated. In its single level storage design, IBM actually developed inherent caching of the system, as all of memory is a cache for all the disk storage.

For those of you schooled in cache, the hardware cache associated with the disk drives themselves is not affected by single level storage. The clear benefit of the cache nature of single level storage is that when one user makes a change to a file in memory, the change is instantly available from its memory location to any other user sharing the file. Swap files need not apply.

No other system uses this phenomenally efficient way of handling objects and data and thus none are as efficient in their virtualization techniques. All other systems use a derivative of the two-level system described earlier in this chapter.

Now, it is a bit easier to understand why IBM and the computer science community have labeled this advanced technique for a one-level storage model as "single-level store." It is hardly new but, it is difficult to implement and this difficulty prevents other vendors, such as Microsoft from making it part of any of their operating systems. That's why it is unique to the IBM i all-everything operating system. Nobody else has invested the resources to get it done.

Auto Managed Disk Pool

As noted in the chapter introduction, there is a notion within IBM i single-level store of an auto-managed disk pool. The fact is that the System/38 and every successor system and operating system of the System/38 right on up to IBM i, actually does use disk drives for hardware. There is no other type of mass storage available. If you are looking for a good reason why disk is still used, it is all that there is. It's that simple.

IBM i has integrated every one of the advanced concepts we have discussed thus far and some that we have yet to discuss. Single-level store started out as the idea of some bright people in IBM and in the computer science community. Then, IBM engineers and scientists developed the concept and designed an implementation. The idea was to deliver an image to a user or a program that the storage hardware resident on the system had very high level characteristics. All storage was to be viewed as main memory.

To help implement such a notion, the OS designers first had to create the notion of system managed disk pools, introduced above. At an OS level, this has had its own set of advantages independent of single level storage. In the

System/38, there was just one disk pool available on the system. Every single disk was in this one pool. On today's largest IBM Power Systems, up to 2,700 internal disks can be directly addressed by IBM. With SANS, IBM i can address even more. At the system level, IBM i is written to treat all disk drives as one big disk. You can think of it as one big set of disks in a huge disk pool, all working together and presenting to the user the illusion of just one disk drive.

That's what makes it so easy for programmers. They don't have to worry about C and D and E and F to Z drives, as is prevalent with all other systems. Through the single level storage abstraction, the system itself carves out space and places objects on the disk platters in a manner that automatically optimizes system storage and performance. To some parts of IBM i, it looks like everything is in memory and to other parts, for the high level developers, it looks like there is one huge disk drive managed completely by the system.

So, the user is shielded from having to assign files to drive letters and drives never run out of disk space. This makes the system much easier to utilize than anything else you have ever touched. Anybody who has been working on larger systems for any length of time knows that when a disk is full and an application needs to write to that particular disk, even if other disks on the system are bare, most systems shut down the application and give the operator a nasty message.

You get to spend a lot of time reclaiming disk space, changing the disk definitions in your code and then running the job again. Since IBM I, out of the box, thinks that it has one big wad of disk appearing as one big disk drive, out of disk drive space messages never happen.

As noted, at a very high level, IBM i thinks it has no disk and that all memory is managed in a flat memory model. This saves implementers substantial amounts of time. There is no denying that whether the platform base is an IBM mainframe, Unix/Linux, or Windows, managing disk and memory is an arduous task for a systems implementer. Not so for IBM i since it is all managed by the operating system.

Large Systems Shops Have Their Special Issues

On larger IBM i systems, to facilitate backup strategies, IBM added the notion of user defined auxiliary disk pools. For those IT shops that do not want all storage drives managed in just one disk pool, IBM i provides an option for users to create a number of separate disk pools. Hardware drives can be assigned to the pools by the operator. This comes in handy as the storage requirement on IBM i systems reaches a very large amount.

In these instances, IBM has provided system administrators the option of segregating journals (logs), archives, transactional data, programs, online hot backup, virtual drives for other operating systems or even applications. Some shops are more comfortable with multiple pools than with just one and over the last ten years, IBM has perfected the notion of multiple disk pools with IBM i.

Managing disk storage is a huge issue on other systems and it steals away much time from a systems programmer. On non-IBM i systems, you do not just set it and forget it. Thus, something as simple as analyzing disk allocations and storage utilization can be a big technical issue. In the mainframe and large server farm or multi-heterogeneous system world, this function alone justifies hiring at least one full time person and quite often more than one.

Detailed Disk Management - OS Function or Not?

To get performance, the systems programmer on other platforms sometimes works at a very detailed level and needs to allocate tracks on a disk to position high use sections of a file to minimize disk and arm movement. If you are not using IBM i then, managing all the disk drives is manual. Every single track of disk space must be manually allocated.

If there is a sudden shift in usage patterns or a major increase in business activity, all the prior balancing work may need to be scrapped and the systems programmer gets to start over using performance reports and brute force analysis. That's why they get paid so much.

Even if you are one of the very best system performance people in the mainframe world, it can take what seems like forever to recover a system that fails and it seems like forever just to keep things right.

The IBM i box does it all; from managing disk allocations to spreading out files, so that they are optimized for performance with automatic allocations across multiple drives. Additionally, IBM i continually rebalances all of the disk segments automatically.

In the Windows arena, Windows, just like the IBM i box, manages a disk pool, but Windows is not so good at it. It has one pool per disk. Even on an individual disk, there are problems that are obvious. If you have high activity adds and deletes, for example, you can lose much disk space until you run a de-frag on your system.

Of course, you must do the de-frag when all users are off the server, including those coming in from the Web. So, there is lost access time, and it normally comes when people need the system the most. Additionally, depending on the volume of adds to multiple files, your files can be fragmented all over one disk causing far greater physical seek times. There are no compresses and no defrags with IBM i. The system manages it all.

Yes, the IBM i box has a few manual disk management facilities such as file "reorgs" and reclaim storage and in theory, operations personnel do run these periodically; but, these are one command operations. And, if operations does not choose to execute the commands, the system still runs fine. You can run an IBM i system for months and months with no measurable degradation in performance caused by disk fragmentation. Try that on other systems.

Single Level Store with High Level Interface - Another Look

At the high-level interface, the single-level store mechanism delivers an image that is unaware it even has disk drives. Memory is viewed as one big continuum, with objects addressed by name. All objects get an address in the continuum.

The microcode worries about where the objects and object pieces actually reside on the disk. This saves programmers and systems managers (in larger installations) tons of time managing system resources.

The Car Analogy

To help gain an appreciation and form a proper perspective for the hugeness of single-level store, this next example uses the analogy of a car and miles per gallon, or better yet, inches per address.

If a car could go one inch per address, then mathematically a car with a 24-bit address space would be able to go 264 miles. Say the address width is doubled to 48-bits. Without doing much work, you might conclude that you should just double the number of miles to 528. But that would be wrong. A car with a 48-bit address space could in fact go 4.5 billion miles. You don't double it once, you double the cumulative value 24 times to get the 4.5 billion value. In other words, the car could go to the Sun and back about 24 times.

Can you imagine where an original AS/400 RISC system with its 64-bit hardware address would take you? How about a 96 or 128-bit address? This would cumulatively double the 64-bit address, 32 to 64 additional times. We can all agree that the result would be a very big number. Anything more would be nothing less than extra very big.

The software address for the IBM i OS in total is 128-bits. Each address portion of a software machine instruction is 128-bits. Thirty-two of those bits on System/38 are used for capability based addressing. See Chapter 14. On IBM i, at the system level, they are still used for security. The other 32 bits (difference of 64-bit hardware and 96-bit software address) are used again to cumulatively double the pointer range to something even larger than humongous.

Additionally, the 128-bit IBM i address was 128-bits back in 1978 with CPF and the System/38. Other than IBM i, nobody in the industry runs with a 128-bit pointer. Yet, this is not a new phenomenon. Many of us who engineered the migrations from 16-bit addressability in System/3 to 128-bit software addressability in System/38 had a hard time understanding why each program grew about 10X.

A good part of that was the 128-bit addresses that got carried around in each virtual single level storage instruction. One thing is for sure. If IBM could up the virtual software addressability to 128-bits back in 1978 with 48-bit hardware, IBM and only IBM knows how to make it 256, 512, or 1024 bits. With single level storage, the sky is really the limit. Watch out for the Eggplants!

Chapter Summary

There are a number of major operational advantages of the single level store as implemented on IBM i besides the obvious. We discussed many ideas in this chapter including system and user disk pools, single disk image for secondary storage, never running out of disk space on an individual disk, as well as not having to dedicate operations time or database administrator time in the management of files and disk/ database spaces. This is besides the inherent benefits of single level storage which were also a big part of this chapter.

As noted, with a single-level store, the entire storage of a computer, memory and disk, is thought of as a single two-dimensional plane of addresses that if brought up on a screen would look like the largest spread sheet ever built. Imagine each cell containing an address pointing to a virtual page. The program or data pages themselves may be in primary storage (main memory) or in secondary storage (disk) but programs or processes that work against those pages are shielded from caring whether the pages are in memory or on disk.

So, this says that the current location of an address is unimportant to a process. IBM i takes the responsibility of locating pages and it makes them available for all processes. If a page happens to be in primary storage, it is immediately available and is used in place. If a page is on disk, IBM i uses the virtual storage notion of a page fault to fire up a link to the IBM i paging routine. The paging routine brings the page into memory where it can be worked on directly by the process.

With single level store, no program does an explicit input or output operation to secondary storage. Instead, the actual reads that occur in secondary storage occur when the page fault fires. The writes to secondary storage occur when IBM i "believes" that modified memory pages need to be written back to their location in secondary storage.

With the IBM i implementation of single-level store, there are two categories of page faults, database faults and non-database faults. A database fault occurs when a page associated with a relational database object like a table, view, or index (within the library / file / member structure) is not currently in memory and it is needed for a process.

A non-database fault occurs when any other type of non-data object is not currently in memory. For example, if a program branches to an address that is of a page not in real memory, this causes a non-database page fault to be fired.

System administrators monitoring IBM i system faults think of many of the non-db faults as program faults. On hardware constrained systems this can be a performance issue at a certain level of faulting. There are faulting ratios to help in this effort and there are standard prescriptions for managing workloads to avoid faulting.

Almost all of this work is performed by IBM i itself though the administrator has the opportunity to override settings for specific job tuning.

IBM i can treat all secondary storage as a single pool of data, rather than as a collection of disk drives, as is usually done on Unix and systems like Linux, Solaris, and Microsoft Windows.

System administrators in shops, which have very large quantities (over 100) of disk drives do have the option of defining user pools of data and assigning a number of specific drives to specific disk storage pools.

In the system pool approach, using one pool as is the IBM i default, the operating system intentionally scatters the pages of all objects across all disks so that the objects can be stored and retrieved much more rapidly. In other words, IBM i pays attention to the location of disk pages so that it places pages on disks in places that improve performance. As a result, an IBM i system rarely becomes disk bound.

IBM's design of the single-level store was originally conceived in the late 1970s as a way to build a transitional implementation to computers with 100% solid state memory.

The thinking, at the time, was that disk drives would become obsolete, and would be replaced entirely with some form of solid state memory such as Bubble Memory. IBM i was designed to be independent of the form of hardware memory used for secondary storage and it still is. IBM i users have been reaping the benefits of this implementation since its first use on System/38 in 1978.

Chapter 14   Advanced Computer Science Concepts: Object-Based Architecture

Object Based or Object Oriented?

In 1978, IBM Systems Engineers spoke of the System/38 as having an "object-oriented" architecture, though technically at the time the term that better described the internal structure for storing things was "object-based." Only in the late 1980s and the 1990s did the term object-oriented take on real meaning on the system with the use of new programming languages such as Smalltalk, C++, and Java.

These use what is known as the object-oriented programming model. As hard as it may be to believe, even the 1978 model System/38 was an object-based system. A good part of what everyone has learned about object orientation over the years is contained within the notion of an object-based system, though there are clearly differences.

The experts' comments on the volatile body of work in the object programming area indicate that people in the know have varying opinions on things. Though the 1995 implementation of the IBM i operating system flavor at the time, known as OS/400, was object-based, as are all IBM i implementations, the tools that IBM used were object oriented. Some experts believe that object orientation transcends languages and goes further to items such as analysis and design methodologies.

All experts seem to agree that there is a hierarchy of "inheritance" in the object-oriented model used in programming languages such that sub-versions of higher level objects inherit the properties of the parent in the hierarchy. Since IBM i objects, when created across the system, do not universally inherit anything from a parent, IBM does not claim that its IBM i operating system is object oriented. However, it is definitely object based.

With all the bold assertions I have made in this book, you know that somebody will challenge me on something. But, as of right now, I have been around so long, I think I am right on all points, including the inherent sloppiness of Microsoft code.

When you take a hard look at the overall design of the operating system, you can see the IBM i unique features. IBM i surely is object based as was the System/38 that preceded it. OS entities are encapsulated as objects. Thus, only operations defined for a specific object are permitted (e.g., program object code cannot be modified via a text editor, etc.). Additionally, objects all possess an attribute called atomicity in that they cannot be split or separated or otherwise manipulated except in part. If you want to work on an IBM i object, you must operate on it as an entire object, and all of its object rules apply.

Believe me, I do not hate Unix or Windows or Mainframes. They just happen to be far more difficult for me to use than IBM i. Object based systems, such as IBM i, however, are in radical opposition to the UNIX model, and if I may add, the Windows model also, which Bill Gates admits is based on Unix. In the Unix model, all objects are regarded as files. Therefore, a file operation is permitted against any Unix system object (e.g., executable code, devices, etc.)

As much as I would like to say that IBM i is everything and can do everything, only half of that is true. IBM i, technically speaking, cannot be regarded as an object oriented operating system. There is more of this to come in this chapter. The reason is that its model—"object based" —lacks some of the basic characteristics of a fully object-oriented model.

I identified a few above but adding to the *can't do list* are subclass creation, and polymorphism. To learn more about these topics that are not part of this book because they are not part of IBM I, just type in the subject into your favorite search engine and you can surely get your fill.

Just as with every other advanced computer science concept that is inherent in IBM i, there are no commercial object-based or object-oriented servers available today from any computer vendor in the hardware or software realm. Only the IBM Power System with IBM i fits the bill. All other servers are thus, legacy, or highly traditional, in their design.

IBM i Provides Many Object Types

Call them classes if you wish but the number of object types supported in the IBM i operating system is huge. IBM has assigned a three to six character mnemonic for each object type. When this object type is written in "English," the mnemonic language of choice for object names, it is always preceded by an asterisk. To give you a brief snapshot of the vast list of object types implemented in IBM i, take a look at Table 13-! It shows a list of the most commonly used objects, their mnemonics, and a short description:

Table 13-1 Object Types Found on IBM i box

Object Type	Object Description
*LIB	Library (where objects are stored. Libraries cannot exist within other libraries)
*PGM	Program (for compiled languages: CL, RPG-IV, COBOL, C, C++, COBOL No interface restrictions)
*MODULE	Module (linkable into a program from a compiled language)
*SRVPGM:	Service program (dynamic set of one or more modules, like a DLL file in Microsoft's world).
*BNDDIR	Binding directory (holds a list of modules and service programs and is used when creating programs).
*CMD	Command (an object used for calling programs – used extensively in the operating system interface)
*MENU	Menu (List of options, accessed with the GO command)
*FILE	File (for both devices, data, and program source; de-scribed with DDS; files can also be created with SQL)

*STMF		Stream file (traditional file that would be familiar to most Unix and Microsoft users and stored only in directories, not libraries.)
*DIR		Directory (part of the Integrated File System that is equivalent to Unix and Microsoft)
*JRN *JRNRCV		JRN & *JRNRCV: Journal and journal receiver (used to journal changes to files, data areas, and stream files)
*USRPRF		USRPRF: User profile (allows users to sign-on to the system)
*JOBD		Job description (used when submitting/starting jobs)
*JOBQ		Job queue (used to queue up batch jobs to run in a subsystem).
*LIND		LIND: Line description (communications line: Ethernet, token ring, etc).
*DTAQ		DTAQ: Data queue (used to queue up data entries for fast retrieval by other jobs).
*MSGQ		MSGQ: Message queue (used to send message to users, can also be used as a data queue)
*OUTQ		Output queue (used to queue up output to a printer or diskette writer).

Metadata and Function Forms an Object

Looking at an IBM i object, you will find two parts, (1) a descriptive part and (2) a functional part. The functional part determines what an object is and what it can do and what it can be used to do and it also provides the object its ability to do it. The greatest trick the hacker has on non-IBM i machines of the Unix or Unix derivative flavors -- Linux and Windows, is their ability to sneak an "object" onto the system as a file and then later change it into an executable. Nothing in either OS stops hackers.

They have had a great time with these operating systems from their inception and the tough part to believe is that they still do. IBM i knows the intended function of an object and when hackers try to use a data file as a program. IBM i shuts the door in their face.

With IBM i, everything, and I mean everything is an object. You saw an incomplete list of objects in Figure 13-1. For our purposes in this chapter, let us consider that database files, programs, job queues, message queues, and a host of other items with unique purposes are what IBM i knows simply as "objects."

We learned above that an object within IBM i has two parts. The first part is referred to as the "descriptive part." We already discussed the second part as it is what gives an object its intended function. The descriptive part contains text in the form of metadata about the object. Between the text description and the functional description an object is documented as being able to perform certain functions and / or to be used in certain operations.

Enforceable Object Rules

Let's look at an example. On IBM i, a program object goes through a lengthy process to be created. Its descriptive part contains information about what it is and its functional part has more rules that are in programming code form affirm that the second part contents are executable, read-only, compiled code. As such, the only operations permitted by IBM i on this object are those that you would expect to be enabled for a program. You can't add records to it. You can't read it in as input to a program. But, if you have the proper authority, you can execute it.

If it were a database object, of course, its rules would permit you to write directly into the middle of the file if you chose, but it were a program, you would not be able to write into the middle of the executable code. The system's program object rules just won't let that happen. Thus, the notion of a two-part object design ensures data integrity for all objects in the system. And, so, again, viruses and other malware cannot hide out in IBM i objects waiting to attack your system. The all-everything OS is designed to swat them down before they have a chance to execute even once. Spawning is a virtual impossibility.

With this simple example of what you can do with a database file and a program, you can see that an object-based design has very important security implications. On a Windows or even a Unix system, as an example, there are no notions of rules for files or programs. Bill Gates was a big fan of Unix so Windows, under it all, looks a lot like Unix. One mechanism by which computer viruses enter an operating environment is by masquerading as data. Since programs are just files in Windows, it is easy for a bad program to be carried around innocently on such systems as if it had some data merit.

Once a bad hunk of malware gets inside a Windows system, and it becomes part of the file structure, the hackers have other methods by which they can flip the name to make it a dot exe and voila, it is executable code. Nothing in the Windows OS checks for that. Once it becomes executable code, it then goes ahead and wreaks havoc on your system and it may even propagate itself to other systems in your network.

Such a change of characteristics from data to program is not possible with IBM i. If the system lets a package enter as data, it must retain the characteristics of a database file forever. It cannot change its mind and become an exe type file as in Windows and take you for an unwanted ride to McAfee or Norton or Kaspersy.

Speaking of McAfee or Norton or Kaspersy, it says a lot about IBM i and its impregnable objects that none of these companies have been compelled to write a virus detection or correction program for IBM i. Object based systems do not lend themselves to viruses or to virus propagation.

IBM i OS Rewritten Using Object Oriented Tools

Though the IBM i box system has always been object based, in 1995, IBM's Rochester Lab rewrote the rules of how far object-oriented programming could be taken. In a major redesign and reprogramming effort, Rochester rewrote the under layer (microcode, low-level code below the TIMI -- sometimes called firmware) of the OS/400 operating system (licensed internal code) as an object-oriented project. The 95 percent of OS/400 that ran above the TIMI continued to work just as before, after some cosmetic changes. Even more importantly, all of the user code (RPG and COBOL programs) that had been compiled more than 17 years prior, continued to work.

IBM used an object-oriented methodology and object programming tools. No other commercial system had ever been written in this fashion. It was a first with new hardware and a new orientation. Somehow, like many IBM i firsts, this groundbreaking computer science event did not make the national news. It didn't even make the local news. The IT press were asleep waiting for Bill Gates or somebody else to discover America and then they were disappointed that it was Columbus, or whomever historians have agreed upon. Most agree that it was not Columbo though Peter Flak in that role could probably unearth many of the continual mysteries of information technology.

The AS/400 in-crowd certainly knew about the rewrite. From a historical perspective, this was a major achievement. The press came back from their slumber six or more years later when Windows was modified (with a little help from AMD) to be able to run on a 64-bit Intel / AMD platform. Yet, 5% of IBM I, under the hardware covers, was completely rewritten in 1995 to achieve the same facility and nobody seemed to care. IBM i accomplished 64-bits so long ago that most IBM i shops now think it's really not such a big deal. They think everybody has been there since 1995.

Can this lack of interest by the press and IBM's unwillingness to pay for the publicity be the reason why the reader of this chapter may be unaware of this capability? Today, the AS/400, iSeries, and the IBM i box are the only object-based commercial systems in existence anywhere.

IBM i provides even greater business value through objects because its integrity never gets compromised and it permits all organizations in which it is deployed to work on business problems rather than fighting the virus du jour.

Chapter 15   Advanced Computer Science Concepts: Integrated Security

What is Security?

Security is the process of controlling access, preventing access, limiting access, granting access, and revoking access. A computer science advanced concept known as capability-based addressing, implemented in the System/38 and CPF in 1978, for years has been acknowledged by computer scientists as the best way to achieve system security.

With the AS/400 family, in the form of today's IBM i operating system, security continues to be built in. The methodology has changed a bit and, it is even better today than just capability based addressing. The most prestigious security clearance for a system and operating system today is given by the Federal government of the US, and IBM i carries that clearance for its built-in security.

Only IBM with its System/38 CPF implementation has ever achieved capability based status in a commercial project. IBM has a number of informal rules that it uses for follow-on products. One of them is that each new product or version must be better than the prior product or version that it replaces. No product is permitted to ever regress to something inferior to its original implementation. So, it would be natural to assume that the AS/400 and IBM i systems, just like the IBM System/38, have continued with capability based addressing and have taken it closer to perfection.

The fact is that with the System/38 as its main product for over eight years, Rochester's IBM lab had done a pretty good job of perfected the use of capabilities within the System/38 architecture. Nobody had ever implemented capabilities on any commercial machine until the System/38 and it was at the top of the "capability" charts until the AS/400 was announced in 1988. Then things had to change because Uncle Sam did not like all the capabilities of capabilities. In this chapter, I will explain why.

Uncle Sam and Capabilities

Of course, you are not going to buy a computer just because it has capability-based addressing or for that matter because it has "integrated security." But once you have an idea of what integrated security using capabilities or what Dr. Frank Soltis refers to as adoption of authority, brings to the business, you'll want your computer to have it. You will then see all other systems that do not have this function as inferior. If they do not have integrated security, they are minimized.

Having once achieved capability based addressing, the highest level of security devised by the top minds in the field, IBM was surprised when it could not get the government's highest security clearance at the time for the future AS/400 because, as noted above, Uncle Sam just did not like capability based addressing. The US government had decided that capability based addressing was not secure.

I am not ready to get into a philosophical discussion about this notion but, the essence of their objection was that once a user or a process or anything on the system had received a capability key for even a temporary act, it could never be revoked.

From my discussions with Dr. Soltis, though he would prefer to move on rather than reflect on what might have been, I got a pretty solid feeling that IBM Rochester could have handled the government's objection within the context of capability based addressing. Uncle Sam held all the cards and IBM was looking for its C2 security clearance for the AS/400 so, it created a different, yet still advanced way of handling security through the object structures on the system. IBM created an impregnable internal security implementation using adoption of authority for its AS/400 and IBM i systems that do not have capability based addressing as the cornerstone for user authority.

It would serve no productive purpose for me to offer commentary about the government's role in what is good and what is bad security. Let me just say that to get Federal C2 level security, IBM had to abandon the beliefs' of the best computer scientists in the world. If you want to stay in business and achieve new markets, there are battles that you must choose not to fight. IBM chose to win the C2 security clearance rather than solve the temporary authority problem with capabilities.

As an interesting side note, when IBM was seeking certification for C2 security (level 50), the team from the Department of Defense acknowledged that they had never seen a system with capability-based addressing that could pass their certification. No matter how much IBM argued our case, the DoD would not budge.

IBM had a mechanism to allow temporary adoption of authority, and this method was acceptable to the DoD team. So, Big Blue moved on and implemented this method, along with internal security-auditing, another DoD requirement when the Company introduced level 50 security in December, 1993 with Version 2 Release 3.

Five Security Levels from Which to Select

IBM i has created a security environment that is as tight as it can possibly be. However, not all of IBM's clients want security at the ultimate level and so, IBM built IBM i with five different levels of security. IBM i shops decide which of these levels they are going to turn on. The five levels of security are as follows

- Level 10 -- No Security -- Everybody is the security officer
- Level 20 -- User profile and password security -- Need password to get on
- Level 30 -- Resource Security -- Need authority to access objects
- Level 40 -- Operating System Security -- access to non standard interfaces is blocked
- Level 50 -- C2 Level Security Department of Defense classification --

IBM ships every new IBM i system at level 40. Security level 10 is no longer supported but, if a shop has been using level 10 it continues to be honored. If an IBM i shops changes from security level 10 to 20, 30, 40 or 50, you will not be able to change it back to level 10. IBM strongly recommends that you leave the security level set to 40. At security level 50, no system internal control blocks can be modified. In comparison some, but not many system internal control blocks, can be modified at security level 40.

IBM i security is so good that even IBM does not recommend that you run at level 50, the C2 level. A big part of the reason is that Level 50 changes the way i5/OS operates to meet the requirements for a C2 certified system. Running Level 50 security has been found to adversely affect performance, so unless you need a C2 certified system for business, IBM recommends that you do not use Level 50. The performance hit is estimated at between 5-15 percent CPU impact.

Computer Science Loves "Capabilities"

Way back in the 1960s and 1970s, computer scientists were planning the future of computing. One of the first advanced capability-based system designs from Carnegie Mellon was called the Hydra operating system. Interestingly enough, Hydra also was object-oriented, and was built with a primitive machine abstraction layer (high-level machine interface), along with a single-level store and a number of integrated functions.

Unlike the IBM i box, however Hydra, and all of the other advanced computer science research projects noted below were / are software-only models. None have ever been implemented commercially and in the labs they were research-only projects. None have had to endure the rigorous hardware and software testing that a commercial product requires. The best that anybody at 10,000 feet can say is that all of the projects achieved some of the advanced computer science notions introduced in Chapter 10 but, none achieved all and more accurately, none achieved more than half.

Thus, no machine ever has been built from the ground up with the advanced facilities nor the unprecedented levels of functional integration as found in the System/38, AS/400, iSeries or IBM i running on the IBM Power System platform.

Security / Advanced Computing Research Projects

The KeyKOS micro-kernel operating system emerged in the mid-1980s and was an improvement over the earlier Hydra. In the mid-1990s, yet another improvement operating system arrived with the help of the University of Pennsylvania's Extremely Reliable Operating System (EROS) project. EROS releases sound much like the story of Linux.

Now on Release 0.6.0, with prerelease 0.8.3 already shipped, the EROS project, spearheaded by Jonathan Shapiro, took the concept of capability-based systems yet another step toward the ideal. Yet, even Shapiro, as bright as he was could not sell his idea commercially and he gave up and he has since moved on to commercial ventures.

Before anybody starts thinking that the System/38 copied any of these projects, please know it was not the case but, there could have been some theory testing from the other side. After all, System/38 was a commercially available product that contained all of these notions and it was commercially available before any of these ideas got off the ground.

More importantly, none of these implementations--Hydra, KeyKOS, EROS or Coyotos, which has become CapROS meaning "Capability-based Reliable Operating System," were implemented on a system that you could buy anywhere.

For thirty years, the IBM i family of machines have been the sole commercial embodiment of how successful the notions in capability-based systems and the notion of adoption of authority could increase the security capabilities of business machines.

The Hydra, the KeyKOS, and the EROS efforts and the later Coyotos / CapROS project, which took over from EROS, are computer science research projects at their best. They may very well be the wave of the distant future for all other machines, but they are not out there today.

From my personal observations, the speed in which these projects move along, and the propensity for today's OS vendors to change to better ways, the distant future is way, way out there.

The System/38 was introduced as a capability-based system way back in 1978 when the notion of capabilities was first being kicked around computer science circles. Due to IBM's desire to achieve the necessary government clearances to market the AS/400 and follow-on units to the government, only system state functions today use permanent capabilities that are similar to those used in the System/38. For the AS/400 to IBM i, IBM had to rework its integrated security model to make it even tighter than that provided by raw "capabilities" alone.

Do "Capabilities" Still Have Value?

Capabilities pertain to objects on System/38 and the notion, though not the full notion, carries on to processes running in the system state on the IBM i platform. System/38 proved that you do not really need a Hydra, KeyKOS, or EROS OS running on DEC, Motorola, IBM S/370 or Intel hardware to be successful with capabilities.

No other operating system tried to use the best from EROS or Coyotos / CapROS to achieve the unparalleled performance and scalability advantages of hardware and software integration and abstraction as done in the 1978 IBM System/38. Today's IBM i system using the phenomenally capable Power 6 processors could surely implement a perfected capability based addressing for user and system state computing.

IBM could handle temporary authority as well as permanent authority within the system pointer in the user state, similar to its work on the IBM System/38. However, as noted previously, it would have been put in a position in which it would have to re-gain the C2 security clearance and this is an effort IBM chose not to pursue. The DoD may not have given clearance, regardless of the proof. Instead, the Company focused on what Dr. Frank Soltis calls *adoption of authority* in order to achieve the same security objectives in the user state.

For IBM i, since capabilities are still used in the system state, they have value but, the value overall to IBM has been diminished due to the DoD's C2 requirements.

In addition to helping the reader understand the innate security that is built into the IBM i operating system at the object level, I felt that it was important to note that IBM had built a fully functional capabilities based machine that was doing quite well and would have continued to do quite well if IBM did not have to change its course to comply with C2 certification. IBM was honored for this achievement. No other operating system from no other vendor ever received such an honor. IBM builds the best operating systems and IBM i is the best that IBM has.

Jonathan Shapiro v. Linus Torvalds

Most everybody in computing circles knows the story of Linus Torvalds and how he brought Linux to the state that it exists today, as a viable operating system for real IT projects. Jonathan Shapiro is in many ways to security notions as Torvalds is to operating systems. Torvalds had a number of issues getting access to technology in this younger days and one of his "distant mentors" was Andy Tanenbaum, one of the most well-known professors of computer science in the world.

Linus Torvalds had many issues with Andy Tanenbaum, regarding operating system kernel design, and these high spirited discussions are documented all over the Internet for the reading. They are quite interesting.

Back in 2006 Jonathan Shapiro got riled up about Tanenbaum and Torvalds taking issue with the security projects that we have lightly discussed in this chapter. Obviously, Shapiro backs these projects implicitly. Baited by the exchange on security by these two gurus, Shapiro stepped into the fray with a post that began like this:

> "Well, it appears to be 1992 all over again. Andy Tanenbaum is once again advocating microkernels, and Linus Torvalds is once again saying what an ignorant fool Andy is. It probably won't surprise you much that I got a bunch of emails asking for *my* thoughts on the exchange. I should probably keep my mouth shut, but here they are. Linus, as usual, is strong on opinions and short on facts. "

You might enjoy a trip to http://www.coyotos.org/docs/misc/linus-rebuttal.html for a look at Shapiro's rebuttal. Clearly these three gurus have had a major influence on today's computing paradigm. For those who had never heard of Jonathan Shapiro until you read this chapter, you now know the level of computer science thought in which he operates.

Additional Information on Capabilities

While Jonathan Shapiro is one of the foremost advocates of integrated security and reliability on computer systems, IBM Rochester can get a major sense of pride from knowing that its groundbreaking System/38 for eight years as a prime commercial product proved that capabilities can be very effective for business systems.

On the System/38 and the IBM i systems, IBM implemented 128-bit pointers which are very similar to high level soft addresses. The system pointers are big enough that besides large addresses, they can also contain information about the types of operations that can be performed on a particular object. The information that would be held would be the object's authority. Dr. Frank Soltis, in his book Fortress Rochester, examines system pointers and capabilities as used in the IBM System/38 and the IBM i. He notes that "A pointer that contains the object address and object authority is called a capability. The S/38 had capability-based addressing because all system pointers contained both the address and the authority. This changed in the AS/400 and was carried forward to the iSeries."

If you are as intrigued by the notion of capabilities as I am, consider reading *What a Capability Is!* by Jonathan Shapiro, available on the EROS Web site at http://www.eros-os.org/essays/capintro.html.

After taking an informal survey, Shapiro concluded that none of his friends, not even the technically savvy, who worked in the computer field, understood what he did for a living. So, he decided to help folks like you and I understand the notion of capabilities by starting from scratch. His article is well written, light in spirit, and assumes little knowledge. It takes the reader on a journey toward a real understanding of the concept of capability-based systems.

Because Jonathan Shapiro has already done a great job in defining the notion of capability, I have chosen not to paraphrase, but to include three paragraphs from his work. I repeat them below, for the technically inclined. If you have no concern for the technical aspects, feel free to skip these.

> "Dennis and Van Horn introduced the term capability in 1966, in a paper entitled 'Programming Semantics for Multiprogrammed Computations.' The basic idea is this: suppose we design a computer system so that in order to access an object, a program must have a special token. This token designates an object and gives the program the authority to perform a specific set of actions (such as reading or writing) on that object. Such a token is known as a capability.
>
> "A capability is a lot like the keys on your key ring. As an example, consider your car key. It works on a specific car (it designates a particular object), and anyone holding the key can perform certain actions (locking or unlocking the car, starting the car, opening the glove compartment). You can hand your car key to me, after which I can open, lock, or start the car, but only on your car. Holding your car key won't let me test drive my neighbor's Lamborghini (which is just as well--I would undoubtedly wrap it around a tree somewhere). Note that the car key doesn't know that it's me starting the car; it's sufficient that I possess the key. In the same way, capabilities do not care who uses them.
>
> "Car keys sometimes come in several variations. Two common ones are the valet key (starts, locks, and unlocks the car, but not the glove compartment) or the door key (locks/unlocks the car, but won't start it). In exactly this way, two capabilities can designate the same object (such as the car) but authorize different sets of actions. One program might hold a read-only capability to a file while another holds a read-write capability to the same file.
>
> 'As with keys, you can give me a capability to a box full of other capabilities..."

IBM i / System/38 Developers Acknowledged

IBM i security is implemented at a system-wide level via code that runs at two different levels of the machine. One layer is under the Machine Interface and the other is above in IBM i proper. All security is object based from the get-go. IBM i uses an authorization scheme to protect objects from unauthorized access and more importantly, unauthorized modification.

Capability-based addressing is a notion that uses the address pointer to provide the capability that permits or denies access to an object. IBM i uses this advanced computer science notion as its object-level security implementation when operating in the system state and it uses the code partners above and below the machine interface for user authorization to objects.

IBM was rightfully so proud of its System/38 implementation that in 1981, at the International Conference for Computer Architecture, Frank G. Soltis, a well-known IBM scientist and the main architect of the System/38, along with Merle Houdek and Roy L. Hoffman, presented the notion of capability-based addressing as implemented in the IBM System/38 to the Association for Computing Machinery (ACM) Special Interest Group on Computer Architecture. Their paper described how support is divided among architectural definition, microcode, and hardware to minimize overhead for this function.

Great plaudits to the innovative IBM System/38 and its designers and implementers for in 1978, it was the first commercial machine that ever used a capability-based model enforced by capability-based properties. On the System/38, the addressability pointers were built to be 128-bits wide, of which 96 bits are the address, and the remainder represented the authority (capability). The System/38 used an architecture known as "tagged," which makes it virtually impossible to counterfeit a system pointer.

The IBM i box therefore, handles system state security by object through its capability-based addressing. User security is via authorization or as Dr. Soltis told me he has always called this, "adoption of authority." Everything on the system is an object. Everything can be secured very easily at this base level, using either the capability-based architecture or the adoption of authority.

You may ask how much integrated fail-safe security is worth to your organization. To answer that, you would have to know your security exposures and how much you were paying at the server level or on internal and external firewalls, including the technical expertise. You might find the cost staggering. IBM i's integrated security does not solve every problem that you can think of but, it is the only machine-based security mechanism available on any computer today, and it helps businesses protect the business value provided by their IBM i servers by keeping them secure.

If you are adding up the business value of IBM i, don't forget to throw a few more tributes into the plus column.

Chapter 16   Advanced Computer Science Concepts: Integrated Relational Database

Integration Is a Common Theme

The System/38, in 1978, was the first computer ever built with a relational database that was integrated within the hardware and the very framework of the system and operating system. Integration is a common theme in the AS/400-iSeries-IBM i architecture.

The integrated relational database was and continues to be a hallmark of the IBM Power System with IBM i. There is no other commercial machine in existence, even today, thirty plus years after the IBM System/38, which comes with its own built-in relational database.

Can you imagine how far ahead of the competition the System/38 was in 1978, when DB2, IBM's leading mainframe relational database product had yet to be announced? And with a System/38, it was just there! You got relational database with every machine. With IBM i of course, you still do.

Moreover, since the notion of relational database was part and parcel of the architecture of the original System/38, it continues to be so with IBM i. In fact, a number of often-used relational DB facilities are built right into the hardware instructions set in the Power 6 chip.

Consider that one of the most frequently used operations in a relational database is index creation. The IBM i family has implemented this function as one hardware instruction. That is why from way-back, the System/38 would outperform all competing systems of its size in the relational DB area.

In fact, to run as well as a System/38, the competition had to execute its benchmark with sequential and indexed file processing to avoid the overhead of an add-on database management system software package. The System/38 had just one performance number, as does IBM i. Both can run database as well as non-database applications with no degradation.

IBM Power System with IBM i Breaks DB Rules

Most relational databases use mathematical set theory and only set oriented operations, implemented through the Structured Query Language (SQL). IBM i can do all this but it actually does even more. Simple features such as the ability to link a compiler read and write operation to the database are not part of the deal on any other machine. Language compilers on other machines are database agnostic.

Not only do they not have database function built-in, they have no idea if a database is even going to be used and if it is, which one it might be - MySQL, Ingress, Oracle, etc... So, nobody else's compilers know anything about databases. In fact, "compiler reads and writes to a database" are anathemas to the spirit of the original relational database model.

Before compilers and utilities such as COPY can be written to use all of the underlying power of any system, those base capabilities need to be defined. IBM built a few new object types with the System/38 and these carry over to IBM i. These object types are as follows:

- Physical Database File Object
- Logical Database File Object

No business system can exist without a strong file system in which to store data. The designers of the System/38, an object based system from the get-go, chose not to create a simple file object that would require an add-on database to give it more business value. Instead, the designers built all the rules necessary for relational database processing into the two object types listed above, and from that moment on, poof, the IBM i heritage operating system had an integrated database.

Since SQL had not fully been perfected at the time, the System/38 designers also built a definition language and a manipulation language into the system. It has a non-descript name called DDS, which is reflective of the fact that it is based on a form type called a **d**ata **d**escription **s**pecification (DDS).

Along with the normal attributes that one would expect in a Physical Database File Object, IBM added support for what has been called a partitioned data set in computer science terminology. Developers for years have been "partitioning" single data files so that they could use one file for multiple sets of similar transactions.

For example, for many years application designers for companies with several hundred order takers would define one file and then partition it into several hundred parts. There would be one file part for each order taker, thereby keeping each order taker's space unique to that order taker. The record shape (format) was the same for all but each had its own space definition.

Object Based Notions Make it Easier

Sometimes operating systems had minimal support for partitioned data sets; other times application designers would take a regular file and divide it themselves to make the application work. Rochester therefore saw the notion of a partitioned data set as a requirement of the database physical file object. And, so they built it into the object. Each section of a physical database file object is called a member and it is of unlimited size and there are unlimited members in a physical database file object. You can't do things like that if you do not have an object-based system to begin with.

Since IBM had designed this nice mechanism for multiple members in database files, the developers decided that they could use this to store source statements for RPG, COBOL, BASIC, and other languages. Additionally, it could be used to store the DDS needed to build the physical file or logical file objects needed for the database. For these special circumstances, IBM Rochester devised a standard file definition with three parts, sequence number, date last changed, and source statement. The three parts were really three defined fields in a database file and this file was used with the Source Editor to store code produced by developers.

So, a source physical database file object called RPG could store RPG code and one called DDS could store DDS statements and so forth. Because each file and each program that was created needed a name, to store the source for the program or for the database, IBM Rochester standardized on the notion of using one member in the source physical database file object for each named program or database file object that would be created.

When the AS/400 came out and SQL became available for the first time in 1988, IBM used the existing physical file and logical file objects to store the database tables and views that are created via SQL. For SQL indexes, the logical database file object already provided the necessary structure so IBM merely mapped the SQL Create Index facility to the native create logical file function. SQL created files and DDS created files use the same structure and another object called a library was called upon to fill the need for a database schema.

Once the underlying database object structure was defined on the IBM System/38, it made sense that the utility programs and the compilers were database aware. This provides the ultimate in integrated services for developers and quite frankly is one of the big reasons why developers who are interested in being productive are annoyed when they must work with other platforms.

IBM Chose the Practical in 1978 Rather than the Theoretical

Rather than worry about upsetting the late Ted Codd, who at the time was perfecting his invention of relational database, the pioneers in the Rochester Labs chose to create a relational database that could do more than work with sets of data. They knew they needed to support set theory but, more importantly, they wanted their database facility to work naturally with the problem and procedural programming languages of the day, using record at a time processing. As a point of fact, most programming is record at a time.

Back then, IBM Rochester did not care if it was different than the theoretical model that Codd had was perfecting. IBM Rochester was happy being better than the standard. Therefore, the System/38 developers built a relational database that could not only read and write naturally to the database, but also the language compilers were made database-aware. Programmers were therefore able to use the database object's metadata rather than having to key input and output specifications for their programs.

Yes, I did say that word "object," again. IBM's integrated database for the System/38, which is now known as DB2 for i, is built on the object notion of IBM i. Every database table, view or index is an IBM i object.

Since the one and only System/38 relational database would always be present on every System/38, as it is on the IBM i box, the compiler writers and the utility writers did not ignore the opportunity to enhance the productivity of the integrated database within their own software offerings. In fact, they built their products to take advantage of the presence of the database, and to make their compilers and utilities, as well as the database, easier to use.

Oh, sure, the Ted Codd database purists hammered the notion that SET theory was not used for all functions and they pointed out that this was not being true to the relational model. Record-level access was never part of Codd's plan; but, programmers needed record level access since there were many record at a time needs in programming, such as looking up a single customer to process an order.

Ironically, this "purist deficiency" is a major advantage of the System/38 and IBM i implementations. Other relational database implementations continue to be plagued with jury-rigged, unnatural facilities within their high-level language (HLL) compilers because their implementers chose not to aid the programming effort with their designs.

For example, to read a record with a traditional system, instead of just issuing a READ command in the natural compiler language, the programmer would have to call a program and pass it parameters. Moreover, the programmer would have to fully describe the input and output in the program and pass it on the program call, rather than have the compiler bring in such metadata from the database itself.

Integrated Database Makes Programmers Productive

System/38 COBOL and RPG programmers by comparison had life easy from day one. IBM i programmers continue to have life easy today. Since all DB products have different ways to call their respective database functions, compiler writers could not include natural links to these databases in their COBOL, BASIC, RPG, or other compilers. So, instead of the compiler writer doing the tough part and leaving the programmer with the easy part, programmers on other platforms need to know the special APIs (application programming interfaces) that are available for each different DB product that can be used on a given system's compiler.

For example, in the Windows client server applications, programmers need something like ODBC and its APIs to gain access to server data. If programs are written in Java going to a servlet server then JDBC APIs are needed. These named APIs mean that the access to data is not natural and thus it is a lot more work than merely telling the compiler to go ahead and get the customer record. That means that for most businesses, programmers are not very productive.

Moreover, a READ using these APIs is not just a READ, it is a specific call to the API with a bunch of parameters including the names of the data fields and the data. Additionally, since there is no guarantee that the reads or updates will actually take place once the request leaves the client or the browser, the programmer also needs to code in some error recovery. All of this is taken care of with an integrated database. The bottom line is that all programmers, other than those working on IBM i nowadays, have lots of work to do for simple everyday database functions.

This was never the case on the IBM System/38 and is not the case on the Power System with IBM i. Since the compiler writers from the System/38 to IBM i all knew about the database ahead of time, since one and only one database was integrated into the system, they were able to devise natural operations within the languages to support database functions at a very high level. Thus, the compiler and the OS does the work, rather than the programmer.

READs and WRITEs to the database are integrated operations just as READs and WRITEs to disk files and tape had been in previous file oriented compilers. Programmers use simple operation codes to access the database with no need for special APIs. Programmers, therefore, do not have to code unnaturally to get their jobs done, so they get many more jobs done than on non-integrated database systems.

Metadata Saves Developer Keystrokes

Besides the pleasure of ease-of-use programming at the device and operation level, the compilers pulled in all of the data descriptions directly from the integrated database object's metadata. Regardless of whether the operations were input, update, or output, the compilers would fetch the data descriptors that previously had to be hand coded at a detail level, and they would pop the input specs and/ or output specs right into the programs at compile time.

They would even show the specs on the program listings as if the programmer had typed them in. When programmers do not have to define input or output in their programs or describe the data fields, they can do lots more productive work. This facility saves development shops an additional ton of tedious I-O coding time.

The traditional Ted Codd databases were often very difficult implementations, requiring high-priced database administrators to manage the systems. Moreover, at the time, databases were either all or nothing. All programs had to use the database if a major file were converted. This created major implementation difficulties. The System/38 database worked first time, every time, with no database administration required. IBM i continues that tradition.

Database Supports File Structures for Other Environments

Besides all the benefits described above, if a file were defined to the database, programs still could use internal descriptions within their programs. Thus, programs could be migrated from System/3 or System/34 or System/36 or Mainframe systems 370 or 390 or z/OS using internal RPG or COBOL data descriptions and the programmer would not have to convert them to use the new database field descriptors.

So, if you called the customer number field "custno" in the program and "customer-number" in the database, your program code could run without caring what the DB field name was. This was a major innovation, but not necessarily Codd-approved.

What this has meant to programmers over the years is that conversions to IBM i are a snap compared to all other systems, mainframes, PCs, or Unix boxes. It will continue to be a snap as IBM keeps making it better. Adding database files is still not an issue on IBM i.

All of this facility permits programmers to build systems and mission critical applications much faster. It also enables them to bring them online faster than ever before in computer history.

Set Theory Operations Not Always Most Productive

Rather than making it more difficult for programmers, by forcing them to use set theory in their program logic, IBM created the easy to learn data description specifications (DDS) language to accommodate the way programmers actually worked. This helped the programmers who used the database to be even more productive than those who chose to continue to use auto report, copy books, or hard-coded input/ output program specifications.

In its product-excellence slide presentations that I often presented to System/38 and AS/400 prospects over the years, IBM suggested a five-to-10-fold increase in programmer productivity would be achieved over traditional methods. Using these powerful, integrated tools, I saw my clients over the years achieve such results. This improvement still holds with the new IBM Power System with IBM i.

All programs written for OS/400 or IBM i in high level languages, even today, continue to take advantage of the productivity facilities of full database integration. In other words, programmers still write code 5 to 10 times faster than on other platforms. IBM just doesn't highlight that part of the machine anymore since the advances are almost thirty years old

Yet, IBM i developers have been enjoying this level of productivity since the System/38 was announced in 1978, over thirty years ago. One would think that by now, the competition would have caught up. Nevertheless, they have not. IBM still has a big advantage in the database area.

No Name Database

This story is funny. In the early 1990's, IBM did a survey of its AS/400 customers to see if they even knew they had a database on their system. It is a fact that many IBM i users even now feel they need no IT staff or they need just a small staff to keep their systems running. In some cases, there is no in-house expertise at all. When IBM polled its AS/400 accounts back then to see if they knew that there was a database on the system, the Company learned more than they wanted to know.

After investing in an integrated database on their premiere midrange machine for years, IBM reported that half of the AS/400 users surveyed did not even know their machine had an integrated database or any database of any kind. Yet, they were using it! IBM thought about it and came to the conclusion that it had to name the database something. That's when the company dusted off its popular DB2 brand and selected it as the moniker for the AS/400 integrated database. It is now known as DB2 for i.

Of course, that marketing move ruined one of my favorite pitch lines that I always felt put the AS/400 integrated database idea in perspective. At one time before IBM named its database, I was able to say, "If it has a name, the machine knows nothing about it. If it has a name, it is not built in; it is an add-on software package." That once was true.

Consider the plethora of databases that fit this mold. The list includes DB2 for all other platforms. Sybase, Informix, Oracle, MS-SQL Server, Ingress, Postgres, and MySQL are also examples. They all have names. With these databases, no language compilers can have any built-in DB hooks. There is no READ or WRITE interface from a compiler to any other database on any other system. Now, the IBM Power System with IBM i database has a name, DB2 for IBM i, but even though it has a name, it is still integrated, and though it is much more capable than the original System/38 database, it is still as easy to use as ever.

Future System Today

When the System/38 was developed in 1978, and deployed in 1980, it was dubbed the "future system today." An honest appraisal by the Windows-loving trade press of the underpinnings of IBM i, which still uses the advanced technology first deployed in System/38, would render a far more complimentary identifier than their current label, "legacy" for IBM i technology.

The facts show that Windows, Unix, Linux, Solaris, and even the IBM Mainframe operating systems are all built using the traditional / legacy approach. I might suggest that in practice this is a patch and add methodology. Fixes and patches are always being made to code that goes back many years. These are the legacy systems of today, not IBM i.

We have demonstrated clearly in this chapter and all of the prior chapters to this point that the IBM Power System with IBM i is built with the most advanced architecture in the industry. IBM i has nine exclusive advanced computer science notions found on no other operating system of today. We looked at the complete list of these in Chapter 10 and we have been discussing them one by one, including this chapter on the integrated database.

Admittedly, IBM i is a bit over thirty years old. If it were human it would be approaching middle age. Listening to the trade press talk about Windows and Unix, you'd think that these offerings are for kids or teenagers. Windows roots go back to 1983. It is over 25-years old. Unix is in its 40's and mainframe operating systems are even older than that.

Now, all of these operating systems are legacy from a time perspective. Considering that all of these operating systems, other than IBM i are based on the traditional, non-integrated piecemeal approach to technology, I would ask their proponents to tell me again about this legacy label that has been slapped on IBM i and somehow withheld from all other operating systems. If you really want a modern, take no prisoners, advanced and complete operating system, there is only one -- IBM i.

MySQL Support

MySQL is one of the most popular open source database packages available today. There are tens of thousands of open source applications which use PHP and MySQL available for download and free to use. PHP is one of the many supported environments on IBM i as is SQL.

These were added in 2005 to the system's full capabilities. In 2007, IBM announced that it was going to do more to integrate MySQL into the overall system by supplying what was then called a DB2 Storage Engine.

Those who have worked with MySQL know that it is a two-piece database. PHP applications use the MySQL verbs and the MySQL syntax to request and update databases. However, MySQL uses at least ten different storage engines from simple to very powerful transaction engines.

DB2 for i is one of the most robust databases in the industry and thus the 2009 availability of MySQL using the DB2 for i storage engine takes IBM i database integration one step further.

This new pluggable storage engine has been developed specifically for MySQL running in IBM i at the V5R4 and V6R1 levels. This storage engine has a name, IBMDB2I Storage Engine for MySQL on IBM i. The IBMDB2I engine works with MySQL version 5.1. Basically, this storage engine allows users to run open source applications on IBM i using the standard DB2 for i backend.

The Best of the Best

It helps to repeat that the IBM i architecture represents everything IBM knows about computers and probably wishes it could have placed into mainframes over the years. At the risk of summarizing with too many superlatives, I am convinced that the IBM i box is the most technologically elegant machine within IBM, and in the entire computer marketplace. Having an integrated database that even integrates MySQL into the picture, makes it all the better.

Summary: Develop Applications Five to Ten Times Faster

Because of the six principles we have discussed so far and those that we will be discussing in the next several chapters, application development using IBM i is still five to ten times more productive than on any other platform. This is the innate capability that made the AS/400 of 1988 the DEC killer. Digital Equipment Corporation and Data General and Wang do not exist today because of the power of the IBM AS/400 as introduced in 1988 and carried forth in IBM i, the all-everything operating system.

Programmer productivity and easy-to-build applications brought the AS/400 and now IBM i to their renowned position in the industry. In 1988, AS/400 programmer productivity not only killed DEC as a company, but there was also some friendly fire. IBM's own 9370 platform and the company's 8100 system, both small mainframe computers, also suffered from the success of the AS/400's immense capabilities and popularity. IBM stopped making them.

IBM i Makes the Power System a Special Mainframe

In a company traditionally managed by mainframe heritage executives, with all products over the years seemingly examined for their mainframe affinity and friendliness, and their abilities to generate revenue, IBM i has not only survived, it has gotten better and now it carries the IBM name. Ironically, the IBM i platform today is a bona fide mainframe, but it is completely unlike the mainframe that IBM builds in its mainframe plants. After all, when teamed with the Power System hardware including the Power 6 chip, it is today's all-everything machine.

IBM acknowledges that it is tough competing against the Microsoft marketing juggernaut. Yet, there is nothing else like this all-everything, "Swiss-army knife" operating system to defeat Microsoft in its own game -- operating systems. It is clearly the best computer technology available and if IBM is ever ready to take on Microsoft, there should be a lot of fun and the world can decide which OS brings the best technology to business. Though Microsoft makes one of the most popular database packages, it chooses to market it separately using a piece parts approach.

Though it may be easier and more profitable for Microsoft to market its database and operating system in that fashion, as you have learned in this chapter it is not good for Microsoft customers and developers. Integration is the key to productivity.

The IBM i database and all of its facility make it the best platform on which to run any business. IBM masquerades the innate complexity of the machine by integrating all of the parts, including the database, into one rock solid system that does not go down.

That's one of the reasons why I wrote this book. I want the best technology to win. The more everybody knows about the all-everything operating system, the better its prospects are to one day rule the world. And a fine and capable ruler it would be.

Chapter 17 Advanced Computer Science Concepts: Integrated Business Language Compilers

It Does Not Have To Be Extra Hard to Program

Integration is the Key Element in Advanced Computer Design. In this chapter, we examine another of the key elements of IBM i integration, Business Language Compilers.

In Chapter 16, we discussed the integrated database provided by every IBM i operating system. The DB2 for i relational database development is now directed from San Jose and Santa Theresa California, where all of IBM's DB2 development work for all platforms is done. IBM changed the focus of the Rochester-designed relational database so that the IBM i community could benefit from all that IBM knows about relational database management systems (RDBMS). Since RDBMS was invented by IBM's Ted Codd back in the 1970's, IBM's storehouse of implementation goodies for DB2 is quite immense and the IBM Corporation is assuring that DB2 for i is as capable as an integrated database as DB2 is for all other platforms.

The inherent object structure of the DB2 for i database make it unique in the industry and it can never be exactly the same as DB2 for platforms that do not have the basic object structure as IBM i. However, function for function the DB2 for i database is just about there with mainframe DB2 and its object structure actually offers more facility and manageability than does any other system.

Among other things that make this possible, there are system commands (CL language) that can dip into the database file objects, physical files and logical files and gain immense metadata about the objects and their usage. Additionally, there is a schema wide catalog as well as a system wide catalog that takes database information and makes it available as it would on any other DB2 system.

Even those databases built by the original data definition language called DDS for IBM i have their metadata held in both forms on the system -- in the object and in the catalog. On top of that, IBM has built routines to go into database files and from the internal metadata, create the SQL commands to build those databases. In many ways this is like the export facilities on other systems without the Insert commands.

My reason for reminding you of the DB2 for i database facilities is that the notion of integrated business language compilers has already been introduced in Chapter 16. In this chapter, we will explore this idea a bit further but we will concentrate on compiler function more than database.

A la Carte Software

A la carte system software has been a mainstay of the mainframe and most OS platforms for many years and the IBM Company has made lots and lots of revenue on a la carte middleware such as VSAM, CICS, MQSeries, WebSphere, and DB2 for platforms other than IBM i. The same a la carte model works for Unix and Windows platforms.

In the 1970's and 1980's, when transaction processing and database features were invented, they were sold as software products to customers with installed systems. To be sold as products, they were given intriguing names. Their function was to sit in the middle (middleware) between customer programming and the operating system.

In the mainframe area, for example, there have always been features that besides the operating system, customer IT shops needed to purchase in order to have a complete operating system. In the Windows and Unix arena, there continue to be the same plethora of add-on products including numerous database offerings such as Oracle, Sybase, and SQL Server and terminal transaction processors such as Tuxedo.

Additionally, compilers began to serve as piece parts at the most common denominator level. As special devices and functions, such as terminals and databases, were developed over time, the compilers were not given built-in device capabilities. Instead, the compiler writers created special interfaces so that programs could be written to control absolutely any device using a generic interface. The interfaces were quite simple however; so, the application program took on the bulk of the work in talking to the devices or the database.

So, programmers could write code in many programming languages to talk to devices but, none of it was easy. There was no language compiler support for any special device or notion that was not basic. Consequently, compilers were built to serve only the simple read / write needs of disk file systems and tape systems.

Application developers, however, were no longer writing programs to use simple disk files or tape files. Data was being stored in databases. Additionally, more programming was written for interactive functions than batch. The terminal devices and the databases, unfortunately for programmer productivity, needed special routines that programmers would either write from scratch or call using complex programming structures. Why companies gave their compiler writers the night off is a puzzle for anybody struggling with the missing pieces in the compiler code.

Windows Is Really Not Multi-User

Windows servers do not foster a multiuser environment. In fact, Windows is really not a multi-user operating system. Client server languages such as C and Visual Basic are used by developers to write programs for the client. To access the server from the client, developers needed to write specific code with facilities such as ODBC (Open Database Connectivity) or JDBC (Java Database Connectivity) for Java programs to be able to retrieve and maintain server databases. Not only is this not very efficient on machine resources but, the fact that it is not built into the Windows compilers cost programmers a lot of unnecessary effort.

Even if they are free or almost free, these products are all separately orderable, separately chargeable, separately installable, and separately maintainable as optional pieces of operating systems that can only be described as shipping incomplete. While we are on the separate theme here, in most cases, the separate products themselves come from separate vendors.

Not to let IBM entirely off the hook, the a la carte system approach is championed by the IBM mainframe division; however, it is also the Unix Way, and the Windows way. These three platforms continue to be ideal spots for piece parts software vendors to sell their wares. With IBM being mostly a services company today, the company makes an awful lot of money assembling these piece parts for its huge customers. Does IBM like Windows? IBM the service company loves Windows and it makes a lot of money when its service customers choose to have Big Blue do the work to assemble a Windows environment for their business.

Does IBM like the IBM Power System with IBM i? Well, it depends on who you ask. Surely the services division and the software division have no reason to especially like anything they do not sell. When you are one of the assembly divisions, a product that needs no assembly cannot be on the top of your list. When you make most of your revenue (over 50% for IBM) on assembly and services vs. the product itself, there is little reason to want an integrated platform. Who can blame IBM or any vendor that sells parts of solutions? The good news is that IBM's Power Systems Division people do want to sell their products and they are healthy as a business and they are pleased when the operating system is IBM i since it inevitably means another happy customer.

As we have been demonstrating throughout this book, the all-everything operating system is integrated with its component pieces, as well as the IBM Power System hardware and the Power 6 chip itself. The opposite of integration, of course, is the notion of piece parts. In an integrated environment, essential elements are included within the hardware and operating system and are part and parcel of the overall computer system experience. With piece parts, well, anybody ever giving a handsomely wrapped box complete with a popular toy to a child knows well those nasty three words, "some assembly required."

The Role of Programming Languages

In today's world, computer science languages such as C, C++, and Java rule the day; however, just about every company has an ERP system or some type of business software package. When those packages run on IBM i or on mainframes and many other systems, you would find that the package is most often written in one of the two best business languages ever created, either RPG or COBOL. A good part of mainframe Y2K work was in COBOL programs, attesting to the language's long-time popularity.

The reason for this is simple. Though a computer science type programmer feels better when he or she has full control of all aspects of the machine – even those aspects that could cause the machine to crash, the business programmer is interested in producing positive results for the company. The business programmer builds business software and wants a business programming language on his or her team to get that job done most efficiently.

There are just two languages, both with origins dating back to the 1950's that were designed from the ground up for business use. Though computer scientists and academics shudder at the mention of their names, the fact is that almost all back room business software on major computing systems are written in RPG or COBOL.

Business Languages for Business Jobs

Years ago, trying to demonstrate the efficiency of the RPG language compared with COBOL, I defined and wrote a database and simple terminal inquiry processing program. I call it Advanced Hello World. All computer programmers at one time have programmed the simpler basic Hello World program in one or more languages as an entrée to learning the language. Advanced Hello World is a rudimentary, but slightly more complex, program that provides both database and screen panel transaction functions.

It is not much more than a program that uses an inquiry panel for a database access as there is no update required in the program. In many languages, simple "terminal" display inquiry is a lot of work and requires as many as one hundred and often more program statements. There is much "systems" coding in these programs as the programmer must form the special device arguments, call the APIs, and after the operation test, that the process completed properly.

The results of this "Hello World" inquiry is brought back to the bottom of the same inquiry panel. The panel itself must be perfectly formatted for full screen processing rather than using a command line interpreter (standard input or stdin) in Unix or an emulated PC DOS session. Besides not taking input from the command line, it is not to present the results using the standard output mechanism or stdout. Instead, this simple application uses a bona fide display format such as that used in Tuxedo or CICS.

The panel is formatted so the program does not need to deal with any of that. For non-IBM i platforms, the routines for this program would have to be written to talk directly to the terminal device sending not only data commands but, also commands to instruct the terminal what to do.

For Unix or Windows programs, what happens in between input and output is also an issue as the input data needs to be parsed and the database access itself is not very simple. ODBC or JDBC does not lend itself to straight-forward operations. As you can see, none of this adds up to programmer productivity on other platforms. On IBM I, it is a snap in RPG and COBOL, and I will prove that to you.

Just as in Tuxedo or CICS, the display format for these programs has been created with a generator so we are not comparing ease of use on the generated panel, just the means of writing the code that works with it.

Before we discuss how to write the program, please examine Figure 17-1 and then Figure 17-2. As you can see, after calling the program with the CL call command, the program launches and sends out a request for input shown in Figure 17-1. The user, in this case, types in GERMAN, one of several key fields in the database file called LANGUAGE. The program gets a hit on GERMAN and puts out the contents of a field that very simply says, "This is "Hello, World" in German."

On IBM i, this program is very simple to write in both RPG and COBOL. Mainframe COBOL and Mainframe RPG, though better than C or C++ are very primitive compared to the IBM i version of the compilers. They too require an awful lot of work dealing with databases and terminal devices.

284 The All Everything Operating System

Figure 17-1 The Advanced Hello World Panel Requesting Input

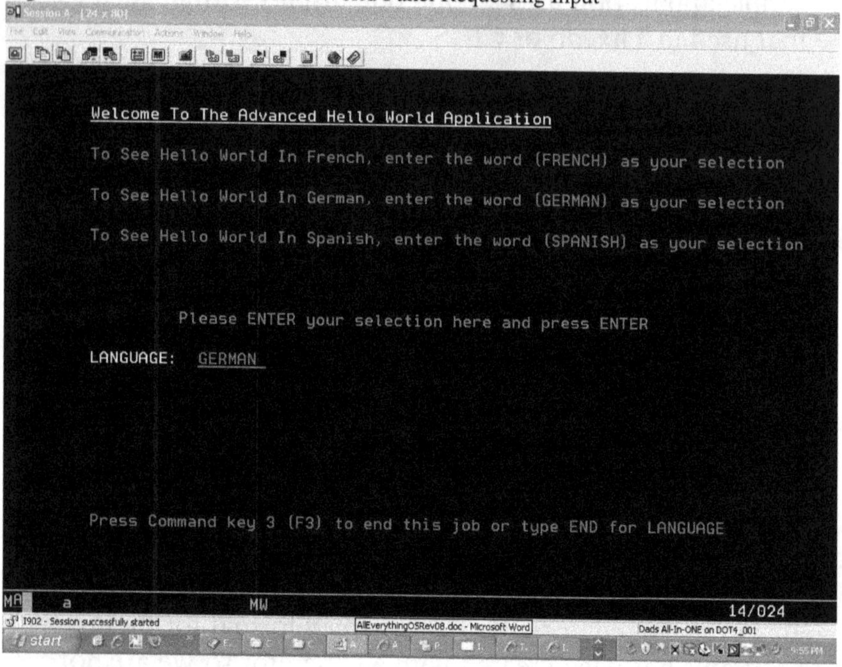

```
Welcome To The Advanced Hello World Application

To See Hello World In French, enter the word (FRENCH) as your selection
To See Hello World In German, enter the word (GERMAN) as your selection
To See Hello World In Spanish, enter the word (SPANISH) as your selection


         Please ENTER your selection here and press ENTER
LANGUAGE:  GERMAN




Press Command key 3 (F3) to end this job or type END for LANGUAGE
```

Figure 17-2 The Advanced Hello World Panel Output for GERMAN

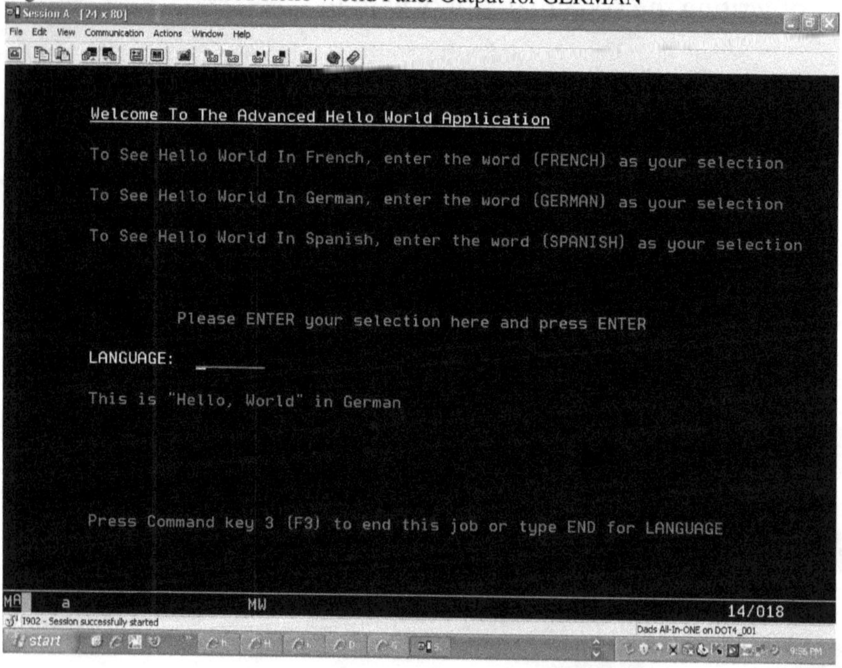

```
Welcome To The Advanced Hello World Application

To See Hello World In French, enter the word (FRENCH) as your selection
To See Hello World In German, enter the word (GERMAN) as your selection
To See Hello World In Spanish, enter the word (SPANISH) as your selection


         Please ENTER your selection here and press ENTER
LANGUAGE:  _____

This is "Hello, World" in German



Press Command key 3 (F3) to end this job or type END for LANGUAGE
```

But, again, there is even more coding with C, C++, Java, and even Visual BASIC because these are not really business languages.

RPG and COBOL are very programmer efficient languages when running on IBM i. That is why programmers absolutely love working with the system. Again, to make my point, they are business languages designed to do business tasks. Reading data and updating business files are natural business computer tasks. T

his Advanced Hello World program in RPG and COBOL are very simple on IBM i and they have to perform nothing more than basic tasks; nevertheless, even with just basic function, this code demonstrates both database access and interactive access in both languages are straight forward and natural.

See Figure 17-3 for the RPG code and Figure 17-4 for the COBOL code for Advanced Hello World and you will see what I mean. If you are non-technical, don't study it too long, but take a peak.

Figure 17-3 RPGIV Version of Advanced Hello World Program

```
1   FPANEL      CF     E              WORKSTN
2   FLANGUAGE   IF     E            K DISK
3   D ERRMSG           C                      CONST('HELLO WORLD TRANSLAT-
4   D                                         ION NOT FOUND, TRY A-
5   D                                         GAIN')
6   C           *IN99        DOWEQ    *OFF
7   C                        EXFMT    SCREEN1
8   C           LANGUA       IFEQ     'END'
9   C                        LEAVE
10  C                        ENDIF
11  C           LANGUA       CHAIN    LANGUAGE
90
12  C           *IN90        IFEQ     *ON
13  C                        MOVEL    ERRMSG         MESSAG
14  C                        ITER
15  C                        ENDIF
16  C                        ENDDO
17  C                        MOVE     *ON            *INLR
```

Figure 17-4 COBOL Version of Advanced Hello World Program

```
.......-A+++B++++++++++++++++++++++++++++++++++++++++++++++++++
0001.00         PROCESS
0002.00         IDENTIFICATION DIVISION.
0003.00         PROGRAM-ID. HELLOACUPD.
0004.00         ENVIRONMENT DIVISION.
0005.00         INPUT-OUTPUT SECTION.
0006.00         FILE-CONTROL.
0007.00             SELECT DB-LANGUAGE
0008.00                 ASSIGN TO DATABASE-LANGUAGE
0009.00                 ORGANIZATION IS INDEXED
0010.00                 ACCESS MODE IS RANDOM
0011.00                 RECORD KEY EXTERNALLY-DESCRIBED-KEY
0012.00                 FILE STATUS IS MF-STATUS.
0013.00             SELECT DISPLAYPANEL
0014.00                 ASSIGN TO WORKSTATION-PANEL
0015.00                 ORGANIZATION IS TRANSACTION
0016.00                 ACCESS MODE IS SEQUENTIAL
0017.00                 FILE STATUS IS WS-STATUS.
0018.00         DATA DIVISION.
0019.00         FILE SECTION.
0020.00         FD  DB-LANGUAGE.
0021.00         01  LANGUA-RECORD.
0022.00             COPY DDS-REFFMT  OF LANGUAGE.
0023.00         FD  DISPLAYPANEL.
0024.00         01  PANEL-RECORD   PIC X(150).
0025.00         WORKING-STORAGE SECTION.
0026.00         01  PNL-INPUT.
0027.00             COPY DDS-SCREEN1-I OF PANEL.
0028.00         01  PNL-OUTPUT.
0029.00             COPY DDS-SCREEN1-O OF PANEL.
0030.00         01  WS-STATUS           PIC XX.
0031.00         01  MF-STATUS           PIC XX.
0032.00         PROCEDURE DIVISION.
0033.00         BEGIN.
0034.00             OPEN I-O DISPLAYPANEL.
0035.00             OPEN INPUT DB-LANGUAGE.
0036.00             PERFORM SCREEN-IO THRU EXIT-SCREEN-IO.
0037.00         CLOSE-ALL.
0038.00             CLOSE DB-LANGUAGE DISPLAYPANEL.
0039.00             STOP RUN.
0040.00         SCREEN-IO.
0041.00             WRITE PANEL-RECORD FROM PNL-OUTPUT
0042.00                 FORMAT IS 'SCREEN1'.
0043.00             READ DISPLAYPANEL INTO PNL-INPUT
0044.00                 FORMAT IS 'SCREEN1'.
0045.00             IF IN99 OF PNL-INPUT IS EQUAL TO B'1'
0046.00                 GO TO EXIT-SCREEN-IO.
0047.00             MOVE LANGUA OF PNL-INPUT TO
0048.00                 LANGUA OF LANGUA-RECORD
0049.00             READ DB-LANGUAGE
0050.00                 INVALID KEY PERFORM LANGUA-NOT-FOUND
0051.00                 NOT INVALID KEY PERFORM LANGUA-FOUND.
0052.00         EXIT-SCREEN-IO.
0053.00             EXIT.
0054.00         LANGUA-FOUND.
0055.00             MOVE CORRESPONDING REFFMT  TO SCREEN1-O OF
0056.00                 PNL-OUTPUT.
0057.00         LANGUA-NOT-FOUND.
0058.00             MOVE 'HELLO WORLD TRANSLATION NOT FOUND, TRY AGAIN'
0059.00                 TO MESSAG OF PNL-OUTPUT.
****************** End of data *********************************
```

RPG and COBOL Are Lots Different

One of the first things that you may notice is that the RPG program is substantially smaller than the COBOL program (17 statements vs. 59). That's one of the reasons why COBOL has always been referred to as a verbose language. Java experts tell me that the same program, written in Java, would more than double the number of COBOL statements. In all fairness to COBOL, once you get through the standard lines that must be in each program, COBOL coding efficiency does get lots better.

What is an Integrated Business Language Compiler?

When the IBM i OS was first being designed, the theme of integration permeated the whole project. Even the compiler writers were involved. In Chapter 16, we described what it means to have an integrated database and how having programs that are database aware makes programmers far more productive.

We will not repeat that in this chapter because there is enough to discuss about how the compilers were built from the ground up to integrate into the advanced database notions being built into the IBM i platform from back when it was the IBM System/38.

The compiler writers for the business languages, COBOL and RPG, were not sitting in other offices when the operating system was designed. They were part of the design team. Consequently, the advanced structures and devices of the IBM i operating system have facilities right inside the compilers to access them.

IBM's compiler writers did the work of writing the input and output control subroutines (the device drivers or APIs as some might call them). During compilation, the compiler injects the necessary code rather than having the programmer write it each time. Therefore, on IBM i, the application developer can operate at a substantially higher level with no concern for the device, the structure, or the database. .

In fact, IBM's compilers took advantage of a feature in IBM i known as device independent data management to enable common routines to behave in a similar / same fashion regardless of the device that was being used. If you look for these features in Microsoft or HP or Sun or IBM mainframe compilers, you won't find them.

So, what are some of the advanced object types and features that are built into the COBOL and RPG languages?

- Database Device
- Workstation Device
- External Data Area Object

Database Device

A Picture is worth a thousand words. The RPG coding to link to the Language Database is shown in Figure 17-6. The COBOL Coding, naturally more verbose is shown in Figure 17-5. The coding to incorporate a database on every other system would include substantially more code and more complex code.

For example if there were five files with fifty fields each, and the RPG program is 17 statements and the COBOL program is 59 statements to start, the programmer would have to type in at least 250 more statements to define the data in the program. With IBM i, the metadata in the database would type those statements for the programmer. That's what you call compiler integration and a major productivity boost for programmers.

Figure 17-5-COBOL File Definition

0007.00		SELECT DB-LANGUAGE
0008.00		ASSIGN TO DATABASE-LANGUAGE
0009.00		ORGANIZATION IS INDEXED
0010.00		ACCESS MODE IS RANDOM
0011.00		RECORD KEY EXTERNALLY-DESCRIBED-KEY
0012.00		FILE STATUS IS MF-STATUS.
0020.00	FD	DB-LANGUAGE.
0021.00	01	LANGUA-RECORD.
0022.00		COPY DDS-REFFMT OF LANGUAGE.

Let's look at the COBOL Code first. This makes the link to the database using the DATABASE prefix to the language file in statement 8. The other thing of note is that there is a COPY DDS in statement 22. This tells COBOL to go inside the database object at compile time and bring in the full description of the file so the programmer does not have to code input or output specifications. Think about what a time saver this is. In COBOL, the field names are immediately available to all functions in the Procedure Division which in Figure 17-4 you can see begins at statement # 32.

Figure 17-6 RPG Database File Definition

2 FLANGUAGE	IF	E		K DISK

So, now, let's look at RPG in Figure 17-3. Actually the code is written in RPGIV but, it is written in RPG style so to the RPG coder it would look the same. Now, ask yourself, is that all there is? The answer is yes, all of the COBOL code equates to the one simple RPG file description statement at line 2 of the program shown in Figure 17-5. This makes the link to the database using the DISK device name and the name LANGUAGE after the F on the left side of the statement.

Just as in COBOL, there are other things of note. There is no COPY DDS like COBOL statement 22 but, there is a little E in position 22 of statement 2. The E says to use the external description of the data and to not expect the programmer to supply input or output specs. This tells the RPG compiler to go inside the database object at compile time and bring in the full description of the file metadata including all the field descriptions so the programmer does not have to code input or output specifications. Since this all happens in one statement in RPG, it is even a greater time saver than in COBOL. The field names are immediately available to all functions in the RPG calculations section beginning on line 6 in Figure 17-3.

Workstation Device

The RPG coding to link to the Display PANEL WORKSTN (terminal) type file is shown in Figure 17-8. The COBOL Coding, naturally more verbose, is shown in Figure 17-7. To incorporate a workstation or terminal file either directly or via a monitor such as CICS or Tuxedo in any other system requires substantially more code and the code is very complex. Moreover, the process is not as efficient because it is not the compiler or the OS doing the work, it is a third party package working as middleware.

Figure 17-7 COBOL WORKSTATION File Definition

```
0013.00              SELECT DISPLAYPANEL
0014.00                  ASSIGN TO WORKSTATION-PANEL
0015.00                  ORGANIZATION IS TRANSACTION
0016.00                  ACCESS MODE IS SEQUENTIAL
0017.00                  FILE STATUS IS WS-STATUS.

0023.00          FD  DISPLAYPANEL.
0024.00          01  PANEL-RECORD   PIC X(150).

0040.00              SCREEN-IO.
0041.00                  WRITE PANEL-RECORD FROM PNL-OUTPUT
0042.00                      FORMAT IS 'SCREEN1'.
0043.00                  READ DISPLAYPANEL INTO PNL-INPUT
0044.00                      FORMAT IS 'SCREEN1'.
```

Just as we did with database, let's look at the COBOL code first. Statement 14 makes the link to the display file named

PANEL using the WORKSTATION prefix to the PANEL device file. The other thing of note is that there is a no COPY DDS required -- even for COBOL.

The WORKSTATION file automatically goes inside the display file object at compile time and brings in the full description of the file, so the programmer does not have to code input or output specifications for the display panels. Think about what a time saver this is. In COBOL, the field names are immediately available to all functions in the Procedure Division which, in Figure 17-4, you can see begins at statement # 32.

From Statement 40 to statement 44 in Figure 17-7, you can see the small amount of COBOL code required to send out (WRITE) the screen panel and then read (READ) it back in. This code not only sends out the panel and reads it back in, it also waits for the reply from the terminal device while the user is typing input. Yet, there is no code required for this as it is handled by the tight integration of the IBM i OS and the generated compiler code.

Additionally, what you do not see in the code is the fact that each and every COBOL and RPG program on IBM i is automatically multithreaded. This too is because of the design cooperation of the compiler writers and the OS writers. Either the RPG or COBOL or both of these programs can be called by thousands of users simultaneously. Through this one program, (RPG or COBOL) many users can interact with their specific terminal device or emulated PC as if they were the only user working with that program. Though IBM i programmers even think this is amazing, they use this advanced capability every single day in their coding -- by not having to for code it.

Figure 17-8 RPG WORKSTN File Definition

```
1  FPANEL      CF    E                WORKSTN

7  C                          EXFMT   SCREEN1
```

So, now, let's look at the RPGIV code again to do the same thing. Ask yourself again, just as in the DB example, is that all there is? The answer is yes, for IBM i.

Of course in other systems that support this type of transaction processing, there would be all the trappings of a middleware (not native) CICS and/ or a Tuxedo or other TP monitor to enable the compiler to communicate with the device. There would be no WORKSTATION device in any other compiler, there would be special APIs with many special arguments and lots of rigorous coding required to pull this off.

Again, if you look at the COBOL example in Figure 17-7, through statement 24, all of the COBOL code equates to the one simple RPG file description statement at line 1 (Figure 17-8) of the program. In RPG, statement 1 makes the link to the display file using the WORKSTN device and the name PANEL on the left side of the statement.

Just as in COBOL, there is also another point of note. The E in position 22 of statement 1 (Figure 17-8) says to use the external description of the data and to not expect the programmer to supply input or output specs.

This tells the RPG compiler to go inside the database object at compile time and bring in the full description of the file metadata, including all the field descriptions, so the programmer does not have to code input or output specifications for the display file.

Since this all happens in one statement in RPG, it is even a greater time saver than in COBOL. The field names are immediately available to all functions in the RPG calculations section beginning on line 6 in Figure 17-3.

On Statement 7 in Figure 17-8, you can see the small amount of RPG code required to send out (write) the screen panel and then read (READ) it back in. This operation is called

EXFMT and it not only sends out the panel and reads it back in, in one operation, it also waits for the reply from the terminal device while the user is typing input. Yet, there is no additional code required for this as it is handled by the tight integration of the IBM i OS and the generated compiler code for the EXFMT operation.

With all due respect to Aflac, as you can see, coding for database and multithreaded terminal applications in the all-everything operating system's best business languages is as easy as duck soup. And even the duck would tell you that is no exaggeration.

IBMi Data Areas

Ted Holt is an IBM i Guru who runs a column for Timothy Prickett Morgan, President of IT Jungle, called "Four Hundred Guru." The Guru gives tips that only a Guru can provide. Holt suggests that "Data areas are as handy as pockets. Maybe that's because they are like pockets in that you can stuff things into them."

What makes these little pockets (the moral equivalent of one record files) very powerful is that they are naturally readable in IBM's business languages, RPG and COBOL. RPG is especially designed again in conjunction with the OS developers to be able to read and manipulate Ted Holt's little stuffed pockets. I can't say the pockets are hot or I'd be in trouble with the *Hot Pockets* people but they are very handy and very usable in RPG.

Data areas are often used to hold system counter information or one record control files for applications. For RPG to read and/ or change a data area, the compiler writers provide two options. You can let the RPG cycle handle the input and output operations, or you can control the I/O using special "IN" and "OUT" and "*LOCK" RPG operations. By far, the easier method is to let the RPG cycle do all the work. I will show you the code for both from one of Ted Holt's works in

IT Jungle. His whole article for those who are interested in data areas is shown at the following IT Jungle URL:

http://www.itjungle.com/fhg/fhg012506-story01.html

Figure 17-9, shows the RPGIV free-form code snippet that uses the RPG cycle to do its work. RPG has advanced itself in the past few years with the introduction of a non-columnar oriented syntax that is known as free-form RPG. Figure 17-10 shows the same function using the IN, OUT, and *LOCK facilities built into RPG in free-form fashion to work specifically with data area objects.

To read in an external data area object in RPGIV, you code using a named data structure with the U option in the definition specs shown in line 1 in Figure 17-9. Note the name of the structure from line 1 is Status.

Figure 17-9 Free Form RPG Data Area DS Snippet Using RPG Cycle
```
0001      D Status                uds
0002      D   Stat                       1      8
0003        /free
0004          Stat = 'BR-549';
0005        /End-free
```

Figure 17-10 Free Form RPG Data Area DS Snippet Using IN, OUT Ops
```
0001      D Status         ds            8    dtaara('STATUS')
0002        /free
0003          in *lock Status;
0004          Status = 'BR-549';
0005          out Status;
0006        /End-free
```

When the program in 17-9 begins to run, it allocates the data area with a lock (U option) shown in lower case in line 1 and brings its contents into storage. When the program ends, it updates the data area and releases the lock. It's about as easy as one could make it. In fact, it's so easy, even a caveman can do it.

The other method shown in Figure 17-10 does not use the RPG cycle. In programming parlance it uses the procedural method. IBM has created three operation codes, IN, OUT, and UNLOCK to control data area I/O in procedural RPG programs. The example in Figure 17-10 does not have a U in the data definition in line 1 and thus the code is controlled within operations.

It retrieves the current value of a data area (IN operation), locks the data area (*LOCK option of the IN operation) assigns a new value, and writes the changed value (out operation) back to the data area object. The Unlock operator is not needed as an unqualified OUT operation to the data area unlocks it after its new contents are written.

The purpose of showing this code in this chapter is not so that you can compete with me for programming contracts in Northeastern PA or so that you can be proficient in RPG. It is to show that the RPG compiler as well as the COBOL compiler not only has natural links to database and workstations but also to other external objects, such as data areas.

Both RPG and COBOL have facilities integrated within their respective compilers that mesh perfectly with the operating system for working with data areas, databases, and terminal devices. Integration at the business compiler level is a grand thing indeed.

Chapter 18   Advanced Computer Science Concepts: Consistent, Intuitive Control Language

Advanced Systems Architecture

Integration is the Key Element in Advanced Computer Design. In this chapter we examine another of the key elements of IBM i integration, a consistent, intuitive control language.

IBM i Control Language is the visible implementation of the IBM i advanced architecture, which we have been discussing in the last several chapters. One of its inherent characteristics is that it allows applications to be built today that will last long into the future. Along with all the advantages cited in previous chapters, it provides a platform for flexibility, ease-of-use, productivity, and growth.

As noted in Chapters 10 and 12, the interface point in the IBM i system is at a high level. Because of this, neither programmers nor users have to learn cryptic machine code for normal functions, since the high level instructions are more English-like.

As an example, one high level instruction can be used to get a database record, perform multiprogramming, handle storage management or even query a data base file. In traditional systems, such functions are handled by multiple software programs. The IBM i all-everything operating system is "smarter" than every other platform, so it does its thing without the need for fancy middleware. Its high level language is known as Control Language.

Operating System Control

Looking at this a bit differently, we can say that machine instructions handle traditional software functions. Control Language is the user interface to the entire machine through IBM i. One of the major advantages, demonstrated in Chapter 12, of the high level interface is that new technology does not affect existing application programs.

Having CL at the point of the interface means, among other things, that fewer programming interfaces overall are needed to work the machine. Through this one simple interface, IBM i CL provides the following functions:

- Supervisor and control
- Language / compiler
- Symbolic interactive debug
- Data base management
- Data communications

CL Can Be Used in Programs

With CL programming and in fact, all programming using IBM i, the programmer has a greater potential for unrestricted growth since the underlying hardware technology does not get in the way. The visual interface to the system through CL means that both you and your programs can move easily into the future. You can take advantage of both new hardware technology and new software technology without worrying about changing your control programs.

Development Software is Hardware Agnostic

Software for IBM i is not written for 16, 32 or 64-bit standards. It is written at an abstraction level that does not care about the underlying bit configuration of the hardware.

Thus, when hardware is upgraded, nobody cares because it does not matter to the functioning of the programs. Of course, the owner of the business whose old CL and other programming now run faster on the new technology -- with no additional work -- he or she cares.

At the machine interface, if you were able to take a snapshot, you would find the point in which CL, the IBM i control language, meets IBM i. IBM i with CL provides a simple and consistent interface to help users and developers alike to learn the system easily while reducing the support staff and costs associated with systems implementation and operations.

CL is the gateway to integrated functions. Overall, CL as a system interface point improves the productivity of programmers. It also increases system performance, and it adds to the system's ease of use. For the business, this translates to programming investments being protected for the long haul. Unlike the Windows environment, when you write a program, with IBM i and CL, you can expect as much as thirty or more years before it needs to change for technology reasons. IBM i does not tie you to any of today's hardware or software technology so even the future is protected.

With an expandable and adaptable interface, IBM i allows you to take advantage of new developments quickly and easily, and it provides a solid foundation upon which to build the future of your business. CL is fully aware of all of the system's features, including the object-based architecture and the built-in integrity and security facilities. Throughout time, CL programs have continued to work to control systems operations and there is no reason on the horizon indicating that the future will in any way impede this capability.

So, now we know how CL is not an afterthought. Just as RPG and COBOL, it has been built to enhance the business value of the IBM i operating system. So, now let's go ahead and learn a little bit more about why it is so special.

CL Objects / Building Blocks

The basic "storage" object on the native IBM i system is called a library. A library is very much like a directory in that it is an entity unto itself that merely is used to locate other objects. However, unlike a directory, the library object is unique as it can hold objects that are not files serving other purposes. In other words, a library does not have the ability to store an executable (exe) file or a .wmf file or pdf file, and for that matter, it can't store even a "boho" file. A library can store only file objects that are real files. Unlike a directory, a library can also store programs and other object types that are not data files at all. They are special objects. Files masquerading as programs need not apply on IBM i.

Every system starts someplace. Every system's storage has a genesis. Most systems have a primary disk with a boot sector and what might be called a VTOC (volume table of contents). This lets the system start the OS and then be aware of the files on the system. IBM i treats all files as single level storage and it groups them into libraries. However, if a file is not really a file but instead is exccutable code, it cannot be stored as a file in a library. The object type rules prevent an object from morphing into another object.

Only program objects, specially tailored to meet the rigorous standards of the IBM i, can be stored as programs. Only the CL compiler or other special IBM i compilers know how to create real program objects. At startup, the IBM i operating system knows all about its objects types and the objects stored on the system.

There is a library on the system in which IBM puts a good portion of the IBM i operating system. Every operating system needs a home. On IBM i this home is called the system library and its official name is the QSYS Library. This is the beginning of the genesis of the actual system table of contents. QSYS happens to be the only "library" on the system which can "contain" other libraries.

How Are Objects Created?

The CL command, **CRTLIB PAYROLL,** when executed, creates a library. Remember, a library looks an awful lot and functions an awful lot like a PC directory but it has much more facility. The library that CRTLIB PAYROLL creates is named PAYROLL. Where was that library created?

All libraries are created in the QSYS library and so I call it the genesis of the system. The letters "CRT" as the first part of the create library command have big-time meaning for CL. CL looks at the beginning of every command as a verb or action word. The three character "verb" that causes all objects to be created on IBM i begins with the letters CRT, for create.

The three letters "LIB" that follows the "CRT" is always the short CL name for library. Thus, CRTLIB makes a lot of sense if you read the verb and noun abbreviations as if they were full words. In CL-speak, the CRTLIB command says, "Create a library." Likewise, the command CRTCLPGM means "Create" "CL" "Program." Just like CRT is always short for create and LIB is always short for library, CL is always short for Control Language, and PGM is always short for program. As you can see, CL is consistent, it is unique, and it is certainly intuitive once you get the hang of it. And then when that happens, it is also, hard to forget.

Library Talk

Unlike other systems; however, when objects are "placed" in a library, such as the PAYROLL library that we would create with the "CRTLIB PAYROLL" command, they are merely located (pointed to) via the library. On mainframes, libraries are physical structures occupying amounts of space on the disk in very specific areas. Moreover, on mainframes, only program forms such as source, routines, and object code cane be in what mainframers like to call a library. The point is no data and actually nothing other than program types can be placed in a mainframe library space. Picture a little corralled off area on the disk, separated from all the data files. To the system managing the disk files on a mainframe, it is very aware that the big file allocation on its disk is really a library for developer type material. It is not used for data or any other notions, including job queues or print queues.

IBM i Libraries Are Special Objects

Structurally, IBM i libraries are far more inclusive than mainframe libraries and are thus completely dissimilar. They are more like PC directories except for two big things:

1. They span disk drives. A library for example can occupy every disk drive on the system if need be.

2. They reference objects, not files.

Since a file is an object in IBM i and it consists of metadata (descriptive) and functional parts, and since objects are not just files to the system, libraries can and do reference files. However, every object stored "in" a library is not viewed at the system level as a file, as is the case on PC servers and Unix boxes. The operating system can differentiate a file from a program, and from any of many object types.

Where Are Libraries?

PAYROLL, like all libraries, when it gets created via the CRTLIB PAYROLL command, links back to QSYS so that it can be located by name through the QSYS library. PAYROLL, when created, is empty. In other words, it points to no objects. When objects are created, the CRT command wants the developer to specify the library to which the object is to be associated. Any library created on the system can physically be placed anywhere on any of the disks by IBM i, however, that does not matter at an operational level.

Nobody, whether they are a user or a system operator or a system implementer or a programmer, cares where anything is physically located. Instead, they depend on IBM i to find whatever they need, and IBM i is up to the task. Of course, if a lower level developer insisted on knowing where all of his or her objects were located physically on the disk drives, it could be done, but I wouldn't hold dinner on it.

IBM i has an innate means of locating any library by name without knowing where (which disk) it is located. Likewise, IBM i can find any object inside of any library merely by knowing its name. As you can see, human beings do not have to manage this system. It takes care of itself; but, the CL language gives the system administrator the tools needed to let IBM i know what to do.

Libraries are Pointer Objects

Let's go back to learn some more about libraries. When you consider that a library actually is an IBM i object created by a CL command, the amount of space, which a library (*LIB object) occupies, compared to all other object types on the system, is minimal. Each referenced object within a library structure consists of not much more than a name and a pointer.

So, in many ways a library is analogous to the Index at the back of a book. If that is the same sense that you get regarding directories, then think of the structure of the library itself as a directory, but the means of dealing with its objects and its multiple object types is completely different and far more intelligent from that of the PC directory scheme.

Creating Objects in Libraries

Once we create our library, say PAYROLL, for review, a library-type object is created in QSYS. CL provides a number of "create" commands that all begin with CRT. When these commands, such as CRTPF for Create Physical File, and CRTOUTQ, Create Output Queue, are executed, they will create their objects "in" a user library such as the PAYROLL library referenced in this section. The CRT command has an option within its command parameters to specify the library. If the developer does not specify the library name for an object being created, the system very nicely places the created object into the current library associated with the user who creates it.

The defaults provided by IBM i permit the unenlightened IT professional to be able to work with the system and perform whatever functions they need to perform unimpeded. As long as they have high enough security they will be unimpeded. If they make a mistake from using the command defaults, they would see the results of the mistake. They would be able to see the results of the mistake and gain guidance for how to execute the command correctly.

On other machines, it is actually difficult to be able to make your first mistake. It is so difficult on a mainframe, for example that when you provide the wrong parameters for a job and you get blown off for syntactical reasons, you typically have no idea why. There are no logical defaults as on IBM i.

You have to figure out which comma is missing or which parm is in the wrong place. So, when you get something through without syntax errors on a mainframe, even if it is three weeks from ever being right, you may feel good. But, you are still three weeks away from implementation. With IBM's CL, it takes so little time to engage the system productively, that mistakes are easily identified and corrected.

Control Language

Now that we have set up the idea for a full command language, or really a Control Language, as it is properly called, from now on, we can refer to it as plain old "CL." CL is a derivative of JCL from the mainframe era and it is a derivative of System/3, System/32, System/34, and System/36 implementations when the word OCL was the term du jour. Since in all of these nomenclatures, the CL part referred to the words Control Language, when System/38 was introduced, and the same language was used for all functions, IBM removed the modifier from CL. The IBM i version carries this through and is known simply as Control Language. Though it is called Control Language, because it is command-driven, it is often, though mistakenly referred to as Command Language.

There are a number of things about Control Language that do not appear as meaningful for 2010 as they did in 1970; but, the language still is impressive. The following list includes many of these factors:

- Requires no system generation
- All functions available at installation
- All functions available on all sized models
- May change default command values
- Configuration changes are Immediately effective without a "reboot"

CL is not an add-on product to IBM i. It is a big part of the IBM i experience. As such, it is the focal point of the premiere operating system of the IBM Power System and it is poised to expand if IBM chooses to let it loose as a full-featured programming language. IBM i, of course is the OS that brings CL to the developer and user community. For its part, IBM i requires no special generation or installation steps.

Consequently, CL requires no such steps either. It's in there on the first IPL. In most cases, IBM i is pre-loaded at the plant and requires no tape or CD or DVD installation time at all. In most shipments of single unit models of the Power System with IBM i, when the plug hits the wall, and the button is pushed, this powerful operating system and its powerful Control Language are ready to go.

All functions of the operating system are available at installation time through a very crisp, concise and HARD TO FORGET Control Language (CL). Some may recall the notion of what was once called a SysGen. This was when all the media from IBM was collected on tapes and/or disk packs, and the system on the specific piece of hardware was configured and loaded at the datacenter, rather than the IBM plant. During the SysGen, the customer's exact specifications would be the input for the process that would generate a custom operating system, as required by the IT shop. It was often a multi-day event.

Every functional mainframe operating system was tailored at the code level by what was, in essence, the compiling of the operating system on the customer premises. Since the language that read in the parms was very low level, the compiling of the customer's customized OS was actually called assembling, and it used an internal assembly language that could be used only for SysGen functions and not for customer work.

System Values vs. System Generation

The IBM i OS, dubbed the all-everything operating system in this book, broke the SysGen paradigm in 1978. Since that time, IBM i users have not had to work with system macros to include or exclude system function. The previous methodology included a shipment of a skeletal operating system that could not be used to run your business. A set of macros had to be assembled and then used in a "no-mistakes-tolerated" weekend work session. The result of the process when successful was a generated system. If you got any of the parameters wrong for that business, you got to do it again the next weekend. From the day the System/38 hit the field, IBM i heritage operating systems did not require compilation/assembly on the datacenter floor. IBM i from its inception has been table-driven.

Operating system functions for IBM i are enabled or disabled or selected or deselected at the system level through a series of options known as "System Values." These values can be changed through CL commands and the impact on the system is either immediate or in rare cases, requires an initial program load or IPL. IPL is the mainframe and IBM i term for "boot." This means that from the first moment of live operation, the IBM i operating system is functional and CL is its guiding light.

My friend, Al Barsa, (Al passed away at COMMON in spring 2008) was in many ways as intrigued by the power of System Values as I. He gave many COMMON presentations about System Values and he would point out how the knowledge of them could help an installation. Al had a major passion for System Values and what they could provide for the user community. COMMON attendees learned everything they ever wanted to know about System Values from Al Barsa from time immemorial. And, I might add, they learned them well.

As a side note, just because they had learned about System Values in an Al Barsa session, does not mean that they did not go back to the very same session at the next COMMON conference just to hear Al speak again.

When the System/38 was introduced, even the most convinced of us, expected that a system generation would be required for such a powerfully capable software machine. Because there was great thought in how a system should be designed, no SYSGEN has ever been required for a System/38, an AS/400, a System i, or any IBM i predecessor OS. IBM Rochester had devised a table driven OS and it works well to this day.

Nobody can present Al Barsa's PowerPoints from COMMON as he can but, I can show you the first page of the WRKSYSVAL CL command so that you can get a sense of all the things these values control. Rather than the OS being built with hard values, the IBM i OS looks to the System Value Table each time it is powered on to set the personality it is to render to a user. Check out Figure 18-1 for the first page of WRKSYSVAL command output and check out Figure 18-2 for a full list of all system values.

Figure 18-1 First Page of System Values Display

```
5738SS1 V2R3M0 931217              RSM                01/05/95  12:56:23
 *...+... 1 ...+... 2 ...+... 3 ...+... 4 ...+... 5 ...+... 6 ...+... 7 ...+... 8
*******************************************************************************
*                           Work with System Values                            *
*                                                              System:    RSM  *
* Position to  . . . . . .  _____ Starting characters of system value     *
* Subset by Type  . . . . .  *ALL_____  F4 for list                            *
*                                                                              *
* Type options, press Enter.                                                   *
*   2=Change    5=Display                                                      *
*                                                                              *
*          System                                                              *
* Option  Value        Type      Description                                   *
*   __    QABNORMSW    *SYSCTL   Previous end of system indicator              *
*   __    QACGLVL      *MSG      Accounting level                              *
*   __    QACTJOB      *ALC      Initial number of active jobs                 *
*   __    QADLACTJ     *ALC      Additional number of active jobs              *
*   __    QADLSPLA     *ALC      Spooling control block additional storage     *
*   __    QADLTOTJ     *ALC      Additional number of total jobs               *
*   __    QALWUSRDMN   *SEC      Allow user domain objects in libraries        *
*   __    QASTLVL      *SYSCTL   User assistance level                         *
*                                                                     More... *
* Command _____        *
* ===> _____        *
* F3=Exit   F4=Prompt   F5=Refresh   F9=Retrieve   F11=Display names only      *
* F12=Cancel                                                                   *
*                                                                              *
*******************************************************************************
 *...+... 1 ...+... 2 ...+... 3 ...+... 4 ...+... 5 ...+... 6 ...+... 7 ...+... 8
```

Because System Values are actually as major advanced notion in computing, just like many of the other ideas we have been studying, please take a look at Figure 18-3. In this Figure, you can see all of the system values that can be defaulted or tweaked on an IBM i system to give it the personality that is needed for any IBM i IT shop.

Figure 18-2 IBM i Comprehensive System Value List

```
QABNORMSW      0                 0                    Previous end of system ind
QACGLVL        *NONE             *NONE                Accounting level
QACTJOB        20                20                   Initial number of active jobs
QADLACTJ       10                10                   Additional number active jobs
QADLSPLA       2048              2048                 Spooling control block addl stg
QADLTOTJ       10                10                   Additional number of total jobs
QALWUSRDMN     *ALL              *ALL                 Allow user domain objects in lib
QASTLVL        *BASIC            *BASIC               User assistance level
QATNPGM        *ASSIST           *ASSIST              Attention program
QAUDCTL        *NONE             *NONE                Auditing control
QAUDENDACN     *NOTIFY           *NOTIFY              Auditing end action
QAUDFRCLVL     *SYS              *SYS                 Force auditing data
QAUDLVL        *NONE             *NONE                Security auditing level
QAUTOCFG       1                 1                    Autoconfigure devices
QAUTOVRT       0                 0                    Autoconfigure virtual devices
QBASACTLVL     6                 6                    Base storage pool activ. lvl.
QBASPOOL    >  518               500                  Base storage pool minimum size
QCCSID         65535             65535                Coded character set identifier
QCHRID         697 37            697 37               Graphic character set and code
QCOMRCVY       0                 0                    Communications recvy limits
QCNTRYID       US                US                   Country identifier
QCONSOLE    >  DSP01             QCONSOLE             Console name
QCRTAUT        *CHANGE           *CHANGE              Create default public authority
QCRTOBJAUD     *NONE             *NONE                Create object auditing
QCTLSBSD    >  QSYS/QCTL         QSYS/QBASE           Controlling subsystem
QCURSYM        $                 $                    Currency symbol
QDATE          01/05/95          ' '                  System date
QDATFMT        MDY               MDY                  Date format
QDATSEP        /                 /                    Date separator
QDAY           5                 ' '                  Day
QDBRCVYWT      0                 0                    Database recovery wait ind.
QDECFMT        ' '               ' '                  Decimal format
QDEVNAMI       *NORMAL           Device naming conventions
QDEVRCYA       *MSG              Device I/O error action
QDSCJOBI       240               Time interval before disc jobend
QDSPSGNINF     0                 0                    Sign-on display info control
QHOUR          12                ' '                  Hour of the day
QHSTLOGSIZ     5000              5000                 Maximum history log records
QIGC           0                 0                    DBCS version installed ind
QIGCCDEFNT     *NONE             *NONE                Double byte code font
QINACTITV   >  120               *NONE                Inactive job time-out
QINACTMSGQ  >  *DSCJOB           *ENDJOB              Inactive job message queue
QIPLDATTIM  >  01/06/95 04:00:00 *NONE                Date/time to automatically IPL
QIPLSTS     >  3                 0                    IPL status indicator
QIPLTYPE       0                 0                    Type of IPL to perform
QJOBMSGQFL     *NOWRAP           *NOWRAP              Job message queue full option
QJOBMSGQMX     16                16                   Max size of job message queue
QJOBMSGINS     16                16                   Job message queue initial size
QJOBMSGQTL     24                24                   Job message queue max inl size
QJOBSPLA    >  4096              1536                 Spooling control block inl size
QKBDBUF        *TYPEAHEAD        *TYPEAHEAD           Type ahead and/or attention key
QKBDTYPE       USB               USB                  Keyboard language character set
QLANGID        ENU               ENU                  Language identifier
QLEAPADJ       0                 0                    Leap year adjustment
QLMTDEVSSN     0                 0                    Limit device sessions
QLMTSECOFR  >  0                 1                    Limit security officer dev acc
QMAXACTLVL     *NOMAX            *NOMAX               Maximum sys 0activity level
QMAXSGNACN     3                 3                    Action to take for faild signon
QMAXSIGN    >  25                15                   Maximum sign-on attempts allow
QMCHPOOL    >  6161              1500                 Machine storage pool size
QMINUTE        57                ' '                  Minute of the hour
QMODEL         D10                                    System model number
QMONTH         1                 ' '                  Month of the year
QPFRADJ     >  3                 2                    Performance adjustment
QPRBFTR     >  SVCDRCTR/SDFILTER *NONE                Problem log filter
QPRBHLDITV     30                30                   Problem log hold interval
QPRTDEV        PRT01             PRT01                Printer device description
QPRTKEYFMT  >  *PRTBDR           *PRTHDR              Print header and/or border info
QPRTTXT        ' '               Print text
QPWDEXPITV     *NOMAX            *NOMAX               Password expiration interval
QPWDLMTAJC     0                 0                    Limit adjacent password digits
QPWDLMTCHR     *NONE             *NONE                Limit characters in password
```

```
QPWDLMTREP      0                 0             Limit repeating chars in pword
QPWDMAXLEN  >   6                 10            Maximum password length
QPWDMINLEN  >   4                 1             Minimum password length
QPWDPOSDIF      0                 0             Limit password character posns.
QPWDRQDDGT      0                 0             Require digit in password
QPWDRQDDIF  >   1                 0             Duplicate password control
QPWDVLDPGM      *NONE             *NONE         Password validation program
QPWRDWNLMT      600               600           Maximum time - PWRDWNSYS *IMMED
QPWRRSTIPL      0                 0             Auto IPL after power restored
QRCLSPLSTG      8                 8             Reclaim spool storage
QRMTIPL         0                 0             Remote power on and IPL
QRMTSIGN    >   *SAMEPRF          *FRCSIGNON    Remote sign-on control
QSCPFCONS       1                 1             IPL action with console problem
QSECOND         23                ' '           Second of the minute
QSECURITY   >   30                10            System security level
QSFWERRLOG      *LOG              *LOG          Software error logging
QSPCENV         *NONE             *NONE         Special environment
QSRLNBR         1034338           ' '           System serial number
QSRTSEQ         *HEX              *HEX          Sort sequence
QSRVDMP         *DMPUSRJOB        *DMPUSRJOB    Service dump control
QSTRPRTWTR      1                 1             Start print writers at IPL
QSTRUPPGM   >   RSMSYS/QSTRUP     QSYS/QSTRUP   Startup program
QSTSMSG         *NORMAL           *NORMAL       Display status messages
QSYSLIBL    >   RSMSYS            QSYS          System part of the library list
                QSYS              QSYS2
                QSYS2             QHLPSYS
                QHLPSYS           QUSRSYS
                QUSRSYS                   ' '
QTIME           12:57:23          ' '           Time of day
QTIMSEP         :                 :             Time separator
QTOTJOB         30                30            Initial total number of jobs
QTSEPOOL        *NONE             *NONE         Time slice end pool
QUPSDLYTIM  >   1800 1800         *CALC         UPS delay time
QUPSMSGQ        QSYS/QSYSOPR      QSYS/QSYSOPR              UPS message queue
QUSRLIBL    >   QGPL              QGPL          User part of the library list
                QTEMP             QTEMP
                GENERAL                   ' '
QUTCOFFSET      +0000             +0000         Coord. universal time offset
QYEAR           95                ' '           Year

Note:  > means current value is different from the shipped value
```

Cl and all other IBM programming functions work on IBM i object structures. The CL command to show the list of all objects on the system is WRKOBJ. The format of this command that permits all object types to be listed is shown in the Print Key output in Figure 18-4 as follows:

Figure 18-4 WRKOBJ Command in Action

```
    5738SS1 V2R3M0 931217                MYMACHINE               01/05/2009 12:57:46
    *...+... 1 ...+... 2 ...+... 3 ...+... 4 ...+... 5 ...+... 6 ...+... 7 ...+... 8
    ******************************************************************************
 01 *                           Work with Objects (WRKOBJ)                        *
 01
 02 *                                                                             *
 02
 03 * Type choices, press Enter.                                                   *
 03
 04 *                                                                             *
 04
 05 * Object  . . . . . . . . . . . . .    *All          Name, generic*, *ALL     *
 05
 06 *   Library  . . . . . . . . . . .     *LIBL         Name, *LIBL, *CURLIB...  *
 06
 07 * Object type  . . . . . . . . . .     ?             *ALL, *ALRTBL, *AUTL...  *
 07
 08 *                                                                             *
 08
 20 *                                                                             *
 20
 21 *                                                                      Bottom *
 21
 22 * F3=Exit    F4=Prompt    F5=Refresh    F12=Cancel   F13=How to use this display *
 22
 23 * F24=More keys                                                                *
 23
 24 *                                                                             *
 24
    ******************************************************************************
    *...+... 1 ...+... 2 ...+... 3 ...+... 4 ...+... 5 ...+... 6 ...+... 7 ...+... 8
```

The specifics of this CL command in Figure 18-4 show that it is not filled in. The object name should be whatever you are looking for or *ALL. The library name can also be *ALL if you want to search all libraries. To get a list of all object types as an example of what this CL command can do as well as to see the plethora of object types on the system, place a question mark for object type as shown in Figure 18-4 and press Enter.

Note in Figure 18-5, that I combined the output of two panels to make it easier for us to read. Each of these object types has a unique purpose on the system. I would bet that there is no IBM i implementer who knows or even cares to know all of these object types. Objects such as *FILE for file and *PGM, and *JOBD for job description and *TBL for table get a lot more play than those unique to lesser used functions.

Figure 18-5 List of abbreviations- all object types on System

```
    5738SS1 V2R3M0 931217              MYMACHINE                    01/05/2009
12:58:44
      *...+... 1 ...+... 2 ...+... 3 ...+... 4 ...+... 5 ...+... 6 ...+... 7 ...+... 8
  **********************************************************************************
  01 *                        Specify Value for Parameter OBJTYPE                   *
  01
  06 * Object type . . . . . . . . . .   *ALL                                       *
  06
  07 *                                                                              *
  07
  08 *    *ALL                           *CSPTBL                                    *
  08
  09 *    *ALRTBL                        *CTLD                                      *
  09
  10 *    *AUTL                          *DEVD                                      *
  10
  11 *    *BNDDIR                        *DOC                                       *
  11
  12 *    *CFGL                          *DTAARA                                    *
  12
  13 *    *CHTFMT                        *DTADCT                                    *
  13
  14 *    *CLD                           *DTAQ                                      *
  14
  15 *    *CLS                           *EDTD                                      *
  15
  16 *    *CMD                           *FCT                                       *
  16
  17 *    *CNNL                          *FILE                                      *
  17
  18 *    *COSD                          *FLR                                       *
  18
  19 *    *CSI                           *FNTRSC                                    *
  19
  20 *    *CSPMAP                        *FORMDF                                  + *
  20
  08 *    *FTR                           *MSGQ                                      *
  08
  09 *    *GSS                           *NODL                                      *
  09
  10 *    *JOBD                          *NWID                                      *
  10
  11 *    *JOBQ                          *OUTQ                                      *
  11
  12 *    *JOBSCD                        *OVL                                       *
  12
  13 *    *JRN                           *PAGDFN                                    *
  13
  14 *    *JRNRCV                        *PAGSEG                                    *
  14
  15 *    *LIB                           *PDG                                       *
  15
  16 '    *LIND                          *PGM                                       *
  16
  17 *    *MENU                          *PNLGRP                                    *
  17
  18 *    *MODD                          *PRDDFN                                    *
  18
  19 *    *MODULE                        *PRDLOD                                    *
  19
  20 *    *MSGF                          *QMFORM                                  + *
  20
  08 *    *QMQRY                         *USRQ                                      *
  08
  09 *    *QRYDFN                        *USRSPC                                    *
  09
  10 *    *RCT                           *WSCST                                     *
  10
  11 *    *SBSD                                                                     *
  11
  12 *    *SCHIDX                                                                   *
  12
  13 *    *SPADCT                                                                   *
  13
  14 *    *SQLPKG                                                                   *
  14
  15 *    *SRVPGM                                                                   *
  15
  16 *    *SSND                                                                     *
  16
  17 *    *S36                                                                      *
  17
  18 *    *TBL                                                                      *
  18
  19 *    *USRIDX                                                                   *
  19
  20 *    *USRPRF                                                                   *
  20
```

Traditional CL Command Functions

CL is used to operate the system as well as a procedural and compilable programming language for job control. The types of functions that can be controlled or manipulated on IBM i with CL are as follows:

- Librarian functions
- Utility Program
- Procedures
- Operator Commands
- File and disk space management

The traditional command structure of other systems with heritage from the 1980 time frame, (System/3, System/34, System/36, and System/370 family machines) consisted of many different types of functions, as well as different formats for major functions. This is one area of life in which variety is not preferred over consistency.

Programmers and operators needed to deal with librarian functions for their program source and object utility programs for certain other tasks, such as copying data. On these systems, procedures have a different format and structure from other command functions and none of the above systems permit grouping of commands, so that an operator or a developer can find the right command when needed. For example, the operator commands for spooling, file and disk management were completely different, in format, from other commands that a system operator would use on these systems.

In fact, on IBM System/34 and System/36, there were operator control commands (OCC) for operation functions such as looking at the spool queue and there were operation control language (OCL) statements for controlling program loads and execution, and then, there were procedures to permit more than one set of OCL to be called at once. If it were not confusing in concept, it would have been confusing in practice.

On top of the different command / procedure structures, though both System/34 and System/36 were known for exceptional ease of use, there was also an independent special manner in which to use the OCC called Console Mode. The Console was hidden in normal mode but, when needed, one could always invoke the special key sequence to get there. With all of the different formats for controlling the system and the notion of regular mode and console mode, System/34 and System/36 may have been easier than most systems to use, but they were far from intuitive.

This mess was cleaned up with the System/38 and its one format Control Language. CL now is one of the hallmarks of the IBM i operating system. Control Language is a single interface to all IBM i functions. IBM i Control Language is made up of many commands that replace the functions of separate commands for programming purposes and for operations on other IBM systems. IBM i commands are consistent in form and they are quite intuitive.

Define Control Language

So, if I was to take a stab at defining Control Language, I would say it is a single consistent interface to all system functions. That is a period back there in case you missed it.

CL can operate in interactive or batch mode. When operating in interactive mode, CL has a consistent prompt facility (Press F4 for Prompt). This feature helps the user avoid many look-ups into reference manuals. Interactive CL also has the ability to list commands in groupings of subject and / or beginning verb. This function is called command grouping menus and is a big aid in programmer/ operator productivity as no command is hard to find. Moreover, once you find a command, all parms are explained within help text and all options are shown by placing a question mark in the parm and pressing Enter.

When operating in batch mode, CL can be pre-translated (compiled.) It is the only system procedure and operator control language, on any system, that can be compiled. Thus, it is very fast, when executing. In compiled mode, CL is designed for controlling application flow and it has powerful arithmetic and logic capabilities, as well as variable interchange and other elements of a full programming language, including direct database manipulation. Additionally, it can interface to the user directly by reading and writing display file panels using IBM i workstation facilities.

CL has one additional facility that is fairly unique for compiled code. Via the question mark facility, as already described for interactive (non-compiled) use, a compiled program with question marks in commands will stop and invoke the prompter so that the operator can select the proper parm at execution time.

Intuitive Command Composition

Our last area of emphasis about the highly consistent and intuitive command interface is its ability to make implementers and operators appear to be smarter than we really are. CL command names are very intuitive. In fact, they are structured like mini English language sentences. Each CL command begins with a verb, followed by one or several adjectives that are also called modifiers, followed by the modified noun or the literal object of the verb. A full command is composed of a command name and from 0 to 50 parameters. Within the command structure, blanks serve as separators between parameters and there can be as many blanks as the developer wants.

The simplest way to demonstrate the consistent command structure is to list the verb, adjective, and noun components of a number of commands. Check out the following list:

VERB:

3 Character Abbreviation	Meaning
CRT	create
WRK	work with
DSP	display
DLT	delete
STR	start
CHG	change

ADJECTVE (MODIFIER):

1, 2, or 3 Char. Abbreviation	Meaning
P	physical
Q	queue
MSG	message
JOB	job
DTA	data

NOUN (OBJECT OF VERB):

1 to 3 Char. Abbreviation	Meaning
D	description
E	entry
F	file
LIB	library
ARA	area

To review the charts above, the IBM i command structure is made up of a 3 character verb which denotes the action to be taken. For example, use CRT for the create action whether you are creating a physical file, a program, or an output queue.

The second part of each command name consists of one or more adjectives. This modifier can be 1 to 3 characters. The modifier distinguishes the type action to be taken. Sometimes, this has to do with the actual type of object to be worked upon and / or created. For example, the modifier can determine whether the action is on a physical file or logical file, or perhaps a COBOL program or an RPG program.

The third part of a command is the noun serving as the object of the verb upon which the action is to be taken. This part delineates that the action is to be taken on a file, library, description, etc... The noun (object of the verb) can be 1 to 3 characters.

Thus, a CL command consists of 1 verb, 0-2 modifiers, and one 1 object. Try to complete the following simple exercise on command names in your head, based on the short lesson we just took.

	VERB	MODIFIER	OBJECT
create RPG program	_crt	_rpg_	_pgm_
create physical file	___	___	___
display library	___	___	___
start print writer	___	___	___

The command to Create an RPG Program is CRTRPGPGM as shown as the first response. If you would like to check your work on the other three exercises above, here are the answers for cases, 2, 3, and 4.

Command Function	Three Parts			Full Command
Create Physical File	CRT	P	F	CRTPF
Display Library -	DSP		LIB	DSPLIB
Start Print Writer -	STR	PRT	WTR	STRPRTWTR

If I were to list all the commands on the system in two columns in 8 point type, there would be over ten full pages of commands in the printout. The fact that the command itself is intuitive makes this plethora of consistent commands quite easy to remember and if I might suggest, something even better, hard to forget.

Command Parameters

It would be nice if CL commands could divine the developers' thoughts and not require parameters. Even IBM i cannot do that, yet! Every command has one or several objects that it operates against and it does things in a certain way, based upon the will of the user / developer. So, there must be human input to help a command know exactly where to find named objects and then, sometimes, where to put them at the end of the process.

Job Control Language on a mainframe and OCC commands on IBM System/3x are positional in nature, meaning that if you miss a comma the whole command is off and the best that can happen is that it detects the error rather than doing something you did not want done.

IBM i command parameters are mostly keyword oriented, though they can be used in a positional fashion if desired or keywords and positional parms can be mixed. Here is the rule on that. Once you begin to use keywords in a prompt, everything after that must be keyword, even if you are positionally correct. So, you can begin with positional parms and switch to keyword parms but, not vice versa. Let's look at a few examples:

All Keyword Command Parameter Structure

```
CRTLIB   LIB(liba)  TYPE(*prod)
AUT(*none)  TEXT(*blank)
```

This says create a library called liba as a production type with no special authority granted and no text used as a descriptor.

Positional then Keyword Command Parameter Structure:

CRTLIB   liba   AUT(*none)

This says create a library called liba with no special authority granted.

Quick Look at S/36 OCL - Comparative Purposes

System/36 OCL was always recognized as being one of the easiest to use in the industry. The following short code snippets first show how a program gets loaded and executed using System/36 OCL and then the code is rewritten to use IBM i CL.

S/36 OCL -- Loading a Program Using Three Files

```
// LOAD PGM1
// FILE NAME-APLVND1
// FILE --------------------
// FILE --------------------
// RUN
```

IBM i CL -- Loading a Program Using Three Files

```
CALL PGM1
```

It's night and day. That's how much easier it is to control the action on an IBM i than it ever was on System/3X.

System/3 Copy Program

System/3 was always recognized as an easy to use system, other than in the terminal support area with CCP. One of its hallmarks was that it had a very nice and very flexible copy file program. IBM i has a phenomenally powerful database aware copy file command called CPYF. Let's compare the two for similarities and differences. It's been awhile for me with System/3 OCL but, I remember it pretty well. There are no System/3 Reference Manuals around that I can find so, you can take my word that this is pretty accurate. First I show the System/3 version of copy file and then the IBM i version to make a point on IBM i simplicity and consistency.

System/3 $COPY Utility -- Popular and Powerful for Its Time

```
// LOAD $COPY,F1
// FILE NAME-COPYIN,LABEL-APPVEND,
   UNIT-D1,PACK-ABCDEF
// FILE NAME-COPYO,LABEL-APPVEND1,
   UNIT-D2,PACK-GHIJKL,RECORDS-500
// RUN
// COPYFILE OUTPUT-DISK
// END
```

AS/400 CPYF-- Copies with One Command and Lots of Options

```
CPYF APPVEND APPVEND1 MBROPT(*ADD)
```

On other traditional systems such as the System/3, as shown above, if you wanted to copy a file you would had to give pack, unit, and file name as well as issue other copy file specific commands for options. On IBM i only the from and to files are required in addition to a parameter in which you specify whether you want the incoming records to be added to the existing file or you want all the records in the file to be replaced. IBM i CL is much easier and simpler to use than any other control language.

Before we close out this chapter on CL, let's show a few other CL commands so you can get a better perspective on the consistency and simplicity of CL for IBM i. Remember the verb/ modifier/ noun format notion as you look at these:

Other IBM i CL Commands

Command	Function
CRTLIB MYLIB	Create library named MYLIB
CHGLIB MYLIB TEXT('MYLIB TEXT'),	Add text to MYLIB
DLTLIB LIB(MYLIB)	Delete Library MYLIB
?CRTLIB	Prompt for CRTLIB keyed interactively or in a program calls the system command prompter
WRKSYSSTS	Work With System Status WRK is a prefix (verb) which provides a vehicle for working with an object (display, change, delete, etc.)
WRKACTJOB	Work with Active Jobs displays the status of all active jobs in the system and allows them to be changed.
CRTDUPOBJ	Create Duplicate Object creates duplicates of objects.
RNMOBJ	Rename Object renames objects
GRTOBJAUT	Grant Object Authority Grants a user authority to an object.
WRKSYSVAL	Work with System Values displays a list of the system values and allows the user to select a value for display or change purposes.
*DO, *DATA, *IF, *GOTO, .. etc.	Some CL program operations CL Programs provide additional commands which only make sense in a programming environment. They cannot be used interactively

CL Summary

The bottom line is that this simple and intuitive scripting language for AS/400 heritage systems from System/38 to IBM i has endured the erosion of time and has emerged as even more powerful than when it was developed initially. Only in its functions does CL bear a resemblance to mainframe JCL and System/3X OCL. Neither of these systems perfected the language necessary to direct the heart of the system's function. CL is far more elegant and consistent than either JCL or OCL.

CL has had to evolve over the years, since it is the language that best understands how to work with all objects on the system. As such as objects have been added to support the ever enhanced role of the IBM i operating system, CL has been enhanced to keep pace.

The vast majority of IBM i commands were written by IBM internal developers to perform system level tasks like compiling programs, backing up data, changing system configurations, displaying system object details, or deleting them. Commands are not limited to systems level concerns; however, and the number of commands can be increased by in-house developers.

For example, when a developer finds that IBM has not created the right command yet for a function that the IT shop needs to perform regularly, IBM has provided tooling to give mere mortals the ability to build their own commands. This makes CL even more powerful and even more customizable for the needs of businesses everywhere.

Additionally, all of IBM's commands can be tailored with a command that I just love talking about. It is the "change command" command, CHGCMD. With the collection of IBM's existing commands, the CHGCMD command, and the ability to create commands that do not exist, CL is by far the most powerful and the easiest Control Language to ever grace a computer panel.

Chapter 19   Advanced Computer Science Concepts: Integrated Transaction Processing

Programmer Productivity Is Still Important

In the 1950's through the mid 1970's, most data processing was done in batch. There were no relational databases and there were no fully integrated systems of any kind. All systems were built from the hardware out. Each new piece of hardware that was announced required its own operating system. Since each new piece of hardware required its own OS, all application programs had to be rewritten to mesh with the new operating system.

In the above sentence, I use the term OS. Even the term OS was new in the 1970's. IBM's 1960's operating system was called DOS (disk operating system). When I went to my IBM training in 1969, the DOS operating system, itself, on the IBM System/360 model 30, an expensive system for its day, took just 6 K.

That's not 6 Meg, and it is certainly not 6 Gig. The Disk Operating System was just 6,000 bytes. The one before it that got scrapped (IBM 1401) took even less space. Moreover, application code was mostly written in Assembly Language and each batch program did just a little work. COBOL and RPG had yet to permeate the IT landscape in a big way.

The 1970's ushered in the second decade of programming. As much of an art as we think programming may be today, back then, it was pure art and little science. There were brainiacs in my day who could actually sit at a keypunch and bang out assembler code that worked the first time. In all fairness to the rest of us, they were few and far between and they were clearly geniuses. Few people were talking about programmer productivity.

However, by the time IBM introduced the System/360 in the early 1960's, Big Blue Knew it could not support a build and junk strategy for application code whenever it introduced new hardware.

Preserving IT Shop Programming Investments

There were no hard and fast rules per se. Any rules that might have been followed were ad hoc and built on the fly. So, the idea of programmer productivity was still to come because machines were still far more expensive than people. Still, IBM knew that its customers were getting fed up with starting from scratch every time a new machine came out. More importantly, IBM wanted to create machines that were compatible and thus, their operating systems could be compatible and thus applications programs could be long-lasting. This made logical sense.

Once System/360 came out with its "architecture," it spelled out the new way of working with computers. Build and junk would no longer make it as a computer strategy. Yet, the 24-bit design of System/360, though huge for 1965, would not sustain the line for the long haul. So, IBM mainframes began a trek of incremental improvement with each leap forward in technology having to be tempered by the inventory of older code that had to be compatible and had to be able to use any new technology.

IBM's investment and its customer's investments in mainframe technology, at least according to IBM, could not be compromised. The retrofitting was painful and IBM's mainframe customers paid dearly if they chose to stay in the past by not being able to take advantage of rapid advances in computing. Or, they paid dearly by moving forward with monumental software conversions.

When database technology arrived, first hierarchical and then relational, they were designed by IBM and other companies as add-ons to a base operating system. There were two reasons for this. 1. IBM did not want to change all of its operating systems to incorporate the new technology and 2. IBM did not want to force its customers to move to the new software technology when clearly it would be an effort to make the transition.

So, companies choosing database software, as an example, could theoretically move one application at a time to the new way and not have to start from scratch. No operating system vendor ever scrapped a whole operating system so that a better way could be developed by starting over.

Consequently on all systems, other than IBM i, database software is still a piece parts solution, available from a number of piece parts software vendors. Moreover, just like database, the new way is piece parts, not integration, because it is easier and more profitable for the vendors to sell one product at a time, than a huge, all-inclusive operating system.

Then again, programmer productivity was not as much of an issue back then; but, soon it would become an issue as the accountants got into the act. It was too late for a complete redesign for the mainframe division but, it was clear what the mission would be if a redesign were ever possible.

Programming Became More Productive

Prior to the System/3 operating system, first introduced in 1969, large IT shops had to be content with running COBOL and PL/1. IBM took a stab at creating a new cycle oriented programming language with its 1401 system and this was brought forward with System/360 with slight improvements. The original RPG language was designed to pretend to have the same characteristics as a big electromechanical 402 or 403, or perhaps even an IBM 407 punch card Accounting Machine. Besides COBOL and PL/1 and this primitive RPG, in the 1960's, there were few other options and large computer customers were OK with that. See Figure 19-1 for a look at an IBM 403 Accounting Machine.

Figure 19-1 IBM 403 Accounting Machine

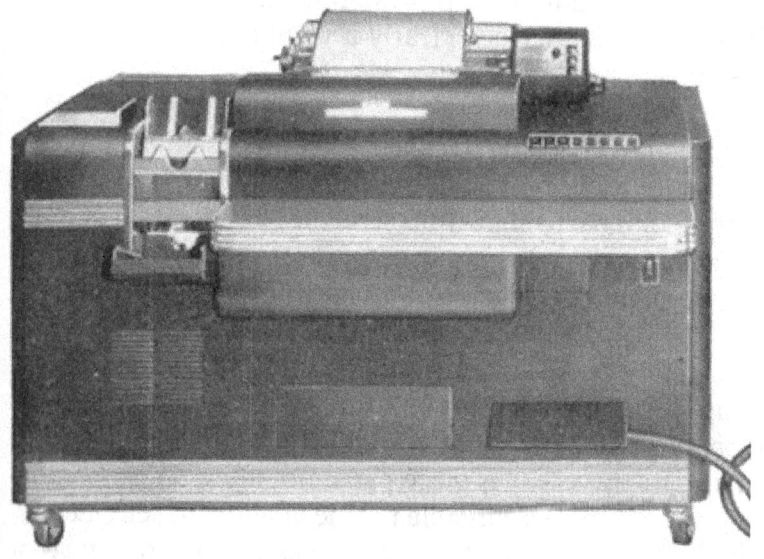

Once programming fully replaced the wired boards of yore, as in the IBM 403 Accounting Machine shown above in Figure 19-1, programmer productivity began to have real meaning. The measurements were crude but, the idea was very right-on. With the 1969 System/3, IBM introduced a substantially more productive language called RPG II and this was the beginning of RPG as a bona-fide business language.

Accountants began to measure the number of lines of code produced by a programmer in a day's work. Programming languages that required more lines of code by definition were therefore less productive than ones requiring less lines. But, programmers got credit for more lines of code with inefficient languages. It was a double edge sword; so, lines of code was a meaningful metric only when using the same programming language.

Early programmers did not like early RPG

COBOL and PL/1 were both very verbose languages and needed many lines of code just to get a full, but basic, program. RPG was always very efficient in terms of lines of code but, many old time programmers rejected it because early RPG was not procedural enough. Instead of the programmers painstakingly mapping out the input > process > output cycle in a program, RPG provided its own cycle. Programmers did not need to spend lines of code on the basic cycle.

Instead of controlling the cycle, RPG programmers had to learn how to make the RPG cycle work for them in order to make the business more productive. The brainiacs never liked RPG because it made programming simple. Most of the gurus of the day liked knowing the internals of computers and using this knowledge to write great algorithms for systems. They really did not like writing business programs in the first place.

With the System/3, RPG had become a very good batch programming language. The language style known as RPG II was much easier than the mainframe version of RPG, which even today looks a lot like the original IBM 1401 version than the IBM i version. By the time IBM in Rochester, Minnesota introduced the System/38, it had perfected the RPG language even further so that it warranted another new moniker, RPG III.

This language was phenomenal and we've got a lot more to say about it. Not only were the operations enhanced but, it was written to take advantage of the advances in OS technology, such as the integrated database and integrated transaction processing facilities. With the integrated transaction capabilities that we are discussing in this chapter, IBM i's RPG at the RPG III and RPG IV level are the most comprehensive, and easiest, to use in a business programming language. Anybody who tells you differently has never worked with RPG. COBOL is the next productive business language. When using an IBM i box, both of these languages benefit substantially from the principle of **Integrated Transaction Processing.**

Bill Gates Hates RPG

As an aside, it may help to better understand why the RPG language is pooh poohed by the academicians and the computer scientists. Being a Business / IT professor, myself, at Marywood University gives me a unique perspective on this dilemma. In a word, RPG is *practical*. In other words it is not theoretical. It is purposeful for business, though not totally multi-purpose in nature.

That is to say, you would not use RPG or COBOL to draw dancing bears or create spinning globes on a display panel or a Web page. I miss the point of why a business person would want a programmer doing that type of nonsense anyway. Just as many academicians want academic freedom over many aspects of reality-- even those that do not apply, computer scientists in academia and outside academia want computer freedom. It's that simple.

Languages written to support business productivity do not fit this model of free thought. Bill Gates is not a business programmer now and he never was. He absolutely hates RPG.

A Bill Gates Story

One of the greatest hybrid computer scientists and marketing geniuses of all time is Bill Gates. He is quite a guy. I bought him a "ginger ale" in a 12 oz. brown bottle one evening in

Florida years ago, when he was 31-years old, and I learned a lot about how he thinks. OK, it was a bottled beer!

When OS/2, an IBM OS originally written by Microsoft for IBM was introduced in 1986, there was a strong rumor that IBM was about to bring out an RPG compiler for its new OS. It never arrived. My perspective is that if it had arrived, perhaps even OS/2 would be a successful operating system in small businesses today.

Back in the late 1980's, Bill Gates, Microsoft's current Chairman and founder of the company, told me over that "ginger ale" that I would never see a Microsoft-built RPG compiler. He kept his word. He said he hated RPG. "It's that language with those... indicators," he told me. As a true computer scientist, he just hated the language. Hating RPG was in his blood.

The C language and the C++ language and the Microsoft developed Visual Basic language have all been pushed by Gates because they were "more functional" than RPG. The fact is that RPG was at too high a level and his languages operated at levels closer to the machine. Bill Gates did not have to worry about rules. Again, computer scientists like languages in which they can do everything unimpeded – even crash the machine if need be.

None can deny that Bill Gates' Windows wares have more than their fair share of crashes. None would deny that Bill Gates is also the master marketer. He outsmarted IBM in PCs and emerged a super billionaire in the software marketplace. It is ironic though, that as much as Gates hated RPG, for many years, Microsoft used AS/400s with RPG to run its business.

Through his superior marketing, most new computer scientists coming from colleges today believe in the Gates notion of computing – via C, C++, C#, and Visual BASIC. Most also even believe that it's OK for computers to crash as often as PCs do. It is not only OK, it is expected. Having worked for IBM for many years, I know that Big Blue never thought it was OK for hardware or software to crash and the IBM Company worked hard to prevent it across all its platforms.

Never being a business programmer himself, Bill Gates either does not understand or does not want to understand that the two most used business languages of all time, RPG and COBOL, are well used in business because they are easy to use, stable, and they are far better suited for the job than computer science style languages. From my own conversation with Mr. Gates, I don't think that would matter. He rejected RPG simply because he does not like it.

Many in the IT industry know that for years Microsoft used AS/400 vintage machines to run its business. At the time of the "ginger ale," that we shared at the cocktail table, Mr. Gates did not need all 14 of the largest AS/400s to run his business, though eventually, Microsoft got so big that they needed 14 AS/400s to keep it all going.

Those 14 AS/400s were not running Microsoft software. They were running ERP application software that was written in RPG and/or COBOL to assure that order fulfillment and the rest of their ERP never failed for Microsoft. The old phrase, "do as I say and not as I do," comes to mind.

Transaction Processing Software

Regardless of how good RPG and COBOL were in the early 1970's for batch processing, the new wave of video terminals that found their way to business desktops in the mid to late 1970's demanded even more than these business languages could naturally provide. IBM answered the call for terminal support early on for mainframes with its Customer Information Control System (CICS).

CICS is a large transaction processing monitor that companies can purchase for mainframe computers. It is a separate add-on to the operating system that enables interactive transaction processing and multi-user terminal support on mainframes.

On small System/3s at roughly the same time, IBM developed the Communication Control Program (CCP), another transaction processing monitor, which brought a lower level of transaction processing than CICS to the System/3. As a small business facility, this package was available as an add-on for free from IBM. But, the company normally sold a lot more System/3 hardware if a customer chose to implement System/3 applications using CCP.

The major transaction processing program for non-IBM platforms today is clearly Tuxedo, which came to life in 1983 at Bell labs and was perfected by 1989. It is now marketed by BEA Systems and it does a good job. It is just not as easy to use as the grated transaction processing on IBM i

Programmers writing for CICS, CCP or for Tuxedo have many more jobs to do in a given program than merely sending and receiving screen panels to and from terminals or PCs pretending to be terminals. For example, the programs must check to make sure that the screens reach the users' terminals and also that the data that is returned is valid.

Such error checking and correction adds many lines of code to transaction processing programs. Terminals are foreign to all other system compilers so, unlike normal disk or tape support in the file section supported by business languages, there is no support for terminals. Thus, non-IBM i programming languages are written to be completely unaware of terminals. With IBM i, it is much easier to write interactive transaction programs, since the terminal is supported as a natural device, and thus it is as easy to work with as disk or tape or even a printer device.

To talk to CICS or CCP or Tuxedo, a programmer must invoke a call to the TP monitor and pass to it arguments directing it to perform a specific operation such as "send a panel" or "receive a panel." Compilers do not support CICS or CCP or Tuxedo or any terminal monitor.

In the case of Tuxedo for example, the compiler writers and the TP monitor are written by different companies. So, compilers do not support Tuxedo naturally but through the same mechanism that all foreign programs are supported -- external calls to APIs. Thus, in this environment, it takes lots more than simple Reads and Writes to display a simple panel or to manage an interactive conversation with a user terminal.

The Beginning of Integrated Transaction Processing

During the development of the System/38, the notion of a workstation (WORKSTN) as a device was brought forth in Rochester, Minnesota. Even before the System/38 was ready to go, in 1977 IBM used the in-process work for the System/38 as the basis for System/34 and its natural way of handling terminal workstations. The company announced and delivered a "WORKSTN" device capability in the RPG Compiler that changed the nature of interactive computing forever on IBM small business systems. The IBM mainframe world was consumed with CICS at the time and thus, it never adopted the integrated approach. There still is time...

Programmers from System/3 who had been toiling with the rigors of CCP (or even CICS and later Tuxedo) were amazed at how simple it was to work with the integrated compilers on this new IBM System/34. In 1978, when IBM announced the System/38, the notion of a WORKSTN device was perfected with the introduction of the *display file* object.

Workstation as a Natural Compiler Device

Just as a tape monitor is not needed or a card monitor or a printer monitor or a disk monitor is not needed in compiler theory, since every compiler is built to talk to those batch devices natively, the IBM Rochester Software Engineering team chose to eliminate the need for a terminal monitor in their operating system and compiler design. In other words, there would be no need for CICS, CCP, or Tuxedo type packages on IBM's new small business machines.

To accomplish this technologically groundbreaking achievement, they wrote the operating system and the compilers to treat a database as a natural disk device, and they used the same medicine to treat a terminal / workstation as a natural device. Anybody in the press paying real attention to what was going on would have inducted these people immediately into the Computer Architecture / Design Hall of Fame.

The IBM Rochester team chose to treat a terminal as a real device that should not and did not require a complex monitor package. It had never been done before and other than the IBM System/38, AS/400 and IBM i lineage machines, it has never been done again. One might say that they integrated the TP monitor such as CICS or CCP or Tuxedo, within the system itself, rendering the monitor invisible. By rendering the monitor invisible, they rendered the systems programmers needed to keep those monitors alive invisible and so companies saved money on people resources.

Workstation as a Natural System Device

Actually as powerful a statement that the last paragraph makes, it is an understatement. IBM did a lot more starting with the System/34 and the Company continues these capabilities with IBM i. IBM Rochester first built the operating system so that it could work with non-standard devices such as terminals/ workstations and databases. Then the compiler writers simply used the operating support built for those devices / facilities, to reach them naturally through the OS. Today, for example, a user can start an IBM i session from any PC or workstation device attached to the system either locally, over communication lines, or even over the Internet. The operating system speaks to the device naturally.

Since the operating system was built to support terminal workstations, no special monitor was needed and the compiler writers were able to provide natural links to the operating system to support these devices directly within the compiler. It literally made programming for interactive display terminals a piece of cake.

It was so easy to write programs for this capability that IBM i shops have been using terminal workstation devices and PCs effectively with IBM Rochester products since 1977.

One has to ask why after 30 years no other system, not even the mainframe, has been retrofitted to permit workstations as natural devices to the system and to the compilers. It sure made life lots easier for IBM i developers and that's why the loyalty factor is so high in the IBM i community.

There are many rumors that IBM is about to do the same thing for Web Browsers and it would have the same historic and marketing impact. Can you imagine not having to deal with the "fifty ways to leave your lover" as found in the Web Development tools of today?

WORKSTN Display File Genius

Unlike the System/34 WORKSTN device, the upgrading of the WORKSTN device as a display file with the System/38 brought along support for multiple users as an innate operating system feature. In other words, when coding for interactive users with a System/34, a programmer had to know how many users, at one time, would be working with the same interactive program. When a program was coded for the System/34 and later the System/36, the programmer needed to designate it as a multiple requester terminal (MRT) program or a single requester terminal program (SRT).

Each SRT request caused a program to be loaded. Program loads cause system performance overhead on all systems. The MRT minimized the program load hit since just the first MRT request caused the program to be loaded. Subsequent requests permitted the new terminal user to be attached to the same user program already executing in memory. In the System/34 MRT environment, the programmer was responsible for keeping track of the data of the various users who were using the program at any point in time. Yes, this caused work, but not as much work as on those systems (Tuxedo and CICS) in which it took lots of work just to talk to the device.

With the display files and the further tailoring of the notion of a "job structure" on the System/38, all programs had the benefits of being MRTs without programmers having to code for multiple users. All IBM i programs are multi-thread by nature. The operating system keeps one copy of a program in memory to be used by all, and it also provides a set of working storage called a process access group for each user who signs on to that program.

All variables and unique processes are in the user's job structure and thus, it does not matter how many users call a particular program, each gets his or her own unique environment, while using the same re-entrant code copy of the program in memory. For something so advanced internally, programmers and users are oblivious to it happening. The management of thousands of users all connected to the same program is something that IBM i does and nobody needs to worry about.

If WORKSTN files made System/34 a cake walk, and to tell the truth, they did, the innate multi user facility of display files in each compiled program added a thick glob of whip cream icing to the cake. There is no easier way to code for interactive transaction processing than to use the integrated transaction processing built into the all-everything operating system. There will be no easier way of sending out and receiving Web pages when IBM chooses to release this often requested facility.

Figure 19-2 RPGIV Version of Advanced Hello World Program

```
1    FPANEL      CF    E                WORKSTN
2    FLANGUAGE   IF    E                K DISK
3    D ERRMSG          C                         CONST('HELLO WORLD TRANSLAT-
4    D                                           ION NOT FOUND, TRY A-
5    D                                           GAIN')
6    C      *IN99             DOWEQ     *OFF
7    C                        EXFMT     SCREEN1
8    C      LANGUA            IFEQ      'END'
9    C                        LEAVE
10   C                        ENDIF
11   C      LANGUA            CHAIN     LANGUAGE                      90
12   C      *IN90             IFEQ      *ON
13   C                        MOVEL     ERRMSG       MESSAG
14   C                        ITER
15   C                        ENDIF
16   C                        ENDDO
17   C                        MOVE      *ON          *INLR
```

RPG Coding for Interactive Work

Take a look at the first line in Figure 17-3, repeated above as Figure 19-2, to see how simple it continues to be to code the WORKSTN display file in an RPG program. Inside of the file named PANEL, in line 1, is a screen panel defined as SCREEN1. This is not needed until line 7 of the program. In line 7 of the program, you can see an operation called EXFMT. Next to it you see the word SCREEN1. This very powerful EXFMT (execute format) operation sends the panel named SCREEN1 to the user, and then puts the program to sleep.

When the user presses a function key or an ENTER key, the program wakes up and processes the returned information from the display screen. Because this is so easy, the life of a programmer is such that when using IBM I, they can concentrate on the organization's "business logic", rather than worrying about bits and bytes.

Yes, that EXFMT operation is both a write to a workstation and a read back. No other compiler in history has had ease of use facilities such as this. That's why programmers using the all-everything operating system have always been the most productive in the universe. They still are and that's a fact.

eCommerce Transaction Processing

With a simple WORKSTN file, IBM eliminated the need for a major cost component and a major customer programming effort, as would have been required with CICS, CCP, or Tuxedo to support interactive terminals. Today, on all other systems to support transaction over the Web, a Web monitor program, such as Bea's Weblogic, or Microsoft's .NET, Apache's Jakarta TomCat, or IBM's WebSphere, is absolutely a necessity. This is a very similar notion to the requirement for CICS and CCP and Tuxedo as much as thirty years ago.

There is no eCommerce transaction processing engine built into any system today, including the all-everything operating system. Though IBM i is staged for it to be announced, it is not here yet. For the all-everything OS, the solutions today for Web transaction processing are Jakarta Tomcat and WebSphere Server and PHP, just as with every other system.

To be fair, IBM does have facilities such as Webfacing, iSeries Access for the Web, and the Host Access Transformation Services (HATS), which permit programs written to the workstation interface to be usable on the Web with minimal alteration. IBM i is clearly ready and well positioned for a major compiler and OS enhancement when IBM is ready to bring this needed function to the IBM i masses. Just as IBM was the first and only company to initiate integrated display file transaction processing, with a WEBSTN (Web station) file, the RPG and COBOL compilers that today work with terminals can simply be retrofitted to work with Web Pages and browsers without even touching the program logic.

Since this is the natural way for an all-everything integrated operating system and an all-everything machine to talk to devices through its languages, I would expect that IBM is working on this methodology as we speak. I hope to see it within the next operating system release or the one after that. It makes sense.

In the meantime, of course, the all-everything machine is positioned well for the Web by being able to use the same or similar Web transaction processing monitors as all other servers out there. Add HATS, iSeries Access for the Web, and WebFacing to the mix and the future is almost here today.

The future for integrated transaction processing from workstations and web-stations on the IBM i box is bright indeed.

Chapter 20 All-Everything Operating System: Extra Ingredients

Integration is # 1

As we have discussed the lineage of IBM i, the all-everything OS, in this book, we examined the history of the hardware and software and the many names, especially those which recently adorned the finest machine and operating system ever built. IBM i is the part of the new IBM Power System with Power 6 technology that gives the machine its AS/400 heritage and personality. And that little "i" in IBM i has always stood for integration. It is the linchpin that provides IBM i its power and elegance.

IBM i Historical Review

Along the way to IBM i, in 1978, IBM first turned its Rochester Labs internal Pacific Project into the IBM System/38, the most advanced system of all time, and it named the operating system simply Control Program Facility (CPF). Then, in 1988, IBM took its Silverlake project and created the Application System/400 (AS/400) and the operating system was re-christened as OS/400. When IBM completely changed the hardware in 1995 from 48-bit CISC to 64-bit RISC, Big Blue chose not to touch the names, even though the system had completely changed.

In 2000, along with all other IBM servers that were renamed, the AS/400 became known as the eServer iSeries 400. This was the first time IBM had chosen the little "i" as part of the nomenclature signifying that the iSeries strength was its integration.

In 2004, when the Power 4 chip gave way to the Power 5 chip, IBM introduced its IBM i5 or simply the i5 and the Company changed the name of the operating system also, this time to i5/OS. In 2006, across the corporation, IBM got religion about the word "system" and got sour on the notion of "servers." During this change, the physical box name changed to the System i and the operating system name remained as i5/OS.

System p Historical Review

From about the year 2000 onward, IBM in Rochester built the frames and all the physical pieces of both "i" boxes and the "p' boxes. At about the same time, the popular IBM RS/6000 Unix machine was renamed as the pSeries. In 2004, it became the p5 and then in 2006, along with the rest of IBM's former servers, it became a system, the System p. The "i" in System i as previously noted was for integration and the "p" in System "p" was for its Power processor heritage.

Powerful RISC processors were always part of the p line from back when it became IBM's second commercial RISC system. The Risc Technology PC or RT PC had preceded the RS/6000 to the line a number of years earlier. That is the lineage of the IBM System p. In 2006, the System p was IBM's premiere system for Unix computing as the Company promoted its own AIX operating system, as well as Linux and an experimental version of Open Solaris.

All of these are either Unix clones or derivatives. Open Solaris is a derivative of Sun's Unix platform known as Solaris. This is an open source version (free) of Solaris that is still in the experimental stage with IBM's Power System lineup.

In 2008, IBM added full support for Unix (AIX) and Linux to the System i machine and thus IBM had in essence eliminated the System p. Since the new System i machine could run Unix or Linux as easily as it could run i5/OS, the name System i no longer made any sense. It was no longer appropriate to bundle i5/OS with universal hardware and call it System i. It would be a little disingenuous to do so.

The IBM Power System -- IBM i, Unix, Linux

So, IBM got its naming book out again and this time the company came up with a hardware platform name that is operating system agnostic. The IBM Power System is the name of the new hardware. It took most of its new name from the name of the chip family upon which it is based, the IBM Power 6 chip line.

Since the engine on the new hardware was no longer based on Power 5 technology, the idea of having i5/OS as the OS name for the "integrated" operating system also needed to be reexamined. With the entire hardware / software line moving to the Power 6 chip, the little "i" still made sense but the "5" for Power 5 had to go.

Rather than start over and re-name the integrated OS as the The Business Operating System or as The Integrated Operating System, IBM chose to change the OS name to IBM i. Though its full logo suggests IBM i for Business, IBM has asked members of the press to use "i" or "IBM i" as the new name for the operating system.

It may seem that "i"-style integration slipped away when the operating system and the hardware were separated in April, 2008. However, this is nowhere close to the truth. The all-everything operating system, IBM I, is no less integrated and no less effective using the IBM Power System as a hardware base than it was using the System i hardware. In fact, since the IBM Power System with Power 6 is more powerful than the Power 5 in System i, the platform actually got a big boost from the change.

The IBM Power System has all the capabilities of the System i and even more as the Power 6 chip is substantially faster and more capable than the Power 5. Moreover, IBM enhanced the components and peripheral devices with its 2008 hardware offering, and so, the Power System is more capable for IBM i and it is also more capable for AIX and Linux. The Power System with IBM i, overall, is actually more integrated, faster, and more functional than the System i. And, that is good for IBM i, not bad.

Learning IBM i and Other Operating Systems

Gaining technical proficiency in a platform is something that takes time. Those technically proficient in AIX / Linux on System p have no problem moving to AIX or Linux on the Power System. The operating system names and the hardware names were never really connected on the "p" platform. Those technically proficient in i5/OS have no problem moving to IBM i on the IBM Power System either.

However, there is a sense of something unsettling about the move for the former System i / AS/400 heritage community. The hardware and the operating system had been connected by a tight umbilical cord for over thirty years and now; to some, it appears that IBM has broken the cord. There are a number of stalwarts in the IBM i heritage community who are concerned that The Power System boxes replacing the System i boxes means that it is the beginning of the end of AS/400-style computing. They are concerned that the only system in IBM that was designed from the outset for programmer and user productivity through functional integration was being sun-setted by the company that brought it to life.

As an IBM i heritage lifer with many side trips to other platforms, I can say that for a while, I too had misgivings about what IBM had done. I am OK now because I have figured out it makes sense. Try this on. If IBM had announced that "the i5/OS operating system was enhanced to run on the Intel x64 and Xeon platform," in addition to System i, I would have been elated.

Most in the IBM i community would feel the same. Removing IBM i from its hardware dependency and onto a platform that is more universal only serves to make the operating system more recognized. Separating the operating system from the hardware, as IBM did in its 2008 platform changes, is the first step in making this happen. So, overall, I think this is a very good move.

Cream rises to the top. IBM i now is an operating system among operating systems and it can be compared as such. It now has its own opportunity to rise to the top rather than be homogenized, along with all of the other same-ole same-ole operating systems. Point by point, it is the best of the best. It is the all-everything operating system. If the trade press takes another look at IBM i when it compares operating systems, it should fare quite well.

With just a little more tweaking, such as a native browser based GUI interface, which I have been told is in the works, as the song goes, "who could ask for anything more." Right now, IBM i is staged for great things. The all-everything operating system is free at last. And, it still is integrated.

Who Could Ask for Anything More?

IBM was once a hardware company with other businesses. Today it is a highly successful services and software company with many other businesses. In fact, it is IBM's new business makeup that has enabled it to survive in a down economy while its hardware / software competitors are flailing.

Hardware happens to be one of IBM's other businesses today as it represents just about 25% of the Company's revenue. So, when IBM's AS/400 heritage clients plead to IBM to make their OS more known to the masses, IBM cannot do that. It is against its successful business model, no matter how much platform zealots want IBM to market IBM i. IBM cannot favor IBM i over its other offerings because it would be bad for business. IBM is a business serving many constituencies and it has chosen to serve them all equally, for the benefit of the corporation.

Big Blue does not highlight one set of IBM products against another set to prop up sales. By now, IBM knows, or certainly should know, that it has the best operating system in the world in IBM i. I certainly did not have to write a book to tell IBM that. IBM knows it. As a business, the fact that the Company makes lots more money with z/OS than IBM i is a good reason not to suggest mainframe clients move to IBM i. IBM has been this way forever and we all must remember that the IBM Company, even in these tough economic straits, continues to be very successful. I would expect IBM to do nothing less than what is best for the Company.

Competing Products Is an IBM Way of Life

IBM history is replete with examples of the best never being permitted to take over the whole banana. For example, Big Blue almost always had two or more competing mainframe operating systems. For the longest time, it also had two or more competing mainframe hardware lines.

IBM's first big operating system was a derivative of the 1964-introduced IBM System/360. Its name, at the time, was simply Disk Operating System (DOS). The other was a derivative of the 1970-introduced, System/370 Operating System (OS). Yes, its name was simply OS meaning

Operating System with no adjectives. IBM viewed this as the beat-all and end-all operating system of the day. No other operating system in the early 1970's could come close to OS for raw system function and power. The IBM Company's forte, from day one, was building phenomenal operating systems. Just look at IBM i for proof of that.

Before the move to z/OS after the millennium change, the name iterations of these two operating systems (DOS and OS) brought forth VSE/ESA and MVS/XA. I don't profess to know much about either anymore but I know more than I probably should. In a nutshell, VSE came from DOS and MVS came from OS. IBM liked having more than one of everything. It never tried to replace all of its VSE accounts with MVS even though MVS was its best offering.

Small Mainframe, Big Mainframe

IBM Systems Engineers (SEs) in the Branch Offices in the early 1980's felt that they had gotten sandbagged, if they needed to work with the purposefully primitive VSE mainframe OS while their peers worked on MVS. When IBM eliminated GSD, for example, and formed NMD for small accounts and NAD for large accounts in the US, some former MVS SEs got to work for NMD. Unfortunately for them, they had been permanently sandbagged as NMD could sell only small mainframes, System/38s and System/36s.

Most very large businesses ran MVS and few very large businesses ran VSE for this very reason. The two operating systems were like night and day. One was rich in function and the other was always purposely limited. One cost a ton and the other was affordable by smaller organizations.

IBM could have promulgated its best OS, MVS to the smaller levels of hardware and provided a one-time conversion and it would have been fine. However, Big Blue wanted two operating systems at a minimum for its mainframe accounts and the Company had a big aversion to conversions that started way back in 1965. As you may recall, in the mid-

1970's, IBM had blocked the introduction of its best operating system design ever, known as FS for Future System, so its customers could avoid a conversion.

In IBM, the Best Must Win for Itself

So, it is easy to understand fully why IBM does not promote IBM i as its beat-all and end-all OS. First of all, as a business, IBM brings in the bulk of its money from MVS and VSE accounts, their associated hardware, middleware, and services.

So, why promote IBM i? Most of the mainframe money comes from software and from services. Having an operating system in the stable such as IBM i, that requires less piece parts software and less services is a concession that IBM makes every day to the IBM i heritage shops by permitting IBM i to exist and then by funding it further development.

Making the Best OS Ever

Pushing one IBM product over another is not how IBM prefers to conduct its business. A rogue Laboratory in Rochester Minnesota better than thirty years ago got IBM into this predicament. IBM had never decided at the corporate level, that it was going to produce a beat-all, end-all system with the best operating system of all time. Computer scientists in Rochester, Minnesota however, had other ideas.

Driven by their desire to achieve the limits of what was possible in computer science at the time, with Dr. Frank Soltis in the lead, Rochester's Scientists and Engineers created the IBM System/38 in 1978. Their work brought major league operating system innovations to IBM for the first and last time in a package that was also easy to use. The successor operating systems from then to now, including IBM i have enhanced the legacy. From a technology standpoint, from 1978 until today, it is clearly the best work IBM has ever done.

IBM never intended to permit this system from the Midwest to become a dominant part of its computing landscape. Companies like Costco, Nintendo of America, and Enterprise Car Rental, and of course the Casinos would have been IBM mainframe accounts if they were not able to find more than they needed in the system that never should have been built.

Yes, in the mid 1980's IBM tried to kill the System/38 with its Fort Knox project and several other times, but it could not. It needed it to fight and win against DEC and the other minicomputer vendors. When it did its thing by the early 1990's and DEC was gone and Wang was gone and Data General was gone, IBM had a touch of buyer's remorse but, it was too late. IBM i continues on and it is better than ever.

IBM i never really fit well in IBM's synergy plans. Neither do Unix and Linux and Windows for that matter. IBM is very smart, however, and it knows well that it cannot exist today without Unix and Linux and it also knows that its large IBM i customers, with 95% penetration in the Fortune 500 would not stand for IBM diminishing the Power System with IBM i in any way. So, not only does IBM keep AIX, Linux, and IBM i as products in its collection of operating systems, the Company continues to invest heavily in all of them.

Business, Not a Computer Science Contest

So, for its part, IBM does its best to support all of its all-everything OS customers, but it is clearly against its business model to try to convince the world that IBM i is the all-everything OS or even that it might be a good choice. The fact is that IBM is not running a computer science contest. It is running a business.

If it were running the former, the contest would already be over and IBM i would have already won hands-down. IBM i loyalists, such as myself, would continue being miffed if there were such a contest and IBM i won; because, IBM as a business would be hard-pressed to publish the results. Since it is running a business and not conducting a contest, and IBM well knows what it is doing, the Company continues to be successful. It finds no need to maintain its success by taking sides.

If you did not know IBM's agnostic stance regarding the members of its system product line before you read this book, now you know. IBM just does not make a big fuss about its outstanding technology. As hard as it is to believe, Big Blue is concerned that taking sides would actually be bad for business.

Having said all that and having given IBM its due for supporting IBM i with investment dollars as it continues to do, I am thankful and so are many other AS/400 heritage loyalists. And, yes, we know that if Corporate IBM ever changed it stance on taking sides, the still revolutionary IBM i all-everything operating system would be its flagship.

The Old Stuff in Review

As we discussed in the nineteen chapters that preceded this, our second to last chapter, IBM i developers have many reasons for liking the operating system. Most of them revolve around the word, productivity. They like getting things done for their respective businesses and IBM i helps them get things done. It does not get in the way.

Advanced Technology Has Its Advantages

IBM i developers, for example, do not write their programs thinking that they are operating at a high level machine interface. Yet, they are. They are not consciously aware of the 128-bit pointers in the operating system permitting objects to be addressed in a huge, almost never ending single level store continuum. Yet they are there. Moreover, they pay no attention to the fact that data really is spread out on numerous A, B, C, D, E etc... drives, since the system handles all that. Yet, that's where the data resides.

They are also not concerned about the innate security of the system, whether rendered by the residue of the System/38's revolutionary "capability based addressing" or the C2 level security inherent in the new operating systems or what Dr. Frank Soltis likes to call the principle of "adoption of authority." Just like everything else, security is just in there and developers take it for granted.

There is something to say about the object-based nature of the IBM i, all-everything OS. Yet, again developers do not have to be schooled in object orientation to use the system effectively. You may know from this book or elsewhere that on Unix and Windows systems, everything is a file, even if it is a program or a Job queue or a print queue.

On IBM i, programmers are not wrapped up all day concerned about everything being an object, even though on IBM i this is not only good, it is lots better than the file system implementations on all other operating systems.

The IBM i objects all have the computer science standard structure that would cause even those with CS degrees to take notice that the objects managed by IBM i are real. They have built-in persistence and garbage collection and all that they need to persevere.

Developers on IBM i find a high level library structure, and another structure as part of the base system that permits Unix applications to run alongside IBM i applications, without the requirement for a Unix operating system. The PASE environment is described later in this chapter. This is another phenomenal feature of IBM i.

What about PC Files with IBM i?

In addition to supporting Unix, IBM created a storage structure that is even more universal. They call it the Integrated File System or simply the IFS. Programmers can use the IFS to hold Windows-like file directories and files when they use the system as a peer file server or they can choose to use it to store html/ xml files for Web access. So, in addition to the more productive library structure, IBM i can support any type of structure that you can throw at it.

How about some Java!

Developers on IBM i are, for the most part, quite spoiled because, whenever they want something, it seems to already be there. For example, Java compatibility is implemented through a native port of the Sun Java virtual machine and many suggest that the IBM i ports at 32-bit and 64-bits are Java's best implementations.

Did you say Database?

Additionally, on IBM i, programmers need not care about other unique integrated features of the operating system such as the RDBMS, now known as DB2 for i. They get to use it with no strings attached. Though the database is not open source, it is free with the operating system. Developers also take for granted the high level CL language; the integration of the compilers into the database and workstation mix, and they especially do not care about the travails of transaction processing with an external TP monitor because all of that is a natural and built-in with IBM i.

Best Business Function in any OS

IBM i developers write their programs thinking that all operating systems should have already advanced to the same level as IBM i. Why would any IBM i developer think that they have not? After all, every other operating system has had more than thirty years to catch up.

IBM i developers are more business oriented than computer science oriented. They write code to solve business problems. They don't want to reinvent computer science solutions every time they need to access a file or a workstation. They do not want to work hard for the sake of computer science. They want to work smart using the best that computer science has to offer, in the form of IBM i.

They love IBM i and they know anybody who gave it the "once over" would feel as they do.

Pass the Menu Please

Besides all these notions that many IBM i developers take for granted, IBM i also includes a natural menu-driven interface, multi-user support and full OS support for any number of workstation devices that you may choose to use -- either on local connections, high speed Ethernet LANS, WANS or the Internet. And, of course, they take for granted the support for natural displays and printers, all wrapped up in a secure, tight package that is just at home on the Web as it is in the home office.

Free Web Facilities

On top of the items needed to run a great in-house operation, IBM provides for free with IBM i, its mainframe and AIX-class IBM WebSphere Application Server. Though it is not integrated per se, it is pre-installed so no SysGen is required for WebSphere and servlet server support. The leading Web server in the industry, Apache, also comes shipped with the base operating system. It's ready to work without any configuration.

I have toyed a little bit with WebSphere on IBM i and I can tell you that it works fine for those that like the Java environment. It is as good as it gets. From 2000 to 2005, I wrote eight books on WebSphere showing how it can be nicely integrated into anybody's AS/400 heritage environment.

Looking deeper into the *goodie* bag for IBM i developers, you will quickly see there is more than just WebSphere. There are also tools that make WebSphere come to life and make the Web as natural an interface as the green screen environment. WebSphere has three major offerings for IBM i that provide natural Web interfaces to the user depending on how they want to connect. These are as follows:

(1) iSeries Access for the Web, a quick way of accessing the AS/400 from your browser, using a client server tool,

(2) WebFacing, a tool that converts green screens into attractive Web pages using cascading style sheets (CSS) templates to add the right level of pizzazz and

(3) Host Application Transformation Services (HATS) which does basically the same as WebFacing without the need to pre-convert the display panels

IBM has no real reason to want the IBM i community to do anything but use WebSphere at the Internet / Web developer level. WebSphere also works for AIX and Linux, and for Mainframes and so. The IBM support for IBM i permits the "i" community to work with the same tools and packages as the other operating systems using the world's most powerful Java application servlet server, WebSphere.

PHP and MySQL for Me

Despite IBM's own business desires in the WebSphere area, the fact is that many IBM i clients are small and can benefit from the plethora of open source Web applications available for PHP on the Internet. Over the last several years I have worked with a number of my clients to bring PHP and MySQL to their shops. During this period, I have written eight books on PHP and I can attest that the environment works well on IBM i. In fact, in early 2009, IBM announced that it had integrated PHP with IBM i and that this powerful scripting environment, along with MySQL, would be shipped with every IBM i system.

IBM arranged with Zend several years ago to bring its award winning PHP to the IBM i platform. IBM now ships this with every IBM i 6.1 version free of charge. This is just another manifestation of IBM doing what is best for its loyal IBM i constituents.

Check out [http://www.zend.com/en/products/core/for-i5os Zend Core for i5/OS] to get a perspective of what is current regarding PHP on IBM i. If you just received IBM i 6.1, like the spaghetti ad, it is in there. You can just begin to use it. PHP uses the native port of the Apache Web server to bring its applications to the IBM i community. It really is neat.

Don't forget that there is now a DB2 for i storage engine for MySQL. Wait 'til you see how that catches on.

Another Look at the Machine Interface

At a programming level it may not be something that your everyday programmer cares about, but it does say something about the power of integration in IBM i. Unlike some other virtual-machine architectures in which the virtual instructions are interpreted at runtime, costing the CPU plenty of cycles that could have been used for more productive purposes, IBM i's machine interface instructions are never interpreted and that means that all code runs better.

To the user, this appears in faster response times or batch jobs completing sooner. To get this done consistently, IBM interjected an intermediate compile time step in which the MI instructions get recoded into the processor's instruction set as the final step in compilation. In addition to metadata, IBM packs a lot of worthwhile components into the compiled object, including both the high level MI instructions and the low level executable machine instructions.

Perhaps you can see the trick. This is how IBM i application objects that may be compiled on one processor family, such as the AS/400 CISC 48-bit processors, could be moved to the next generation processor, such as a RISC based IBM Power System with a 64-bit chip without requiring a re-compilation. In fact, in this environment, the shop does not even have to find its source program libraries.

The trick, of course, is that the application object (in MI instructions) is saved in the older "metadata." When that object is restored onto the new platform, the OS discards the old machine instructions and it re-encapsulates the TIMI instructions into those required for the new processor.

Pointers to Excellence

As a computer science buff myself, with my very own degree in Data Processing from King's College, in Wilkes-Barre, PA, at a time when only King's, Penn State, and Temple were offering such degrees in PA, I like to point out that IBM i's instruction set defines all pointers as 128-bit. That's a pretty wide pointer. Since the pointers are a fabrication at the MI level, they can be made to be 256 or bigger some day in the future. Some might call pointers addresses; but, since they do not exist at the machine level, pointers seem to be a good term for them.

The 128-bit notion was in the original IBM System/38 of 1978 and CPF was aware of every one of those bits. It's only gotten better over time. Moving to Power processors, there are 16 additional hardware bits (from System/38's 48) with which to work. With capability based addressing taking 32-bits of the System/38 pointer, it never really had all 128-bits for addressing but then again, it did not need them. Virtual addresses in the 64-bit range are already humungous in size.

I no longer suggest that anything is so big that you'll never need the large size. I learned my personal lesson years ago. I bought a 16K PC in 1981. The max sized PC available at the time was 64K. In my early IBM years, I had worked with 8K System/3 card systems and 12K System/3 model 6 boxes and so 16K seemed like a lot to me so I did not go for the 64K of memory. I wondered why anybody would want such an oversized PC. I now know that humungous today is not necessarily humungous tomorrow as tomorrow may bring another need. Yet, 64-bits is an awful lot of address space for today and tomorrow.

The Library Has All the Information

The IBM i all-everything OS includes an extensive library-based operating system. In addition to the natural library structure, the IBM i OS can also manage virtual partitions. These can support additional copies of IBM i or they can run other operating systems such as Linux and/or Unix. This is gee-whizz stuff for sure and IBM i has had this built in support for many years. Many small IBM i shops do not care as much about these gee-whizz facilities but, they are glad that IBM keeps making IBM i stronger.

IBM i Does Windows

Long before 2008 and the IBM Power System with IBM i introduction, i5/OS and even OS/400, could support multiple instances of AIX, Linux, Lotus Domino, Microsoft Windows 2000 and Windows Server 2003. Some of this was via partitions that could split the processor into up to ten parts and some of this was done by using the frame of the IBM i as a Blade Server and adding as many Wintel x64 blades as were needed for the load.

At the time, i5/OS, AIX, Linux and Lotus Domino were fully supported on the Power processors but, Windows was supported with either single-processor internal blade servers (IXS) as previously noted or via an extension link. This notion, called "externally-linked multiple-processor servers (IXA and iSCSI)," provided Windows PCs a way of each appearing as blades to the i5/OS operating system. Making it even more impressive, IBM provided virtual SAN support via i5/OS so that the Windows PCs were able to be fully supported without using any internal disks. It was all done within the frame of what was then the System i. All of this works even better with today's IBM Power System.

IBM i Blade Servers are Outstanding

As part of the 2008 hardware change on up to 2016, IBM introduced and enhanced the Blade Servers package that can now mix Power and x64 blades (Intel and AMD) in the same blade server package. Meanwhile, the IBM Power Systems continued to support the SAN-like facilities noted above enabling remote and local Windows OS "blades" to be directly attached and controlled by IBM i.

Now, IBM Power Systems or IBM Power blade models running on any of the supported IBM Blade Centers can be configured with LPAR (Logical Partitioning) on IBM i. Blades controlled by IBM i with configured partitions can run various operating systems in those configured partitions.

When in operation, each LPAR is given a portion of system resources (memory, hard disk space, and CPU time) depending on the allocation formula. The LPAR technology in IBM i itself is smart enough to find unused resources and allocate them as needed for a given time.

Long before IBM invented the Power System for IBM i, the AS/400 heritage operating system supported i5/OS, AIX, and Linux. The i5/OS operating system was always the boss; however, but the other operating systems controlled their own workload as if i5/OS was not even in the picture. IBM i provided a SAN interface to the other operating systems and it virtualized the I/O before virtualization was even a buzz word. That's how well done partitioning was done and continues to be done on the IBM i heritage platform.

Client Server and More

Back in 1994, Lou Gerstner said that IBM was going to be a full participant in server-centric activities. When he had learned that only the PC Server and the RS/6000 machines supported client server and the Internet shortly after his arrival, while saving the entire IBM Corporation, Lou Gerstner set out to change that.

Though he had come from a company (Nabisco) that, among other things, created nourishing, non-contaminated peanut butter, Mr. Gerstner intuitively knew that if you were into server-centric, and client-server was the technology of the day, then your server offerings better match the needs of that client. In this regard, Mr. Gerstner was brilliant.

He directed all server divisions to become both server compliant (as in client-server) and he said that IBM's servers needed to not only participate but, needed to rule the Internet. Even with Lou Gerstner's insight, IBM's mainframe division and the AS/400 heritage divisions entered the foray a few years late but, they soon caught up.

Thus, the System i and now the IBM i OS supports common client-server-based technologies such as ODBC and JDBC for accessing the DB2 for i database from client software such as Java, Microsoft .Net languages and others.

Before the IBM Power System existed, Unix programs could run on a non-partitioned IBM i system. AIX (IBM's Unix) programs are binary compatible with IBM i when using the Portable Applications Solution Environment, nicknamed PASE by IBM. PASE is essentially "a Unix run-time operating system within an operating system."

When IBM Rochester began to create the hardware for IBM's only all-Unix box, known at the time as the pSeries, it was lots easier to do since PASE had been running on the iSeries for years. The AIX development team continues to provide the most recent and most stable version of AIX to run under PASE using the Unix KORN shell.

Programming

There are a number of chapters in this book about how programming integration helped make IBM i the all-everything operating system. As noted, the basic languages for IBM i include RPG and COBOL. The fact is there are many more languages on the list below but, most are not available anymore for ordering.

- RPG
- Assembly language
- C
- C++
- Pascal
- Java
- EGL
- Perl
- Smalltalk
- COBOL
- SQL
- BASIC
- PHP
- PL/I
- Python
- REXX
- etc...

As shown in the list, support on IBM i includes the Java language, including a 32-bit Java Virtual Machine (JVM) and a 64-bit JVM.

The CL language is not on the list but, in many ways, it is a bona fide programming language. With CL, commands can be prompted using the keyboard F4 function key. Moreover, as discussed in Chapter 18, commands also provide cursor-sensitive help to make specifying command parameters easier for the developer.

IBM i commands are constructed in a very intuitive way. As you learned in Chapter 18, all command names are based upon a 3-letter abbreviation standard for "verbs" and "objects." Using this standard means of forming a command, IBM i commands are hard to forget.

On other operating systems, OS commands are not quite so simple or intuitive. All other operating systems use cryptic and inconsistent command names for related functions or command parameter switches. As an example of how bad this can get, try to interpret the next command. If you love finding things in Unix, you should have no issues with the grep command:

`grep -v bash /etc/passwd | grep -v nologin`

Another Look at Common CL Commands

But, if you are a normal human being, you will crave the built-in ease of use of the IBM i CL command set. To review and to highlight the power of CL for programmers in the IBM i environment, I have included a few of the most necessary of the many CL commands that IBM has built into the IBM i OS. When you begin to use CL, you will see that this language makes operating system communication better than it would be in any other OS environment:

Common CL Commands:

- **CRTUSRPRF** - Create user profile
- **DSPUSRPRF, CHGUSRPRF, DLTUSRPRF** - Display, change, and delete user profile
- **DLTLIB** - Delete library
- **CRTLIB, DSPLIB, CHGLIB** - Create, display, and change a library
- **ADDLIBLE, CHGLIBL** - Add to or change library list
- **CPYF, CRTF, DSPF, CHGF, DLTF** - Copy, create, display, change, and delete file
- **WRKACTJOB** - Work with Active Jobs
- **WRKSYSSTS** - Work with System Status
- **STRSST, STRPASTHR, STRSBS** - Start System Service Tools, start pass through (remote login), start subsystem
- **VRYCFG** - Vary configuration, bring interfaces up or down
- **PWRDWNSYS** - Power Down System
- **WRKSPLF** - Work with spool files

Programming Languages Welcome

The Compiler writers for IBM i made all the compilers easier to use than on other systems. Even without the non-traditional add-ons for special devices for terminals and databases, the IBM i based compilers would still be deemed clean and highly usable. For traditional business programming purposes, RPG and COBOL are most often selected. Yet, because the IBM i OS is also a sophisticated operating system for computer science types, it has a very powerful C Language and the C++ language is also available. These are also built to the natural device facilities within the IBM i operating system.

The interface to the integrated database permits languages to treat database files in much the same way as other platforms treated ISAM or VSAM files. ISAM and VSAM are mainframe terms for file systems but, the Windows FAT systems or other file systems can easily be substituted to get the same meaning.

The IBM i platform has integrated security at the operating system level. It is as good as it gets and IBM has achieved the business compliance level C2 rating from the Federal Government. IBM's AS/400 was the first general-purpose computer system to attain a C2 security rating from the NSA, and in 1995 because the Power chip changed the internals of the platform, the C2 rating was extended to employ a 64-bit processor and operating system.

Other Goodies that Many Care About

Computer Science brings you the best that scientists and engineers are working on. Experts operating at this level rarely are thinking about the best way to line up an order record with a customer in a DB transaction. That's a fact. When you get outside of prevailing computer science for a bit, however, IT managers do things for practical reasons, not for the pure computer science of it all.

In the late 1990s and into the new millennium, you would still find a large number of IBM's smallest clients who had not yet made the leap of faith to the AS/400. They were still running on the Advanced 36 model of the AS/400 that IBM introduced in 1995 with the first batches of Power RISC chips. There are still IBM clients running on these machines. Several years ago, for example, I had the pleasure of moving one of these clients from one of the older model System/36 RISC boxes to the IBM i5.

The System/36 was always IBM's most successful small business computer; but, in the late 1980's, it had reached its architectural limit. Many of the executives in the small businesses that ran the System/36 did not care about the architecture as long as the machine showed up for work every day. And, it did, every day.

Eventually, as these machines got older, IBM's System/36 client executives decided that they too would move to the AS/400 technology. As noted above, my client moved from the Advanced 36 RISC model to the IBM i. The new system cost just over $20,000 and it ran the pants off the old system, supporting a mixture of 100 users on terminal workstations, and PCs emulating workstations.

IBM i today still has the System/36 environment as part of its offerings and many users, including my client, have never chosen to convert their code to native and it seems they never will have to. This is just another example of how IBM protects its customers' investments.

In this case by continually updating an environment that enables non-native coding to run unchanged on IBM i, my client runs their business every day and they have an active development environment. They just don't want to go back and fix something that isn't broke. With IBM I, they do not have to do so.

Many Users Admire IBM i OS

Before the departure of deposed CEO John Akers from IBM in 1993, Mr. Akers had been whittling down a lot of IBM's businesses, either selling them off or preparing them to be sold. He was clearly positioning IBM to become less, rather than more. During this time, there was a lot of speculation about who should succeed John Akers to the IBM throne. Steve Jobs the Apple and Pixar Entrepreneur was frequently mentioned and overtures were made but, Jobs did not accept.

Bill Gates, then Microsoft's CEO, was noted as being on the short list if you can believe the rumors. Another big rumor was that as IBM was seemingly being auctioned off, Gates was asked which part of IBM he would be interested in. His reply was the "AS/400 Division." It is my personal opinion that if Gates was permitted to buy the AS/400 Division from IBM, IBM would be exclusively a software and services business today. The IBM i line, free of all of its IBM encumbrances of having to treat all systems fairly, would have been used by Microsoft to wipe out IBM hardware, Sun, HP, and all the rest of the contestants from the large to the small. Bill Gates would be the richest man in the world. Oh, he already is.

It does speak great volume about Gates' opinion of the IBM i line of systems. Over the years since 1993, Microsoft struggled to move its own business systems from the AS/400 platform to Windows Servers. Nobody really knows if they were successful in doing this. You may recall that in the 1990's as Microsoft was trying to move the world's biggest players to Microsoft "Server" technology, its biggest issue was that it was still using IBM's AS/400 systems to run its own business.

Actually, the fact that Bill Gates expressed interest in AS/400 while, at the same time, he was trying to beat it in the marketplace begs the question for all time. "Why use Windows when Bill Gates would rather have his business run on IBM i? The answer to that question should provide all business managers with enough information to know the course of action they should

Chapter 21   The All-Everything Operating System in Perspective

The Platform to Run Your Business

Real businesses choose real computer systems with real operating systems to support business-critical applications. The focus of this book has been the all-everything operating system, which is about as real as it can get. It is the best operating system ever designed and unlike all other operating systems that are sold today, it was designed for business.

The IBM i operating system running on IBM Power System technology is a cut above the norm. When business value from IT is the objective, no other OS can answer the call like IBM i. IBM i is designed to help all businesses meet the highest service levels defined by your business. Moreover, as an all-everything platform, it can be readily adopted to handle every new business opportunity that comes your way. While the competition is discussing the problem, an IBM i programming team can be working on your solution and have it up and running before the competition knows the problem can be solved.

The "i" in IBM i as you know by now stands for integration. This all-everything operating system integrates a trusted combination of relational database, security, Web services, networking and storage management capabilities. With its advanced functions and integrated database, it provides the foundation for efficiently deploying high payback business processing applications. There is nothing like it.

Though your aged trial balance and your critical inventory reports won't be coming off the printer the very moment the IBM i is installed, it will seem that fast. IBM i consists of a full complement of business enabling facility, fully tested, and pre-loaded up front. Unlike IBM i competing systems, this work is done before the system is shipped complete so it does not have to be built piece meal, software and hardware, in your company's data center. You get the advantages of the advanced functions of IBM's largest mainframes packaged with small system ease of use.

With IBM i, everything is more efficient and so along with its pre-integration and testing, IBM i is built to enable your company to develop and/ or deploy high value applications faster. Additionally, because the components are integrated and the right tools are supplied with the package, you can maintain your applications with substantially fewer technicians on your staff. The bottom line is that IBM i is built for business and using IBM i in your business will help your bottom line.

Reviewing the Lineage

IBM i is the most functional business operating system ever developed by IBM. It runs on IBM's best Power System platform. It is a descendent of the most advanced computer ever built, the IBM System/38. Way back in 1978, this system was the brainchild of Dr. Frank Soltis, who served as IBM's Chief Midrange Computing Scientist until he retired in December, 2008.

IBM had a future systems project underway, in the early 1970s, in which the corporation designed, on paper, the greatest system that could ever be built. Because IBM's large customers had developed an aversion to machine conversions, IBM never developed this design into a system for its largest customers. Instead, Dr. Soltis and others in IBM's Rochester, Minnesota Lab picked up this design, dusted it off, added their own favorite flavors and developed the System/38 as the embodiment of all the IBM knew about computer science at the time. But, because the System/38 was the product of the "Small Computer" Division, until the late 1990's, it was underpowered compared to the IBM mainframes.

Today, no other system or operating system is as advanced as the combination of the IBM Power System running the IBM i all-everything operating system. Though the System/38 offered more capacity than the previous IBM small business computer systems, namely the System/3, System/32, System/34, it was designed to not compete, size-wise, with IBM's large mainframes that were built in Endicott and Poughkeepsie NY.

When the IBM System/38 came out, everybody wanted one. At the time, IBM's General Systems Division knew how to sell computers to new businesses and to existing IBM customers. The specs were so good and the price was so right that orders were buzzing through the computer systems in IBM branch offices across the world.

Unfortunately, the computer science complexities and integration built into the original machine, the ease of use form that the machine needed to present, and the small system frame that it was permitted to run in, created a huge problem for the Rochester Lab engineers and scientists. In fact, it was so sophisticated and so unique and so powerful of an operating system with matching sophisticated hardware that, as hard as it tried, the Rochester Lab could not get the job done on time.

It took over a year from when the system was promised until it began to ship regularly to IBM Branch Offices. The Regional Data Center System/38 machines that IBM's own Systems Engineers trained on were often buggy in the beginning. To many, such as myself, it was a miracle that all the work was done well enough for IBM to authorize first customer shipment.

Our IBM Office in Scranton, PA had tons of orders for the box. However, customers got antsy because it did not come out right away and they needed to do other things, rather than wait. Many went with small mainframes while others tried to cram their work into the System/34 platform. So, IBM more than likely lost about 80% of its orders as just about 20,000 System/38s were sold in the first five years of availability.

When IBM's infamous Fort Knox project that was to eliminate the System/38 was canceled, IBM in Rochester hustled through its famous Silverlake project and it announced the AS/400 in June 1988. Unlike the System/38, the AS/400 was enabled to grow large. Eventually AS/400s became as powerful as mainframes with today's IBM Power System model 595 being even more powerful than the most powerful mainframe in terms of workload capacity. The IBM i operating system of today was enhanced many times on the road to Power Technology

All of the advanced computer science notions that were conceived with the System/38 are still prevalent in today's IBM i operating system. Plus, over the thirty years, many, many additional enhancements have been added making IBM i the only all-everything operating system in existence.

IBM I, as noted throughout this book, is IBM's greatest success story. The operating system is widely installed in large enterprises at the department level, in small corporations, in government agencies, and in almost every industry segment. It is the finest operating system in the business and it is built for productivity and ease of use. Businesses just love it when they get over that it is made by IBM and not Microsoft.

"The Eggplant That Ate Chicago"

by Norman Greenbaum
(Dr. West's Medicine Show & Junk Band)

You'd better watch out for the eggplant that ate
 Chicago,
For he may eat your city soon.
You'd better watch out for the eggplant that ate Chicago,
If he's still hungry, the whole country's doomed.

He came from outer space, lookin' for somethin' to eat.
He landed in Chicago. He thought Chicago was a treat.
(It was sweet, it was just like sugar)
You'd better watch out for the eggplant that ate Chicago,
For he may eat your city soon (wacka-do, wacka-do, wacka-do)
You'd better watch out for the eggplant that ate Chicago,
If he's still hungry, the whole country's doomed.

kazoo solo

He came from outer space, lookin' for somethin' to eat.
He landed in Chicago. He thought Chicago was a treat.
(It was sweet, it was just like sugar)
You'd better watch out for the eggplant that ate Chicago,
For he may eat your city soon (wacka-do, wacka-do, wacka-do)
You'd better watch out for the eggplant that ate Chicago,
If he's still hungry, the whole country's doomed ("It's in trouble"

If he's still hungry, the whole country's doomed

Books by Brian W. Kelly
www.letsgopublish.com; Sold at

www.bookhawkers.com
Email info@ letsgopublish.com for specific ordering info. Our titles include the following:

Great Moments in Notre Dame Football The story about the beginning of US football and ND football in the US as well as the great moemnts and great coaches and players ove the years.

Thank You IBM The story of how IBM helped today's technology millionaires and billionaires gain their vast fortunes

WineDiets.Com PresentsThe Wine Diet Learn how to lose weight while having fun. Four specific diets and some great anecdotes fill this book with fun.

Wilkes-Barre, PA; Return to Glory Wilkes-Barre City's return to glory begins with dreams and ideas. Along with plans and actions, this equals leadership.

The Lifetime Guest Plan. This is a plan which if deployed today would immediately solve the problem of 60 million illegal aliens in the United States.

Geoffrey Parsons' Epoch... The Land of Fair Play Better than the original. The greatest re-mastering of the greatest book ever written on American Civics. It was built for all Americans as the best govt. design in the history of the world.

The Bill of Rights 4 Dummmies This is the best book to learn about your rights. Be the first, to have a "Rights Fest" on your block. You will win for sure!

Sol Bloom's Epoch ...Story of the Constitution This work by Sol Bloom was written to commemorate the Sesquicentennial celebration of the Constitution. It has been remastered by Lets Go Publish! – an excellent read!

The Constitution 4 Dummmies This is the best book to learn about the Constitution. Learn all about the fundamental laws of America.

America for Dummmies!
All Americans should read to learn about this great country.

Just Say No to Chris Christie for President!
Discusses the reasons why Chris Christie is a poor choice for US President

The Federalist Papers by Hamilton, Jay, Madison w/ intro by Brian Kelly
Complete unabridged, easier to read version of the original Federalist Papers

Bring On the American Party!
Demonstrates how Americans can be free from Parties of wimps by starting our own national party called the American Party.

Saving America
This how-to book is about saving our country using strong mercantilist principles. These are the same principles that helped the country from its founding.

RRR:
A unique plan for economic recovery and job creation

Kill the EPA
The EPA seems to hate mankind and love nature. They are also making it tough for asthmatics to breathe and for those with malaria to live. It's time they go.

Taxation Without Representation Second Edition
At the time of the Boston Tea Party, there was no representation. Now, there is no representation again but there are "representatives."

Healthcare Accountability
Who should pay for your healthcare? Whose healthcare should you pay for? Is it a lifetime free ride on others or should those once in need of help have to pay it back when their lives improve?

Jobs! Jobs! Jobs!
Where have all the American Jobs gone and how can we get them back?

IBM I Technical Books

The All Everything Operating System:
The story about IBM's finest operating system, its facilities, and how it came to be.

The All-Everything Machine
The story about IBM's finest computer server.

Chip Wars
The story of the ongoing war between Intel and AMD and the upcoming was between Intel and IBM. This book may cause you to buy or sell somebody's stock.

Can the AS/400 Survive IBM?
Exciting book about the AS/400 in an IBM i / System i5 World

The IBM i Pocket SQL Guide.
Complete Pocket Guide to SQL as implemented on System i5. A must have for SQL developers new to System i5. It is very compact yet very comprehensive and it is example driven. Written in a part tutorial and part reference style, this book has tons of SQL coding samples, from the simple to the sublime.

The IBM i Pocket Query Guide.
If you have been spending money for years educating your Query users, and you find you are still spending, or you've given up, this book is right for you. This one QuikCourse covers all Query options.

The IBM i Pocket RPG & RPG IV Guide.
Comprehensive RPG & RPGIV Textbook -- Over 900 pages. This is the one RPG book to have if you are not having more than one. All areas of the language covered smartly in a convenient sized book Annotated PowerPoint's available for self-study (extra fee for self-study package)

let's go to www.letsgopublish.com to see the full list of LetsGoPublish creations--- including Chip Wars!

www.ingramcontent.com/pod-product-compliance
Lightning Source LLC
Chambersburg PA
CBHW071359050326
40689CB00010B/1691